The 0.5 Generation

The 0.5 Generation

CHILDREN MOVING FROM THE UNITED
STATES TO MEXICO

Víctor Zúñiga and Silvia E.
Giorguli

UNIVERSITY OF CALIFORNIA PRESS

University of California Press
Oakland, California

© 2024 by El Colegio de México, A. C.

Library of Congress Cataloging-in-Publication Data

Names: Zúñiga, Víctor, author. | Giorguli Saucedo, Silvia Elena, 1970-
    author.
Title: The 0.5 generation : children moving from the United States to
    Mexico / Víctor Zúñiga and Silvia E. Giorguli.
Description: Oakland, California : University of California Press, [2024] |
    Includes bibliographical references and index.
Identifiers: LCCN 2023025977 (print) | LCCN 2023025978 (ebook) |
    ISBN 9780520398597 (cloth) | ISBN 9780520398603 (paperback) |
    ISBN 9780520398610 (ebook)
Subjects: LCSH: Immigrant children—Social aspects—Mexico—21st
    century.
Classification: LCC JV6344 .Z86 2024 (print) | LCC JV6344 (ebook) | DDC
    305.23086/91209720905—dc23/eng/20230630
LC record available at https://lccn.loc.gov/2023025977
LC ebook record available at https://lccn.loc.gov/2023025978

33 32 31 30 29 28 27 26 25 24
10 9 8 7 6 5 4 3 2 1

Dedicamos este libro a Galilea, Génesis, Angélica, y
Beto, de quienes hemos aprendido tantas cosas.
Thank you so much for sharing with us your
fascinating journeys between the United States and
Mexico.

Contents

Illustrations

FIGURES

Acknowledgments

The authors would like to thank and recognize the excellent work by Catalina Panait for translating this book from Spanish to English and by Jennifer Stacy for carefully editing the whole manuscript. Catalina and Jennifer worked with passion because they love child migrants. We are also grateful for the support of the Mexican Federal Consejo Nacional de Ciencia y Tecnología for funding the different phases of our fieldwork from 2004 until 2018. Finally, we would like to express our appreciation to Adela Angoa and Montserrat Yong, who helped us during the different stages of the statistical data processing and organized the final manuscript, and to Dairee Ramírez and Eduardo Carrillo, for the support they have provided since the earliest stages of the preparation of this book.

Introduction

OVERVIEW OF RESEARCH PROJECT AND PARTICIPANTS

This book is devoted to the study of children between the ages of zero to seventeen who have arrived in Mexico from the United States since the beginning of the twenty-first century.[1] We specifically discuss two groups of migrant youth: those who were born in Mexico, migrated to the United States, and then came back to Mexico and those who were born in the United States and moved to Mexico. Their experience crossing the border between Mexico and the United States categorizes them as international migrants. This term, "international migrants," most accurately defines and describes these minors from both a sociological and demographic perspective. This book analyzes multiple aspects of the migratory experience of these children and adolescents, including their integration or reintegration into Mexican society and its institutions.[2]

Why are these children and adolescents in Mexico? Why did they move from the United States to Mexico? Essentially, these migrant children have arrived in Mexico as a result of changes in patterns of Mexican migration: in recent years scholars have documented a decrease in emigration from Mexico to the United States and an increase in return migration (Giorguli and Gutiérrez 2011a).[3] As a result, in 2010 the net migration flow from Mexico to the United States fell to zero and may have even reversed in subsequent years (Passel, Cohn, and González-Barrera 2012). Thus, Mexico has transformed from being a country of emigration to being one of immigration and transit. Quantitatively, the proportion of child migrants arriving in Mexico is important and must be considered a social priority.

Why are these children in Mexico? Why are they in a country that historically has been a migrant-sending country? (Fitzgerald 2008). Why are they not living in the United States, which is a prototypical country of immigration? The answer to these questions involves macroeconomic and macropolitical dimensions that we briefly outline hereafter. As previously stated, since 2005 Mexico has transformed into a migrant-receiving country after having been a predominantly migrant-sending country for more than a century (Hernández-León and Zúñiga 2016). The majority of migrants who began arriving in Mexico were Mexican adults who, after residing for several years in the United States, returned to Mexico accompanied by all or some of their family members, including children born in the United States. This information led scholars to identify the macrostructural dimensions (i.e., economic trends, political stance, and legal framework) that caused the reversal of the traditional migratory flows. David Leal, Néstor Rodríguez, and Gary Freeman (2016) defined this phenomenon as the "era of restriction and recession" and illustrated how these macrostructural dimensions were interrelated. In the United States, anti-immigrant political and legal measures were associated with the effects of the Great Recession (2007–9). These measures weighed on the lives of Mexican migrants and their families and generally explain the displaceability to which they have been subjected. It is within this context that hundreds of thousands of children arrived in Mexico from the United States. Inasmuch as these children are sons and daughters of the Great Migration (1990–2005), they are also a part of the Great Expulsion (Boehm 2016; Hernández-León and Zúñiga 2016; Valdéz Gardea, Ciria, and García Castro 2017).[4]

This book is devoted to the study and analysis of the migratory experience of international youth migrants who have arrived in Mexico from the United States during the past fifteen years and to their integration into Mexican society. To address these children's migratory experiences, we take into consideration the geographic, familial, and subjective elements of their migration process, as well as the heterogeneity of their migratory trajectories. Some of these children return to Mexico (if they were born in Mexico), and others come to the country for the first time in their lives. After revealing the heterogeneity of these migratory trajectories, we address several crucial questions: How many international child migrants are there in Mexico? Has their presence in Mexico increased in number? Where do they come from? For how many years did they live in the United States? How do they explain their arrival in Mexico? How do they experience these transitions and changes? Do their families live in Mexico, or are their families divided by borders? Through these questions we aim to capture the myriad facets of these children's migratory experiences.

To account for the integration (or nonintegration) of children into Mexican society and its institutions, we analyze the existing data on the transitions, ruptures, and contradictions that children experience when they enroll in Mexican schools. Some of these children enroll for the first time in a Mexican school, while others reenroll because they had previously attended school in Mexico. In all cases school is the mediating institution that can facilitate the social and political integration of international child migrants.

INTERNATIONAL CHILD MIGRANTS IN
THE UNITED STATES AND MEXICO

We find it essential to define the category of "international child migrants," especially because this concept can lend itself to different interpretations. In their introduction to *Children of Immigration,* Carola Suárez-Orozco and Marcelo M. Suárez-Orozco (2001) explain that the categories of "children of immigrants" and "immigrant children" are not interchangeable, and they delineate clear distinctions between the two. The first category, "children of immigrants," refers to children born in the destination country to immigrant parents. The literature on migration refers to these children as the "second generation" (Portes 1996). In many countries children of immigrants are granted birthright citizenship by jus soli, the rule that the place of children's birth determines their citizenship. This is the case of the children of Mexican immigrants who were born in the United States. Their birth on U.S. soil granted them citizenship, and, as such, they are U.S. citizens, not immigrants. The children are considered members of the second generation of immigrants, while their parents belong to the first generation. It is important to reiterate that, in this context, the children of immigrants are not immigrants.

On the other hand, "immigrant children" are immigrants just like their parents and relatives. These children participated in migration: they moved to a different country than the one in which they were born, just as the adults did. In the literature on migration, these children are referred to as "second-half children" (Thomas and Znaniecki 1958) or as members of the 1.5 generation (Rumbaut 2004; Harklau, Losey, and Siegal 2009; Rojas-García 2013). Scholars emphasize the fact that age matters—and it matters a lot—when trying to understand the phenomenon of migration and the social integration of migrants. Migrants who arrive in the destination country at an early age undergo a process of primary socialization known as the internalization of social worlds (Berger and Luckmann 1991). Simply put, immigrant children were first educated in their parents' country of origin and, after they arrive in the destination country, they restart their primary socialization process. This happens first when they come into contact with the new social environment and then, predominantly, when they enroll in school. Once in school, they undergo a new socialization process that aims to transform them into both national and local members of the receiving society, the country to which they were brought by their parents or relatives.

The most visible element in this new socialization process is language. Children often arrive in a society in which the dominant language is different than their parents' language (Spanish or Indigenous languages), which they spoke on a daily basis when they were living in their countries of origin. In the case of Mexican children who arrive in the United States, the acquisition of English as a second language—or third or more language—is a highly complex process (Hamann, Zúñiga, and Sánchez García 2022). Children continue to use Spanish at home with their family, and many had already started learning to read and write in Spanish while in school in Mexico. In other words, they already have the ability to communicate with their parents, siblings, relatives, and other people in their community. They have already developed a complex language system consisting of phonological awareness, morphology, and an enriched vocabulary, among other skills. When immigrant children enroll in schools in the United States without having any knowledge of English, they face a double challenge: they must learn the English language while they are expected to learn academic content in English (Valdés, Capitelli, and Alvarez 2011).[5]

Migration scholars have pointed out that age is a central component in analyzing the integration of international migrants into destination societies. Roger Waldinger (2008a) presents both expected and unexpected evidence as to why age is relevant in the process of international migration. For example, it is expected that individuals who move to another country at an early age acquire the dominant language spoken in the destination society and perhaps become as proficient as native speakers. However, it is less expected to learn that migrants who came to the United States as children send fewer remittances to their relatives in countries such as Mexico, El Salvador, or the Dominican Republic compared to those who arrived as adults. Furthermore, this group travels less frequently to their country of origin. To paraphrase Waldinger, migration has a stronger impact on the lives of individuals when they become involved in this process at an early age. In the case of child migrants, it is more likely that the destination society will become their "new home," whereas the society of origin will gradually grow subjectively distant.

Ruben Rumbaut (2004) proposes even finer distinctions regarding the relevance of age in international migration by nuancing the category of first-generation immigrant. He refers to youth who arrived in the United States between the ages of thirteen to seventeen as the 1.25 generation. These adolescents are likely to enroll in middle or high schools. Those who were between six and twelve years old when they arrived in the United States are considered part of the 1.5 generation and enroll in elementary schools. Lastly, migrants aged zero to five who arrive in the United States belong to a generation that is very close to the second generation: the 1.75 generation. While they were not born in the United States, these children arrived at a very early age and essentially underwent the entire primary socialization process in the destination country, first as members of their families and later as students in schools (often beginning in preschool). Within all of these categories, these children are international migrants.[6]

None of the aforementioned categories—1.25, 1.5, 1.75, or second generation—accurately describes the children we study in this book. Our subjects are child migrants who have the right to Mexican citizenship based on the principle of jus soli or the principle of jus sanguinis. As previously stated, they are international migrants because they have crossed the national borders at least once, if not more. To shed light on these children's situation and to capture the distinctive features of this new migratory flow, we put forward the concept of the 0.5 generation. The term "0.5 generation" seeks to grasp the characteristics of this particular type of mobility to Mexico as a destination country and highlights the fact that the children who move from the United States to Mexico cannot be included in any of the established generational categories used in the literature on migration.

METHODOLOGICAL NATIONALISM

It is paradoxical that international child migrants who are living in Mexico after having been born or having lived in the United States have received little attention in the literature on migration. First, consider the category of "children of immigrants," as explained by Carola Suárez-Orozco and Marcelo Suárez-Orozco (2001). Before coming to Mexico, these children were not considered immigrants because they were living in the country in which they were born—the United States. Once they arrive in Mexico, the children can no longer be considered second generation: their parents are Mexican nationals and no longer considered immigrants because they have returned to live in the country in which they were born. So the children must now be categorized as international migrants because they have moved from one country to another. Next, let's consider the category of "child migrants"—those who were born in Mexico and migrated to the United States. As explained earlier, when these children were living in the United States, they were categorized as the 1.5 generation. However, once in Mexico they become "return" migrants because they returned to the country in which they were born.

The focal children of this book have long been invisible to migration scholars in countries that historically have been destination countries (such as the United States, Canada, Germany, etc.). The invisibility of these child migrants in the scholarship is surprising because scholars are acutely aware of the fact that international migration has always included both return and circular migration.[7] It is likely assumed that these migrant children and the children of immigrants arrive in the destination countries and stay there permanently. This book shows that this is not necessarily true. Many children born in the United States (who were considered members of the second generation when they were living there) are now living in Mexico and are being educated in Mexican schools.

This book also shows that numerous children who were considered members of the 1.5, 1.25, or 1.75 generations when they were in the United States are now living in Mexico. These children were born in Mexico and later moved to the United States, usually accompanied by one or more of their parents, and then returned to Mexico as minors.[8] Three important aspects of their migratory identification emerge. First, the categories of "second generation" and "1.5 generation" no longer make sense when these international child migrants arrive in Mexico. Second, these children are underage when they engage in these migratory movements and are still in the midst of the primary socialization process. Third, and consequently, Mexico is increasingly becoming a receiving country for international migrants (Giorguli and Gutiérrez 2012; Hernández-León and Zúñiga 2016), a topic we discuss in more detail in this book.

It is through this lens that we ask the following: Why are these child migrants absent from the research about international migration? Why are these particular migration flows absent, even though migration scholars are aware of the fact that circulation and return have been a constituent component of international migration since the nineteenth century (Perlmann and Waldinger 1999)? To address these questions, we draw on theoretical and methodological frameworks of "methodological nationalism" (Wimmer and Glick Schiller 2002; Llopis Goig 2007). Scholars who study both the second generation and the 1.25, 1.5, and 1.75 generations of immigrants assume that children and adolescents do not circulate, they do not return, and they do not move from the destination countries. This is likely because they are looking at facts from the traditional destination countries and making interpretations only from those data.

Hence, these authors' scholarly pursuits—and findings—are limited to domestic issues. Rarely do they show any interest in what child migrants face in their countries of origin, nor do they wonder whether these children (who are either children of immigrants or immigrants themselves) have lived in their parents' countries of origin, at least for a period during their childhood or adolescence.[9] For example, scholars in the United States wonder what language these children speak at home, if they are learning English, and if they are doing well in school. They are curious as to whether or not these children identify with U.S. society, if their allegiances lie within the United States, if they'll get good jobs when they reach adulthood, if they'll achieve upward mobility vis-à-vis their parents, among other topics. All of these are legitimate academic and political concerns, but they are relevant to the society of the United States, where the specialists in these fields work. If the children leave the United States, what happens next is no longer deemed relevant to the field.

Methodological nationalism has paradoxically shaped the field of migration and, specifically, that of the social integration of child migrants. Demographers, who are very much aware of the diversity of migration flows and have highlighted that migration is not and has never been unidirectional, have pointed out that many children born in the United States spend their entire childhood, or part of it, in Mexico. Michael Rendall and Berna Torr (2008) studied cohorts of child migrants and estimated that in the 1985–90 and 1995–2000 cohorts, one in ten children born in the United States to Mexican mothers spent their childhood in Mexico. Thus, the fact that most of the research on the social integration of child migrants does not acknowledge this phenomenon is problematic.

TWO DECADES OF INDUCTIVE RESEARCH

We became interested in studying international child migrants living in Mexico when we were in the United States, in Dalton, Georgia, to be exact, in the company of Rubén Hernández-León and Edmund T. Hamann. From 1997 to 1998, we conducted research about Dalton, the most prominent carpet-manufacturing hub in the country, which was—and still is—a destination for Mexican migration (Zúñiga and Hernández-León 2005a). We conducted surveys and carried out fieldwork that included site visits, observations, and participation in numerous work meetings in the city of Dalton. During those years our research focused on schools because the local education authorities were concerned about the rapid changes in student enrollment in their districts. The arrival of large numbers of Mexican children, as well as Guatemalan and Salvadoran children, was completely changing the dynamics and demographic composition of school districts in this region of Georgia (Hamann 2003). Authorities and teachers were going through a difficult period of adjustment and adaptation to effectively working with migrant populations. It was through this lens that we had numerous opportunities to talk with school principals. They often told us, "These children disappear." We assumed that this meant not that the children actually vanished but that they moved elsewhere—that is, they migrated. One possible scenario is that they moved to a different place in the United States, while another possibility is that they returned to Mexico or went there for the first time, had they been born in the United States. In December 2004 we began our research in Mexico, where we found the "missing" children. And that is where the disappeared children appeared.

Beginning in 2004, a collaboration of scholars has been investigating the migratory trajectories of these focal children. The research group is composed of Eduardo Carrillo (Tecnológico de Monterrey), Michaël Da Cruz (Université d'Aix-Marseille), Edmund "Ted" T. Hamann (University of Nebraska–Lincoln), Rubén Hernández-León (University of California, Los Angeles), Shinji Hirai (Center for Research and Higher Studies in Social Anthropology), Catalina Panait (Tecnológico de Monterrey), Betsabé Román (University of California, San Diego), Anabela Sánchez (Universidad de Monterrey), Juan Sánchez García (Escuela Normal Miguel F. Martínez), Rebeca Sandoval (Ford Foundation) and María Vivas-Romero (Université de Liège). Our work has spanned several Mexican states over the years, including Nuevo León (2004–5), Zacatecas (2005–6), Puebla (2009–10), and Jalisco (2010–11). The first survey was carried out in Nuevo León due to the access and infrastructure that the state education authorities provided. We continued in Zacatecas because we were interested in doing research in a state well known for its long migratory tradition and high migratory density. In Puebla and Jalisco, we responded to the request of state education authorities.

While conducting fieldwork in Jalisco, the first group of researchers (composed of sociologists, anthropologists, and linguists) asserted the need to collaborate with experts in the demography of international migration between Mexico and the United States. As we were conducting, presenting, and publishing our research, readers and decision-makers representing public institutions frequently asked us questions like "How many international child migrants are currently living in Mexico?" and "Since when have they been arriving in Mexico?" Our answers to these questions were incomplete because our surveys were based on state-level samples and were limited to data that had been collected in schools. In 2010, within the *Binational Dialogue on Mexican Migrants in the United States and Mexico* initiative (Giorguli et al. 2021), we began a fruitful dialogue with Edith Y. Gutiérrez (El Colegio de México), Frank Bean (University of California, Irvine), Susan K. Brown (University of California, Irvine), Bryant Jensen (Brigham Young University), and Adam Sawyer (California State University, Bakersfield). Ever since, we have coordinated these two groups of researchers to participate in a continuous exchange of information and ideas. This book encompasses the research that emerged from these partnerships.

In 2013, with more robust demographic data about international migrants in Mexico, we embarked on a multisited, longitudinal research project in the Mexican state of Morelos. This project, unlike the previous surveys, no longer attempted to count the number of international child migrants enrolled in schools but rather to depict their life histories. This ongoing project aims to grasp the ethnographical richness of the migratory and education trajectories of ten children and their families.

In a strict, nonmetaphorical sense, this book is the fruit of an empirical and theoretical journey that began in 1997 in Dalton, Georgia. Rubén Hernández-León, Ted Hamann, and Víctor Zúñiga were conducting quantitative and qualitative research that included surveying Mexican and Central American parents whose children were enrolled in Dalton public schools. Additionally, Ted was completing the fieldwork for his dissertation about the demographic changes in Dalton and their influence on educational experiences, which he defended in 1999. During those years (1997–2007), we had regular contact with second-generation children, but more frequently with 1.5 generation children, and began inquiring into their experiences on both sides of the border. Shortly after, our research journey in Mexico commenced in 2004. Throughout these twenty-five years, our research has followed an inductive approach: we have allowed ourselves to be guided by the methodological principle, as put forward by Ted Hamann, that "we don't know what we don't know." The methodological positioning is useful in any field of study, but it is imperative when it comes to adults studying the experiences of children and, in this case, child migrants.

Traditionally, studies on migrants have relied on adult-centered understandings and perspectives, which is why Madeleine Dobson (2009) urges us to "unpack" migrant children who, until recently, were comparable to "luggage" transported by migrant adults. To unpack these children and overcome an adult-centered perspective, we use the inductive method that invites us to ask provisional questions without having all the answers within reach. From this lens we learn directly from the children involved in migration. While we better understand the contexts that produce, reproduce, and condition these children, we also learn about the decisions that they make as agents and strategists in their own migration process. By invoking methodological humility, we privilege the voices of those who really know and understand the migratory experience: the migrant children (as well as their parents and relatives). As researchers, we must let the children show us the way and refine our preliminary questions in the process, developing new and better questions, creating different and more robust categories, and, ultimately, generating more appropriate research methods.

Four examples demonstrate our inductive approach to research and, at the same time, explain the way in which this book is structured. In our first studies, we noticed that very young children (six to eight years old) not only had difficulties answering the questionnaires but also were often unable to provide accurate information about their migratory experiences. They did know in which country they were born (all children knew this piece of information), but they did not remember or did not know the specific town or state. Often they did not know in which country their parents had been born or in which schools in the United States they had studied. In short, the children, especially those who had come to Mexico when they were very young, did not remember or did not know a great deal of information. Because of this, we made the decision not to ask children to answer a questionnaire and to rule out young children from the interviews we conducted.[10] This was a mistake that we recognized when we ultimately decided to interview three children, ages six, seven, and eight, in the Mixtec region of Puebla. We found their narratives fascinating: Itzcalli (six years old) was born in the United States but did not remember exactly where; Manuel (seven years old) was born in the suburbs of Chicago; Jessenia (eight years old) was born in some town in New Jersey. These children's perspectives were captured, analyzed, and ultimately published in a journal article (see Sánchez, Hamann, and Zúñiga 2012).[11]

A second example of inductive methodology occurred when we were conducting interviews in different municipalities of Puebla. Ted Hamann and Juan Sánchez came up with the idea of using the children's answers from the questionnaire during the interview to more authentically dialogue with each of the children about their written responses. The interviews were conducted months after the questionnaire was given. When we returned to the schools in Puebla, we had already identified the international child migrants and arrived with the questionnaires in hand for these children. Annexed to the survey were questions created exclusively for migrant children, including the question: Would you be interested in talking to us about schools in the United States? The options were "yes" and "no." If the children answered affirmatively, their full name was requested. This way we could link the children's questionnaire with their interview. To our surprise, in many cases we found contradictions between one source and the other but soon realized that this was not the result of the children's "lies" or "errors" but rather a consequence of the instrument used (questionnaire or in-depth interview). This is how we discovered that using mixed methods (which, in common jargon, is a combination of quantitative and qualitative methods) is not a simple task. The pieces of information collected from different methods do not fit together like the pieces of a jigsaw puzzle but rather forced us to admit that the views and perspectives of children (and of all human beings) are not necessarily coherent. Together, the quantitative and qualitative data allowed for contradictions, nuances, and tonalities, which were very useful and permitted us to gain a better understanding of what we wanted to know. Hence, the complex findings resulted in an article that was published in 2017 (see Hamann, Zúñiga, and Sánchez García 2017).

The third example of the heuristic potential of this inductive method emerged when we decided to analyze migratory trajectories in detail to understand how children and adolescents explained their return to Mexico. By doing this, we realized that the initial information we gathered from the children (when they answered the questionnaire, or when we interviewed them) was like a photograph capturing one instant out of the whole trajectory. Certainly, that photograph was accompanied by a story about what they had experienced before, but we were entirely ignorant of what happened after they returned. We regretted the fact that we had no idea of what had happened to many of the children who had shared with us their complex—and risky—experiences as migrants. This is why we decided to change our methodological strategy when we started the project in Morelos.

As mentioned earlier, we selected a small number of child migrants to follow across several years so that we could capture their entire story through adulthood. Through this longitudinal approach, we discovered that the children who were enrolled in schools later dropped out. We also found that these children often returned to the United States, mostly those who have dual nationalities or those who have relatives living there, and that it was not unusual for them to move from one place to another within Mexico, thus combining international migration with internal migration. In a nutshell we discovered that the trajectories of child migrants are much more complex than we had assumed and that only a longitudinal study could holistically capture this complexity. The initial findings of this study were published first in Betsabé Román González's doctoral thesis (2017) and then in an academic article published in 2016 (see Román González, Carrillo, and Hernández-León 2016).

Last, the fourth example of our inductive research journey can be observed by comparing a paper presented by Silvia Giorguli and Edith Gutiérrez in May 2011 at an academic conference with their article published on the same topic at the end of the same year. The researchers' initial presentation raised the question: "Is there any evidence of changes in the patterns of Mexican migration to the United States?" The question stemmed from intuition based on the preliminary analysis of data from the Mexican 2010 census (Giorguli and Gutiérrez 2011a). Proceeding in an inductive manner, the analysis went on to compare Mexican and U.S. official data sources, which ultimately allowed the researchers to affirm that "the change in the migratory pattern is illustrated by the sharp fall in the annual number of emigrants and by the unexpected return of a great number of Mexicans and children of Mexicans to national territory" (2011b, 21). By 2012 the conclusions were firmer and more nuanced because the patterns were combined:

> There is a historical process of emigration [from Mexico] that is character-ized by the loss of circularity and increased settlement in that country [United States], as well as by the incorporation of women and children into the migration flows. On the other hand, the outflow from Mexico has decreased substantially and, in the last five years, there has been an unprec-edented return and entry of Mexicans and children of Mexicans from the United States. (2012, 1)

Consequently, there is not one single answer to the question that Giorguli and Gutiérrez (2012) raised. Rather, this question could be answered in various ways because migration patterns are multilayered, much like sedi-mentary geologic structures in which layers are juxtaposed against one another. While older layers are hidden underneath more recent layers, they are no less real and must be incorporated in our understanding of migration patterns.

This book is the result of a research journey that addresses the migra-tory experience of children who move to Mexico from the United States and their process of integration (or nonintegration) into Mexican society and its institutions. These two specific research areas are included in each chapter, although, depending on the subject, in some chapters the migra-tory experience is privileged, while in others we give priority to the inte-gration process.

Chapter 1 summarizes the conceptual path we followed, guided by the theoretical tools that each of us possess according to our disciplinary backgrounds. This chapter ends with a synthesis of the theoretical per-spectives that have guided us for more than twenty years. The remaining chapters present the research findings and are divided into thematic sec-tions. Chapter 2 focuses on the migratory experience of children from zero to seventeen years of age, while presenting the chronology of the migra-tion process from the United States to Mexico. The analysis begins with the 1990 Mexican census, includes the 2000 and 2010 censuses, and ends with the data from the 2015 population survey (INEGI 1990, 2000,

2010, 2015). It reveals a sociodemographic profile and the geographic distribution of children born in Mexico and in the United States who migrate from the north to the south.

Chapter 3 presents a typology of the migratory experiences of children. Specifically, we seek to define the different types of international child migrants living in Mexico and explain why it is important to differentiate among them. This chapter focuses on school-age children and explains how the typologies have been constructed and modified. Chapter 4 shifts attention to the migratory experience of children by addressing their geographic itineraries from the United States to Mexico. This chapter intends to provide answers to questions specifically about geography and child migration. Some of these questions apply to all children in our study, such as where had the children been before they arrived in Mexico? And where did they live and study in the United States?

Chapter 5 focuses on the migratory experience of both U.S.-born children and "return" migrants. We use quotation marks for the term "return" because, in the case of the children born in the United States, moving to Mexico is not a "return." They arrived for the first time in a country unknown to them. This chapter seeks to capture the migratory experience from the United States to Mexico from the perspective of children. The children experience not just a change of country but often an abrupt change of context (for example, moving from Brooklyn to Xayacatlán de Bravo, in Puebla). Drawing from the children's experiences, this chapter synthesizes the social integration (or nonintegration) of child migrants into Mexican society and into the communities to which they arrive. However, the integration of children into Mexican society and its institutions is addressed in detail in chapter 6, where we discuss the "institutional reception" of international child migrants in Mexico. We focus on the most important mediating institution in the socialization of children: the school. Here we try to summarize the key findings from our research over the past twenty-five years.

Chapter 7 also discusses the integration of children, but this time we focus on their families, with special emphasis on the dispersion of families, an aspect that we believe is quite significant. International child migrants are much more likely to live apart from their parents than nonmigrant children. We present evidence that living apart from their families for a period during childhood or adolescence is a constitutive part of these children's migratory experience. Integration into Mexican society is hampered by the fact that families are still divided by the border. This information about families serves as a preamble to chapter 8, which specifically explores the integration of children as a "subjective itinerary." For this we drew inspiration from the analysis carried out by Shinji Hirai and Rebeca Sandoval (2016) about the subjective trajectories of young people pertaining to the 1.5 generation who returned to Mexico by their own decision (before or after coming of age).

Last, in our conclusions we present public-policy issues that emerged from our findings. Mexico has gone from being a migrant-sending country to becoming a migrant-receiving country, and, as such, questions about political, educational, economic, and social integration should be incorporated into the public agenda regarding migration. Before tackling each of these issues, we want to delineate the characteristics of the methodological dialogue that made this book possible and to inform the reader of the sources used throughout the different chapters.

THE METHODOLOGICAL DIALOGUE

Over the course of two decades, a team of anthropologists, pedagogues, linguists, psychologists, sociologists, and demographers have carried out diverse studies about child migrants who arrive in Mexico from the United States. All of these researchers are familiar with methodologies specific to their discipline: standardized linguistic tests, participant observations, in-depth interviews, surveys, census databases analysis, focus groups, and ethnography, among others. As Louis-André Gérard-Varet and Jean-Claude Passeron (1995) point out, each of these methods refers to equally valid and valuable scientific rationalities. This understanding of methodological complementarity led Bruno Péquignot and his colleagues (2022) to invite social scientists to emulate physicists and biologists by building methodologically ecumenical communities:

> We are under the impression that if sociologists have failed to recognize the principle of noncontradiction, if their conflicts resemble those that destroyed

biologists a century and a half ago, and physicists more than fifty years ago, that is probably because they invest too much effort in explaining *all* the phenomena and *all* the processes while conducting all the research procedures with the help of one single battery at their disposal. (2022: 281; translated, emphasis added)

The dialogue that we have tried to encourage throughout these years and in this book is reflective of our "ecumenical" scientific community, a concept coined by Bruno Péquignot and Pierre Tripier (2000) more than twenty years ago. They assert that the principle of noncontradiction lends researchers to defining and valuing "truth" based on a certain scale and through a certain perspective: this "truth," though, can also be seen as "false" when seen from another scale and through another perspective. However, these contradictions need not necessarily turn into methodological rivalries but rather can be understood as complementary to each other once researchers accept how the different "truths" operate and are applied in the natural sciences.

DATA SOURCES

The surveys carried out in the months of December 2004, 2005, 2009, and 2010 constitute, as a whole, our primary data source. Over the years we have surveyed 57,422 children, among whom 1,486 are migrants from the United States and 865 were born in the United States.[12] We asked children and adolescents with no international migratory experience about the migration of their family members and about their relationships with the child migrants enrolled in their schools. We asked the migrant children about their migratory itineraries, their families' involvement in the migration process, their arrival in Mexico, and their school career. Nonmigrant children answered thirty-seven questions (thirty-three multiple-choice questions and four open-ended questions), while migrant children answered seventy-one questions (sixteen of them were open-ended questions). At the beginning there was a clear reason for using the survey as the initial method for the project: none of the participating researchers had any idea whether there were international child migrants from the United States living in Mexico (we were six years away from the 2010 Mexican population census). We began this journey exclusively because of our intuition that arose during the fieldwork we carried out in schools in Georgia. The survey was the most suitable instrument to provide evidence that children from the United States were living in Mexico. Not only would the survey prove that they existed, but it would also provide an estimated number of child migrants enrolled in primary and secondary schools (public and private) in a certain federative entity (i.e., a state) in the country during a specific school year. The first survey was conducted in the state of Nuevo León in 2004 and the last one in Jalisco in 2010; both surveys utilized representative samples. In all the cases, schools, groups, and children were selected through a stratified random sampling method.

Three main reasons guided our decision to conduct surveys about child migrants in schools. The first is methodological in nature: by defining schools as a research site reflective of society, we could easily select a manageable stratified and representative sample size. The second is political in nature: if children from the United States were enrolled in schools in Mexico, then the findings of the research could have an impact on educational policy by supporting decision-makers in creating programs that meet the needs of these children and that take into account their unique identities and experiences as international migrants arriving to Mexico. We hoped that the information provided by the students enrolled in schools would capture the attention of education authorities. The third reason is rather scientific in nature: at the beginning of the project, we decided to engage in a dialogue between the sociology and anthropology of international migration as well as the sociology and anthropology of education. In other words, we sought to know both the migratory trajectories of the children and their school trajectories—and the interplay between these trajectories. For this reason the initial phase of our research focused on the schools, on children's educational trajectories and fragmentations, and on the complex transition from the U.S. to the Mexican school system. By doing so we wanted to emphasize the fact that, for child migrants, migration implies migrating from U.S. schools to Mexican schools (Zúñiga and Hamann 2008; Valdéz Gardea 2011). Over time the emphasis on schooling gave way to other aspects of the migratory experience of children.

We now acknowledge that conducting surveys in schools was a practical, wise, and methodologically valid decision that, at the same time, brought on an important limitation: not all children and adolescents who move from the United States to Mexico enroll in schools. For some (we do not know how many), migration leads to school dropout, defined as a permanent or temporary interruption of the child's school trajectory. Others do enroll in schools in Mexico when they arrive but then drop out at a later time. (In this case we know how many because of a project we are currently carrying out in the state of Morelos.) We now know that these children do not actually abandon school, but rather the Mexican school abandons them.

Our secondary data source comes from unstructured interviews with 191 children. All the interviews were transcribed and compiled in a database of narrations, responses, and testimonies of more than one thousand pages. The interviews sought to reconstruct the children's migratory and school trajectory in the United States and in Mexico in an understandable format. Some of these interviews depict eloquent stories because the children we interviewed trusted us and because they possessed outstanding narrative skills. Others are concise and limited to brief answers. Most of the interviews were conducted in Spanish; approximately one-sixth were conducted in English or alternated between both languages. In a few exceptional cases, the interviews were curtailed as we realized that the children felt uncomfortable talking about events in their life or their relatives, most of them painful experiences associated with migration.

The third data source is composed of information we collected from the interviews with teachers and school administrators. We conducted 83 interviews across the five Mexican states. In all the unstructured interviews, we addressed five topics that we considered important: (1) the visibility of the child migrants (we wanted to know if the teachers or principals were aware of the presence of these children in their schools); (2) the challenges these children were facing in schools (according to the teachers); (3) how the teachers and principals explained the challenges the children were facing; (4) the kind of relationship that the children's parents had with the Mexican school; and (5) educational policy recommendations to better serve these children's needs.

The fourth data source is less systematized but still very valuable. It consists of the field notes taken by all researchers who participated in these projects: notes on schools, school relationships, and localities where the children lived. In the first four states, we did not visit the child migrants at their homes. As of 2013, when we began our research in the state of Morelos, we started taking field notes about their homes, communities, parents, grandparents, siblings, and other relatives.

Last, our analysis of surveys and interviews is complemented with nationally representative data from Mexico and the United States. While this data does not provide information on children's mobility, it does offer a general view of our focal population and the changes over the past twenty-five years. Starting with the data collected from the samples in the 1990, 2000, and 2010 Mexican *Population and Housing Census* (INEGI 1990, 2000, 2010) and the 2015 Mexican *Intercensal Survey* (INEGI 2015), we analyzed the changes in volume, sociodemographic profiles, geographic distribution, and household data of children born in the United States and of Mexican children who returned to the country after having lived in the United States. U.S. databases were also used to identify the presence of Mexican and second-generation children in the United States. In this case, we used the nationally representative data collected by the U.S. Census Bureau for the *American Community Survey* (U.S. Census Bureau 2016). Finally, we revisit Mexican data sources to provide a comprehensive picture of the school situation (attendance and completed education) of international child migrants in Mexico.

1 Theoretical Journey

From a demographic perspective, international migrant children and adolescents currently living in Mexico are individuals aged zero to seventeen years who, at some point in their lives, moved from the United States (or other countries in the world) to Mexico. This demographic definition responds to both legal (status as a minor) and geopolitical (crossing national borders) criteria. The latter part of the definition, that of "international migrant," can sometimes pose problems for demographers because an international migrant must be a person who resides in the destination country for a reasonably long period. An accurate definition will ensure, for example, that tourists or commuters are not counted as a part of the migration flow.[1] From the anthropological and sociological perspectives, this demographic definition is only a point of departure—it is not complete. In this chapter we synthesize our attempts to elaborate this definition by incorporating political, geographic, symbolic, and social dimensions that emerged throughout our research in efforts to theoretically capture the unique experiences of international migrant children and adolescents.

GEOGRAPHIC DISLOCATION

Let us return to Georgia, where school principals told us that, to their astonishment, "Hispanic children disappeared" (that is, after they had been enrolled in school). This apparently paradoxical trait of the children, who were migrants and children of immigrants, led us to question two somewhat contradictory aspects about their experiences: their geographic migration trajectory and their integration into the destination society. The first stems from studies about the geography of migration, focusing on territorial mobility. The second comes from the theoretical discussions about the integration of migrants, centering on their sense of belonging to a particular society. Because international migrants come from and belong to a society different than the one in which they arrive, they must undergo a process of integration. Since the beginning of the twentieth century, this has been referred to as the "assimilation process" in U.S. sociological literature—a concept that emerged from the work of sociologists at the Chicago School during the first half of the twentieth century (Park and Burgess 1921; Fuller 1939; Park 1950).

First, we look at the process of assimilation of migrant children and the children of immigrants. Since the nineteenth century, school in the United States has been conceived as a mediating institution between society and the state (Orfield 1998; Lamphere 1992a; Goode, Schneider, and Blanc 1992). In this role the school gives meaning to the national society while also legitimizing social stratification and interethnic borders (Hamann 2001). For all children, but especially for migrant children and children of immigrants, school is authorized as the primary means of assimilation. As Paula Fass so eloquently explains,

> Too little attention had been paid to schools as social sites and lively arenas for experience, to those who inhabited the schools, or the populations served by the schools. Moreover, those populations were often and repeatedly composed of immigrants, and the experience of immigrants and their children at school was, I believed, the necessary subject of understanding how American society was created and how the nation came to be defined. Immigrants, and minorities more generally, were critical to the American social experience. (2007, 3–4)

Through this lens, school in the United States not only imposes language, political principles, and axioms of social interaction as essential elements of belonging to the nation but also progressively prepares children and adolescents to become responsible and productive adults in a local society. This second mission of the school in the United States is a special characteristic of the country's school system, as K–12 schooling is decentralized and funded by local taxes. Within this context the institution is committed through its resources, personnel, and programs to an assimilationist approach that encompasses both the national and the local spaces in which the children will function when they reach adulthood.[2]

The second defining aspect of these focal children is that they are migrants—that is, they accompany adults in their migratory mobility: they cross borders, and these movements are a constitutive part of their socialization experience (i.e., they move away or "disappear"). It is not settlement and belongingness to a territory that defines them but geographic dislocation. Their parents and families participate in what Michael Peter Smith and Luis Eduardo Guarnizo call "transnationalism from below" (1998). That is to say, as large transnational companies move within different national and regional spaces seeking the best conditions for return on capital (i.e., transnationalism from above), migrant workers move and disperse, strategically seeking to maximize their opportunities and minimize their risks.[3] Children participate in this game, and, as a result, multilocalization is part of their life experience.

Taking into consideration both of these conceptual components (assimilation and mobility), Edmund Hamann proposed that international child migrants be defined as sojourner children or students: "I take the term sojourner from Hackenberg's (1995, 248) referral to the sojourner versus settler debate that has been ongoing in international migration research circles for several decades (e.g., Chavez 1988). That debate focuses on when/whether transnational newcomers to a receiving community should be considered permanent members" (2001, 37).

The sojourner population is made up of people who are not necessarily permanent residents. This means that sojourners are the product of vicissitudes inherent to the place to where they migrated and to their own decisions. Be that as it may, this population is not deeply rooted in their place of residence and can easily remigrate or be dislocated. Often sojourn-ers' "life worlds are neither 'here' nor 'there' but at once both 'here' and 'there'" (M. Smith 1994, 17). As Hamann (2001) pointed out, sojourner students and their families are clear examples of what Smith and Guarnizo (1998, 18) call "the new transnational working class," a term that empha-sizes the fact that crossing and recrossing borders are the social practices that ontologically define sojourner children.

At the same time, Hamann (2001) clarifies that common categories used in the U.S. literature to describe these children (e.g., "Latinx," "poor," "undocumented," or "English learners") do not capture the essential, defining element of child migrants' experiences: their geographic disloca-tion. Still, dislocation cannot be understood as a notion that fits into the demographic dichotomy of "emigration / immigration" because an emi-grant is someone who moves away from a place and an immigrant is someone who has settled in a new place. The geographic mobility of sojourner children appears to be somewhere in between this dichotomy, and they should be understood as semipermanent immigrants or perma-nent immigrants. This ductility of children's experience indicates that their lives are multilocal and the ties that they have to their geographic origins and destinations must be delineated accordingly. Children will develop multiple allegiances and will become vulnerable especially because, according to the state, they do not exist (or their existence is noted only when they "disappear").

Such is the case of Abel, whom we met in Jerez, Zacatecas, in November 2005, when he was fifteen years old and enrolled in a local high school. He was born in Jerez and, when he was nine months old, moved with his parents to a city in the United States whose name he did not remember. He knew that he lived in different places throughout the United States until they settled in Saint Louis, Missouri, when he was old enough to enroll in kindergarten. There, he attended primary school through the sixth grade. When he was twelve years old, his mother became seriously ill and passed away. Due to these circumstances, intensified by the fact that Abel was not authorized to reside in the United States, his father decided to send Abel to the city of Chihuahua. Abel's father, who was suffering from diabetes, and Abel's younger sister, who was born in the United States, continued living in Saint Louis. Abel arrived in Chihuahua to live with his aunt (his mother's sister). After two years in Chihuahua, he was sent to Jerez to live with his older cousin's family "because here I have more relatives." After that we do not know what came next for Abel, who is now an adult. What we do know is that, at age fifteen, he had a keen awareness of how dislocation was inherent to the lives of international migrants.

Once child migrants are envisaged as sojourners, the assimilatory function of school is nearly disabled. Schools require habitual and permanent attendance to properly fulfill this function. Thus, sojourner children challenge the antonymy between "settler" and "sojourner," giving way to categories of students that institutions cannot assimilate, such as "potentially mobile resident" and "almost-settled sojourner," like Abel. He was a resident of Missouri, or at least that was what he and his teachers believed. In fact, for many years (too many considering his young age) and due to familial and legal circumstances (he was born in Mexico and was not authorized to live in the United States), he became a sojourner. But when we met him in Jerez, he was still thinking of a way to return to Missouri not only because his father and sister lived there but because he still considered Saint Louis his home. Educational institutions, both in the United States and in Mexico, do not acknowledge or incorporate Abel's reality as a sojourner in any way in the curriculum or in the schooling experience writ large.

It could be argued that not all international child migrants are sojourners, as many become more or less permanent residents of the destination countries to which they were brought by their parents. Certainly, this is valid, but such a narrow geographic perspective ignores the current sociopolitical and legal context in which child migration to the United States occurs (and which also explains the children's presence in Mexico). Their parents, with very few exceptions, are foreigners in the destination country. Documented or not, they are potentially deportable, and therefore the condition of "dislocability"—the state of being subject to dislocation—will always be present in the children's lives, even for those who are considered citizens by jus soli (Genova 2005; Dreby 2015).[4] Many children born in the United States are in Mexico because their parents and some of their older siblings decided to return to Mexico due to fear of deportation.

In the United States, the legal, law enforcement, and political contexts regarding the deportability of migrants, especially Mexicans, are framed by several pieces of federal legislation: the Illegal Immigration Reform and Immigration Responsibility Act of 1996, the Antiterrorism and Effective Death Penalty Act of 1996, and the Patriot Act of 2001. Together these constitute a triad of federal regulations created to identify, criminalize, incarcerate, and deport noncitizens living in the United States who are deemed to be "undesirable" or "dangerous" (Hagan, Castro, and Rodriguez 2010). These legal regulations were accompanied by operational initiatives that have had devastating effects on migrants and their families, two of which stand out: the Safe Communities Program and the 287(g) Program. The Safe Communities Program is a deportation program enforced by U.S. Immigration and Customs Enforcement (ICE) agents and allows local city and county police to identify and expel undocumented people. The 287(g) Program is named for Section 287(g) of the Immigration and Nationality Act and authorizes local police agencies to enforce immigration laws, consequently turning them into immigration agents trained and supervised by ICE (Hernández-León and Zúñiga 2016). Within this institutional context, the dislocability of children of immigrants or of migrant children is not a hypothetical question but a constant and threatening possibility.

Dislocability does not end when the children arrive in Mexico. Mexican society and its economy and institutions create their own dynamics of expulsion. Low-paying jobs, schools unable to respond to the needs of migrant children, families divided by the border, and discriminatory local environments sometimes force children to remigrate, especially those who have dual citizenship.

FRAGMENTED SOCIALIZATION

Hamann's (2001) concept of migrant children as sojourners was further strengthened when we came into contact with child migrants in Mexico. In Nuevo León and Zacatecas, we found children who were born in Mexico and moved to the United States when they were very young. We also found those who were in the United States and arrived in Mexico before reaching school age. Some migrated when they had already entered adolescence. Most had passed from one school system to the other at least once or twice. Many of those born in the United States began their schooling there and later came to Mexico, undergoing a school transition. Many of those born in Mexico began their schooling in Mexico, then migrated to the United States, enrolled in schools there, and then, after a period, returned to their country of birth. They changed school systems twice. We also found children who had gone through school transitions three or four times. A few of them transitioned from one school system to the other every year. These children participated in their families' circular and seasonal migration, as is the case with the children we met in the northern municipalities of Nuevo León and in some places in Zacatecas.

We also discovered that children often lived apart from their parents for short or long periods. Some child migrants were living in Mexico with their grandparents, aunts, or uncles. Other children had lived in the United States with only one parent while the other was absent. In short, all of this led us to discover that the label of "sojourner" (i.e., dislocation) did not encompass all of these children's experiences. In an effort to fully capture what the children were going through, we coined the term "fragmented socialization" (Zúñiga, Hamann, and Sánchez García 2008). Fragmented socialization speaks not only to the migrant children's geographic dislocation but to their fractured school and familial trajectories. Or, to put it differently, geographic dislocations almost always involve institutional and symbolic fractures.

Theories of socialization (Durkheim 1922; Mead 1972; Berger and Luckmann 1991; Dubar 2000) are based on the premise that, in a society, members of new generations (children and adolescents) internalize a relatively unified symbolic universe that makes it possible to maintain a mostly stable social order—that is to say, a social order that reduces anomie, friction, and conflict. Through the work of the aforementioned authors, we can infer that the symbolic universe to be internalized is one imposed by the state. Thus, for new members of society, internalizing the dominant symbolic order includes the formation of citizenship, the inculcation of national precepts, and the imposition of shared beliefs. And it is school—the state's ideal institution—that is charged with instilling citizenship, beliefs, precepts, and national loyalty.

Socialization theorists do not consider child migration and assume that minors do not come into contact with opposing symbolic worlds throughout their socialization process. In fact, Peter Berger and Thomas Luckmann (1991) argue that, to be effective, a necessary condition for socialization is limited contact with other possible social worlds that compete with the symbolic universe that is to be inculcated. For socialization to be completed successfully, children should not have contact with other possible societies, and, if they do, this contact must be supervised by adults to avoid contamination between the social worlds. The purpose of socialization, then, is for children to internalize their parents' social world as the only world, not as one of many possible worlds. But when exposure to opposing worlds is unavoidable (a crucial component of an international child migrants' experience), then the "naturalness" of the social world in which children are trained, educated, and socialized is called into question. As a result, migrant children navigate between different worlds that do not necessarily complement one another.

With this in mind, it can be argued that the principal condition for an international child migrants' successful primary socialization—avoiding contamination from other social worlds—is not met. Generally speaking, their socialization process unfolds like this. For children of immigrants (children born in the United States to Mexico-born parents), contradictions arise between family socialization and school socialization. Amid these contradictions school may come out victorious and the children, who are U.S. citizens by birthright, will subjectively identify with the U.S. citizenship and proclaim their allegiance to the United States, and English will be their dominant oral and written language, if not their only language. If their parents' approach to socialization is capable of resisting the symbolic power of the school, second-generation children may develop bicultural and bilingual competencies that will allow them to comfortably move between two symbolic worlds. However, due to the demands of everyday life such as friendships and social discourse groups, second-generation youth are likely to identify more with the society in which they were born and educated than with the society from which their parents originate. One issue of concern is that members of the second generation are also members of segregated, and sometimes linguistically isolated, minority groups (Valdés 2001). The quintessential conditions of belonging to minority groups lead these second-generation children and young people into processes of "segmented assimilation" (Zhou 1997). According to theories about socialization, adults who are members of the second generation simultaneously identify with the segments of the national society (i.e., the United States) and segments of the society from which their parents came (i.e., Mexico).

The same thing happens to child migrants, especially those considered 1.5 and 1.75 generations, who are taken to destination countries by their parents or relatives. The substantial difference between these children's experiences and those who are considered second generation is that these children are not citizens of the destination country. The socialization process becomes even more complicated if migrant children have entered the destination country without authorization. When they become of age, they discover their "illegality" (Gonzales 2011) and become aware of the fact that this will always function as a glass ceiling that will prevent them from fully integrating into the society in which school has prepared them to live as adults (Hirai and Sandoval 2016). If they return to Mexico, their birth country, these young people enter into a process of resocialization because they have been socialized in the United States and thus Mexican society is objectively and subjectively unknown to them (Anderson and Solis 2014).

International child migrants in Mexico also experience the discords and segregation that we described earlier as members of the second generation or the 1.5 generation; however, when they arrive in Mexico, they are no longer considered members of those generations and undergo their own fragmented socialization. Fragmentation occurs to different degrees of intensity. For now, let's look at the extreme cases: children who come to Mexico to live with relatives in small rural towns after having been schooled for several years in a metropolis in the United States experience more abrupt fragmentations in their socialization than those who arrive in Mexico at an early age and are accompanied by their parents. For the latter the symbolic influence of U.S. society and its institutions is practically nil. Even more contrasting are the experiences of children who participate in seasonal circular migration. They spend a few months in the United States and the rest of the year in Mexico for every single year during their childhood and adolescence (Panait and Zúñiga 2016). Many international child migrants living in Mexico find themselves in between these two extremes. However, in all cases the foundational components of the children's primary socialization are altered to a certain extent and in varying ways. These foundational components include social meanings that are created and sustained through language, local and national affiliations, the construction of the self, and the internalization of plausibility structures (the definition of what is sanctioned, permitted, and acclaimed by a local or national society).

To illustrate fragmented socialization, we present an excerpt from a conversation we had in September 2016 with Lulú, a fifteen-year-old girl, from Higuerón, Jojutla, in the Mexican state of Morelos. She arrived in Morelos when she was thirteen, after having lived most of her life in San Diego, California. Upon arriving in Morelos, she enrolled in junior high school, and shortly thereafter the teacher gave an exam that included drawings depicting some of Mexico's national heroes. The students had to identify them and write their names in a box under the drawing. As one would expect, Lulú did not recognize any of them, but she did feel confident enough to write the word "Indian" under the drawing representing Cuauhtémoc and the word "British" under the drawing representing Hernán Cortés. This anecdote causes all of Lulú's family members to burst out laughing during the numerous family gatherings to which we have been invited since 2013.

Fragmented socialization does not equate to truncated socialization. International child migrants are not mutilated human beings: Lulú is not "broken" or "defected," in spite of the humiliation she suffered in junior high school. They are children who learn how to negotiate different adult worlds. All these worlds are equally legit: those represented by their families (in the United States and in Mexico) and those represented by schools (in the United States and in Mexico). Their experiences in learning how to negotiate social worlds are mediated by their changing social circles and local contexts. These children are much more than bilingual individuals—some of them are binational individuals—they are children and adolescents who learn to move between competing ritual and normative worlds.

TRANSNATIONAL STUDENTS

As our research progressed and our knowledge about migrant children's school trajectories deepened, we became aware of the fact that focusing on the fragmented aspects of the socialization process left out an important component to these children's migratory experiences: they move from one school system to another school system, and, in the eyes of the children and their parents, both systems are equally legitimate.

Transitioning between school systems inevitably causes fractures in children's linguistic and cognitive development, teaching and learning experiences, and national affiliations. However, at the same time, these transitions foster the development of metacognitive skills that permit children to link the formal learning that happens in schools with the informal learning provided by the social contexts in which they are immersed. Acknowledging the integral role of transitions from the U.S. education system to the Mexican education system, then, led us to adopt the concept of "transnational students."

We made this decision, recognizing the theoretical risks involved. The theory of transnationalism has received strong criticism since 2004, particularly from Roger Waldinger (2006, 2008b) and Waldinger and David Fitzgerald (2004). These authors are quite clear in their critique: "Many international migrants may engage in trans-state social action on one form or another, but transnationalism is a relatively rare condition of being. . . . Likewise, 'transmigrants', understood as a 'class of persons', generally do not exist" (Waldinger 2008b, 9). The authors' critique of transnationalism stems from myriad sources and lines of thought, of which we highlight two. First, they assert that all present and past international migrants maintain ties with their communities and countries of origin, and this permits the circulation of goods, information, and people. These ties are inherent to the international migration process, and therefore the labels "transnationalism" or "transmigrant" add nothing novel to understanding this experience. Rather, they mislead us to believe that only contemporary international migrants have created networks of connections with their countries of origin and suggest that national boundaries have been gradually fading away.

Second, a hallmark characteristic of the twentieth and early twenty-first centuries is the fact that national boundaries have not disappeared. In fact, borders have been strengthened, and federal efforts to prevent foreigners from entering national territories have become increasingly severe and effective, to such an extent that it is widely accepted that our age is characterized by the "obsession" to transform national borders into hermetic dams (Foucher 2007). Drawing on these realities, Waldinger and Fitzgerald (2004) conclude that international migrants are foreigners and that their ties with their countries and communities of origin are inevitably conditioned by the rules and ordinances established by the receiving countries. Consequently, they assert that the idea of "transnational spaces" is naive at best.

These criticisms of transnationalism are irrefutable. So why do we refer to international child migrants in Mexico as "transnational students"? What does this label add to our understanding of these children? First, it is essential to clarify that we do not use nouns (transnationalism or transmigrant) but rather the adjective "transnational," which indicates the quality—real or potential—that an individual has for moving from one national space to another. In words such as translucent, transport, transcend, trans-Siberian, the meaning of the prefix *trans* means "to cross" and "to pass through"—that is to say, it means "to move to the other side." The adjective "transnational" cannot be replaced by "binational" because the latter indicates the right to two nationalities, a status that only some of the international child migrants living in Mexico possess (those born in the United States). Second, the noun being qualified is "student" (not "child," "boy," or "girl"), thereby indicating that it is the school experience that enables children to pass through two national societies, not their familial upbringing.

With these clarifications, we argue that the category of "transnational students" adds value to understanding migrant children in Mexico. On one hand, it highlights the subjectivity of primary socialization: when children are enrolled in schools within a particular country, they not only learn the "national" language but also are instilled with national loyalty and a love for that country. They have contact with legitimate agents— their teachers—who, while exercising symbolic authority, convey the importance of belonging to a national community and of learning to respect the nation's founding myths. These are essential to creating and maintaining the social fabric in societies made up of millions of people and to reproducing the tacit social habits and rules valued in the dominant society. Of course, all this occurs to varying degrees due to students' acceptance or resistance and their individual beliefs. However, the symbolic authority of the school succeeds in producing cultural citizenship with internalized affiliations, standards, beliefs, and values shared to a greater or lesser degree by all or by many members of the national society. As such, acquiring "transnational" characteristics, the ability to transit between nations, depends entirely on children's exposure to the influence of the schools in those nations. While school has the capability to inculcate national concepts, this does not necessarily always translate into reality.

The following vignette from field notes taken during school visits in Georgia in March 1998 provides a snapshot of how the process of education influences children's subjectivity. In a classroom at a school in the city of Dalton, where most of the students were from Michoacán and San Luis Potosí (or their parents were from Michoacán and Potosí), the teacher was explaining (in English) the origin and meaning of the Thanksgiving holiday:

> In the year 1620, a little ship came to America. It was called the Mayflower. There were one hundred people on the ship. The people were called Pilgrims. They came from England. The Pilgrims wanted to have their own church. They could not have their own church in England. The first winter in America was very cold. The Pilgrims did not have much food. . . . The Pilgrims got sick. Many Pilgrims died. It [w]as [a] terrible time. In the spring, Indians came to visit. They were friendly. Two Indians could speak English! And say: hello! The Indians showed the Pilgrims how to plant corn. The Pilgrims worked hard. . . . They learned to hunt the turkeys that lived in the woods. When fall came, the Pilgrims were very happy because they had a lot of food for the winter. They made a big dinner. They invited the Indians to come and eat with them. The Indians brought deer for the dinner. . . . They ate and ate for three days. The Pilgrims were thankful for the good things they had. This was the first Thanksgiving in America.

We do not know the extent to which these narratives resonated in the students' subjectivity or to what degree the students identified with the narrative of the first Thanksgiving. What we do know is that the teacher's symbolic authority served its socialization function by narrating to the students the U.S. national origin myth. As these children subjectively begin to assimilate that narrative, they gradually gain eligibility to belong to the national community. But if they do not, they will remain partially excluded from it. For some of the international child migrants in Mexico, the educational process of the schools in the United States has left a significant and lasting print on their minds and souls, while others spent short periods (one or two years) in these schools. For those who were born in the United States and came to Mexico before school age, while they are international migrants, their subjectivity lacks transnational characteristics.[5]

Distinctly, the objective aspects of the adjective "transnational" are determined not by children's school trajectories but by their right to citizenship by jus soli. International child migrants who are living in Mexico and were born in the United States have the right to both nationalities. They can move across the border in both directions just like any citizen and do not need to apply for visas or worry about being repatriated. They can enter—and they do—the United States or Mexico as full members of both nations. This privilege is independent of the education they have received. Thus, children born in the United States who arrived in Mexico before starting their schooling will enjoy these perks even without knowing how to speak English.

Dual citizenship is an advantage that is not without drawbacks. Waldinger (2008b) points out repeatedly how, throughout history, dual citizenship has been in conflict with the concomitant loyalty expected of members who belong to one—and only one—nation. Holders of dual nationality may be viewed as potential traitors. While national laws are not explicit on this issue, and dual citizenship is not prohibited, mononational citizens tend to be skeptical about people who claim to also belong to another national society. This skepticism, as Waldinger explains, becomes an exclusionary force when the "other" citizenship is that of an enemy or potential adversarial country. In the event of war, as the history of the United States shows, dual citizenship is untenable: in this case, dual citizenship holders must decide their loyalty and renounce one of their two citizenships.

International child migrants living in Mexico are protected from these reactions because Mexico is not an enemy or potential enemy of the United States. Objectively speaking, it is very likely that they will make use of their dual citizenship. These children frequently refer to their dual citizenship and are able to move freely between both countries, brandishing their U.S. citizenship when entering the United States and their Mexican citizenship when entering Mexico. In this sense they are transnational individuals, because they can transit within and between both countries and enjoy the political rights each nation grants its citizens. Here, it is worth revisiting Waldinger and Fitzgerald's (2004) position: the movement of people across national boundaries is essentially a political act because it implies the presence of foreigners within a specific national space. From this perspective children living in Mexico with dual citizenship embody a different political performance when they cross the border: objectively, they will not enter either of the two countries as foreigners, and, as they were educated in both countries, they do not feel like foreigners in either Mexico or the United States. The U.S.-born children being educated in Mexico are becoming true transnationals through a process that is not only de jure but also de facto.

THE 0.5 GENERATION

When we were conducting fieldwork at a junior high school in Lagos de Moreno, Jalisco, in February 2011, we interviewed Karla, who was thirteen years old and enrolled in her first year of secondary school (i.e., seventh grade). She came to the room where we were interviewing students who had been enrolled in schools in the United States and had returned to Mexico. After some small talk and jokes, we began the interview and soon found out that Karla had actually began her schooling in Mexico: she was born in Los Angeles and came to Lagos de Moreno when she was four years old. Consequently, Karla had no schooling experience in the United States. However, we decided to continue with the interview. To our surprise, despite the fact that she did not speak English and was largely unfamiliar with Los Angeles and that her parents and sisters lived in Lagos, she had a very clear vision of her adult life: she would study tourism or hotel management in Los Angeles or in Las Vegas, because her cousins, her father's cousins, and her uncles (her mother's brothers) were all living in those cities. Later during the conversation, she recalled that she also had relatives in Chicago. Karla finished the interview by confidently stating, "That's why I have my American passport." How is it that these dreams and aspirations are able to manifest, even though Karla's subjectivity and symbolic world had been constructed exclusively in Lagos de Moreno? Karla's perspective of her future is indicative of her belonging to the

0.5 generation, even though her knowledge of the United States has been limited to her first four years life and to the information that her relatives in the United States have relayed to her.

Based on this finding, we began to discuss the uniqueness of the migration process of children with dual citizenship, regardless of whether their schooling was carried out in both countries or exclusively in Mexico. These children are U.S. citizens—and well aware of this fact—who are being educated in Mexico. The vast majority of these children feel Mexican and identify with Mexican society (at the national and local levels); nevertheless, many of them are imagining their future in the country where they were born. Like Karla, these children are not deceiving themselves because they have a network of connections in various parts of the United States by way of family members, and they also have an U.S. passport.

With our findings we returned to the literature on the categories of generations of migration and suggested revisions to better represent these children. The labels "second generation" and "1.5 generation" lack empirical validity once children arrive in Mexico. Both labels relate to another society: those born in the United States are considered members of the second generation in U.S. society but not in Mexico. Those born in Mexico are members of the 1.5 generation, but only while living in the United States: back in Mexico this category in invalid. The children residing in Mexico are international migrants in every sense of the term. They migrate during their childhood or adolescence—that is, they cross national borders while still being schooled.

These are sojourner children. They are transnational students, and they also experience fragmented socialization. However, none of these categories reflect what Karla revealed to us. While living in Mexico (understood as the receiving country), they can imagine living their adult life in another nation. This is how we developed the new category of the 0.5 generation, which takes into consideration all the elements from the research on migrant generations, including country of birth, age of migration, stage of life, country where socialization is carried out, and dominant language (Warner and Srole 1945; Rumbaut 1994; Rumbaut and Ima 1988). The children's adjustment and integration into Mexican society depend on these elements (Rumbaut 2004), even while they may be imagining living their adult lives in the United States.

The expression "0.5 generation" encompasses both the mobility of these children and the fact that they belong to a generation of migrants while simultaneously calling attention to the reality that these children are not members of a migrant generation that has been previously conceptualized in the literature because they are Mexican by birth and the receiving country is Mexico. These children are not return migrants even though, theoretically speaking, those born in Mexico, who spent a period of their lives in the United States and then returned to Mexico, could be considered return migrants. However, the category of "return" dilutes their experience and disregards crucial elements that make them unique: they migrate while still children, they partially undergo socialization in the United States, and often English is the only language that they know how to read and write (see table 1).

Labeling all these children as return migrants (as their parents generally are labeled) can be misleading, especially when referring to those who moved to the United States at an early age and were socialized in that country and in its schools. These children, despite being Mexican by birth, often feel like foreigners in Mexico—at least initially upon their arrival. In the case of the U.S.-born children who had never been to Mexico, there would be even fewer reasons to classify them as return migrants.

The category of "0.5 generation" contains two important characteristics. The first is represented by the "zero," which indicates that these children, once they arrive in Mexico, have to start practically from zero. The "zero" expresses the fact these children's migration to Mexico makes the immigrant/emigrant dichotomy meaningless: while in Mexico, they are immigrants and emigrants at the same time. This is particularly relevant for children who lived in the United States without authorization and whose mobility is limited. If, in their adult life, they fail to obtain authorization to reside in the United States, they will be limited to living only in Mexico even though they have been educated in schools in the United States. They will remain immigrants/emigrants for a long portion of their life, if not forever.

The second unique characteristic is represented in the "point five." This is suggestive of an embryonic state, something that is in gestation and thus still unknown. A sort of uncertainty is entrenched in the migratory experience from the United States to Mexico of children aged nine, ten, or eleven, especially those who have the right to both nationalities. All the

Table 1 Comparison of second generation, 1.5 generation, and 0.5 generation
migrants between Mexico and the United States

Category	Definition	Characteristics	National context
Second generation	Children of Mexicans who migrated to the United States	Right to dual citizenship	United States
		Schooling in the United States (with exceptions)	
	Children born in the United States		
		English with native speaker proficiency (with exceptions)	
1.5 generation	Children of Mexicans who migrated to the United States	Right to Mexican nationality only	United States
	Children born in Mexico	Schooling begun in Mexico or the United States and continued in the United States	
		Varying English proficiency	
0.5 generation	Children who lived in the States United and arrived in Mexico before adulthood	Right to dual citizenship for those born in the United States	Mexico
		Right to Mexican nationality only for those born in Mexico	
		Arrival in Mexico after school enrollment in the United States	
		English as dominant language	

U.S.-born children we interviewed were aware of fact that, from a legal
perspective, they were both Mexican and U.S. citizens. As such, they could
study, live, and work in both countries without any legal restrictions.
However, both "zero" and "point five" apply to all international child
migrants in Mexico, regardless of their country of birth. There are chil-

dren who were born in the United States but do not plan to live there; for some this is because they witnessed how their parents were humiliated in that country. There are also children who were born in Mexico and who hope for the possibility of a visa to authorize their "return" to the United States, the country in which they were socialized.

The embryonic or gestational component of the 0.5 generation contains objective elements, such as the children's bilingualism, their practical knowledge of the two societies where they were educated, the academic knowledge acquired (history and geography of both countries), and the skills needed to negotiate multiple contexts. It also contains subjective elements, such as feelings of belonging, attachment to certain symbols, multiple affiliations, and multiple allegiances and loyalties. These children have experiences that distinguish them from their peers in schools and in their neighborhoods or in their local communities. Had they stayed in the United States and had been educated only in U.S. schools, these children would have been considered "Mexican Americans." But when they migrated to Mexico and enrolled in Mexican schools, their objective and subjective trajectories were substantially modified. The children and adolescents of the second generation or the 1.5 generation became children of the 0.5 generation: international migrants living and studying in Mexico, who are at the same time Mexicans raised in the United States and, some, U.S. citizens educated in Mexico.

It will be important for future research to address a series of comparative approaches for identifying the differences between second, 1.5, and 0.5 generations (Waldinger 2021). It is very likely that we are going to find substantive differences between immigrant children and children of immigrants who remained in the United States and those who belong to the 0.5 generation. It is very likely that these studies will offer evidence about the significant role played by bilingual skills, bicultural competencies, and binational statuses on the lives of these children.

CONCLUSIONS

Our intellectual journey over the past twenty years has been one of inquiry into and dialogue with various theoretical sources, which in turn have nurtured how we envisage and represent the uniqueness of child migration from the United States to Mexico. The first data we collected regarding children's geographic mobility led us to revisit the notions of "sojourner" and "settler," making it clear that spatial dislocation, be it real or potential, is one of the distinctive features of international child migrants living in Mexico. This feature opened the door to new inquiry into the fragmented socialization processes, both in a family context and at school, inherent to these children who now live in Mexico after having lived part of their lives in the United States. These symbolic, cognitive, emotional, and social fragmentations were not understood as deformations or weaknesses but rather revealed the transnational characteristic of the children's learning experiences. It is very likely that children who were enrolled in schools in the United States and are now studying in Mexico develop distinct competencies that help them feel at home in both countries.

The ability to move within and between both societies seemed to be a characteristic of those who had been exposed to educational processes in both countries, likely because it is in school where the skills necessary to integrate, at least partially, into each of these societies, are acquired. However, to our surprise, Karla showed us that a thirteen-year-old girl, born in Los Angeles and raised in Jalisco since the age of four, could wisely use the resources provided by her extended family living in the United States and by her birthright U.S citizenship. This component of the migratory experience that combines country of birth, age during migration, and stage of life led us to include international child migrants living in Mexico in the generational framework and to coin the category of "0.5 generation." This category emphasizes, first, the fact that Mexico represents a new starting point and, second, uncertainty about what the future will bring for these children especially, but not exclusively, for those who have the right to both nationalities.

After having thoroughly presented the theoretical foundations that frame the experiences of child migrants who came from the United States and are now living in Mexico and, particularly, having defined the concepts that capture these children's shared experiences, we will analyze national data from Mexico about this population's main sociodemographic characteristics and tendencies. To do so, we draw on the 1990, 2000, and 2010 Mexican censuses (INEGI 1990, 2000, 2010) and the *2015 Intercensal*

Survey (INEGI 2015). One limitation of these data sources is that they do not allow us to delve into the particularities of migratory movements such as age when migrating, family situation upon arrival in Mexico, and number of trips between countries, among others. Nevertheless, the size of these databases, their geographic coverage, and the compilation of multi-dimensional information throughout Mexico allow us to clearly illustrate the profile of child migrants, their regional distribution, and how they have changed over the past fifteen years.

2 The Demographics of Child Migration

It was not until very recently that migrant researchers began to pay attention to children's cross-border mobility. Up until this point, traditional Mexican migration had been described as a labor-driven migration pattern consisting predominantly of young, single males, while the others involved remained largely invisible. After the implementation of the Immigration Reform and Control Act (IRCA) in the late 1980s and early 1990s, new migration patterns emerged that combined labor movements with family movements. As a result, the proportion of women and children in the migration flows to the United States increased.[1] Additionally, the loss of circularity in migration flows during the 1990s (a result of reinforced of border security) led to the establishment of migrant family communities that included both U.S-born and Mexican-born children. As the population of both authorized and unauthorized migrants increased, mixed-status families formed and included both children who were U.S. citizens and those who did not have legal documents to be in the United States (Zúñiga and Hernández-León, 2005a).

In 2011 nearly eight hundred thousand children who were born in Mexico resided in the United States. In the same year, slightly more than four million children were born in the United States to Mexican parents, and, of these, nearly all (3.4 million) had both mothers and fathers who were born in Mexico (Giorguli et al. 2021). Given the size of this population and its rate of growth, studying children's integration into the school system(s) and their social mobility (as it was attached to both their parents' work and their schooling) became even more relevant to the research on migration. However, scholars almost exclusively focused on migrant children's trajectories and experiences in the United States. Essentially, the children of Mexican parents in the United States—regardless of their country of birth—were thought of as a settled population with low mobility toward Mexico. From this research we did not anticipate what the 2010 Mexican census data would show regarding the number of children who migrated from the United States to Mexico as a result of the Great Expulsion, a movement triggered by the development of strict immigration policies and by the 2008 economic recession.

Who are these school-age migrants? How many are there and how have their demographics and characteristics changed throughout recent decades? Data from the Mexican census and the *2015 Intercensal Survey* permitted us to trace the evolution of this focal population—children and adolescents ages zero to seventeen—from 1990 to the present. The Mexican census and the *2015 Intercensal Survey* were the best data sources to support delineating an overall portrait of child migrants in terms of number, geographic distribution, and some of their sociodemographic and household characteristics. Although not representative at the national level, the case studies of five Mexican states that we present in the following chapters provide greater details about the children's migratory trajectories in terms of the stage of life during which they migrated and their age when they arrived in Mexico as well as other relevant aspects to our study, such as school experience in one or in both countries. Despite the limitations of the Mexican census and of the *2015 Intercensal Survey*, these sources allow us to observe changes in the population of school-age child migrants in Mexico over time. These data capture all the child migrants, whether they were born in the United States or in Mexico, who were living in the United States five years prior to the census or to the *2015 Intercensal Survey*.[2]

THE MIGRATORY MOBILITY OF THE 0.5 GENERATION

Since 1990, data show that there has been a certain degree of migratory mobility of children from the United States to Mexico, though smaller in number compared to that of adults in migration flows. The 1990 census captures approximately 150,000 child and adolescent migrants, the majority (90 percent) of which were born in the United States. The child-migrant population in Mexico continued to increase over the next two decades, albeit at different rates, depending on place of birth and age group. The total number of migrant children almost doubled between 1990 and 2000, and it doubled again by 2010 (see table 2). After that there has been a decrease in the number of migrant children in Mexico, a statistic that coincides with the same trend in the return rate of adult migrants (Giorguli and Angoa 2019). In other words, in 2015 there was still a significant number of children arriving from the United States to Mexico, but this number was smaller than what was reported in 2010. This decrease is most clearly observed among the Mexican-born population and the population of children up to five years old, which diminished in size between 2010 and 2015. It is worth making a clarification about the U.S.-born population of children in the category of ages from six to seventeen. This age group has not significantly declined because this category is not limited only to children who arrived in the country within the past five years. The data for this category, then, includes the child-migrant population documented in the previous census because these children have been residing in Mexico for more than five years. Thus, the *2015 Intercensal Survey* includes migrant children who arrived in Mexico before 2010 as well as the new arrivals between 2010 and 2015.

The dramatic increase in the number of children with migratory experience in the United States between 1990 and 2010 is consistent with the greatest number of child migrants who moved to the United States since IRCA and who spent time in the United States before returning to Mexico. The percentage of U.S.-born children within this population of migrants who arrived in Mexico also increased, but at different rates depending on the age group. The growth of this population can be explained by the increase in family migration after the implementation of IRCA and is con-

Table 2   Population, ages zero to seventeen, residing in Mexico, by birthplace and
residence five years prior to the Mexican census or *Intercensal Survey*,
1990–2015

Migratory experience	1990	2000	2010	2015
U.S. born				
0-5 years	52,910	127,997	249,292	138,246
Percentage of change		141.9	94.8	−44.5
6-17 years	81,430	132,595	320,851	412,246
Percentage of change		62.8	142.0	28.5
Mexican born, living in the United States five years before the census*				
6-17 years	13,580	33,538	62,981	32,520
Percentage of change		147.0	87.8	−48.4
Total (U.S. born and Mexican born)	147,920	294,130	633,124	583,012
Percentage of change		98.8	115.3	−7.9

SOURCE: Our estimates are based on census samples (INEGI 1990, 2000, 2010) and the *2015 Intercensal Survey* (INEGI 2015).

NOTE: The percentage change refers to the 1990–2000 and 2000–2010 intercensal periods and to the 2010–15 quinquennium.

*The children in the age group zero to five years were not asked the question about their place of residence five years prior to the census date. As such, this information is not available for this population.

sistent with the joint experiences of couples, with or without children, who migrate to the United States.

The first decade of the twenty-first century saw the fastest growth in the number of Mexican migrants moving to the United States. In the years 2000 and 2005, the number of Mexicans who traveled north reached a historical high. While these figures are debatable, it is estimated that approximately 770,000 migrants left Mexico during 2000 and 670,000 in 2005 (Passel 2011). Between 2006 and 2010, the migration flow reversed. Emigration decreased and return migration increased considerably, reaching almost one million Mexicans between 2005 and 2010 (Masferrer 2012; Giorguli, García, and Masferrer 2016; Giorguli and Angoa 2019).

Demographically speaking, the first decade of the twenty-first century was one of turmoil in terms of migratory flows between Mexico and the United States. As paradoxical as it may seem, this decade began with the highest levels of migration from Mexico to the United Sates and ended with the most significant population flow in the opposite direction in the history of the Mexico-U.S. migratory circuit. Thus, it is critical that we ask, What happened to child migrants during these years? The number of entries of minors from the United States to Mexico continued to rise, but at different rates among two population groups—the U.S-born and the Mexican-born children. The number of Mexican-born, and U.S.-born migrant children under the age of six grew between 88 percent and 95 percent during the 2005–10 quinquennium. However, the category of U.S.-born children between the ages of six and seventeen stands out with the most dramatic increase. This group increased 1.4 times, partly due to the demographic inertia of the previous decade and partly due to new arrivals.

In 2010 the number of U.S.-born minors and of Mexican-born minors who returned to Mexico reached a historical level of 633,000 children. Most of these children came to Mexico to live with their parents (Giorguli and Gutiérrez 2012; Aguilar Zepeda 2014). In reference to the total migration from north to south, minors accounted for a third of the migration flow during the quinquennium, had the highest return rate between 2005 and 2010, and continue to represent the same proportion of migrants in the most recent data (2010–15) (Giorguli, García, and Masferrer 2016). The 2010 data highlight unprecedented proportions of this phenomenon and sparked a discussion in Mexico about the disadvantages that these children and adolescents face during their incorporation or reincorporation into the country, especially regarding integration into schools and access to health services.

As we previously stated, the data from the *2015 Intercensal Survey* show that the return rate from the United States to Mexico continued, yet slowed from 2010 to 2015. After the Great Expulsion and at the end of 2010, the number of Mexican-born school-age children who returned to Mexico decreased, although this number was still higher than that of 2000. In the case of Mexican-born children, it should be noted that the data indicate the number of minors residing in the United States five years before the census. Considering the trends form the previous decades, the number of children with migratory experience from the United States to Mexico would likely be considerably higher if the information were not limited to the five-year period. However, this is the way in which the questions are structured in both the Mexican census and in the *2015 Intercensal Survey.*

SOCIODEMOGRAPHIC CHARACTERISTICS OF THE 0.5 GENERATION AND CHANGES OVER TIME

The educational experiences of children and adolescents who come from the United States to Mexico vary according to their place of birth. While we assume that the population presented in table 2 share the experiences of having lived and possibly studied in the United States, and all these children were living in Mexico at the time of the census or *Intercensal Survey,* there are differences in their sociodemographic characteristics and in their location throughout the country, which suggest that their experiences upon arrival to Mexico and enrollment in Mexican schools may differ. Perhaps the first and clearest difference between the two groups lies in the age distribution. The available demographic data suggests that the general profile of child migrants born in the United States is younger than that of those born in Mexico. Particularly in 2010 the data show that the number of U.S.-born child migrants was highly concentrated within the age group of zero to five. Comparing the data on figure 1 with figure 2 (both focus on child migrants ages six to seventeen) clearly shows that the age profile of children born in the United States tends to be younger than those born in Mexico. In 2015, the last year of study, the majority of migrant children are concentrated within the age range of six to eleven, which is precisely the age range for primary school enrollment, according to Mexican regulations.

The concentration of migrant children in the younger age groups, especially in the year 2000, is illustrative of the U.S.-born children's arrival to Mexico even before they reach school age. The relatively lower presence of U.S.-born adolescents in Mexico could also indicate the fact that this population returns to the United States once they reach a certain stage in their educational trajectory (for example, enrolling in high school), and, due to

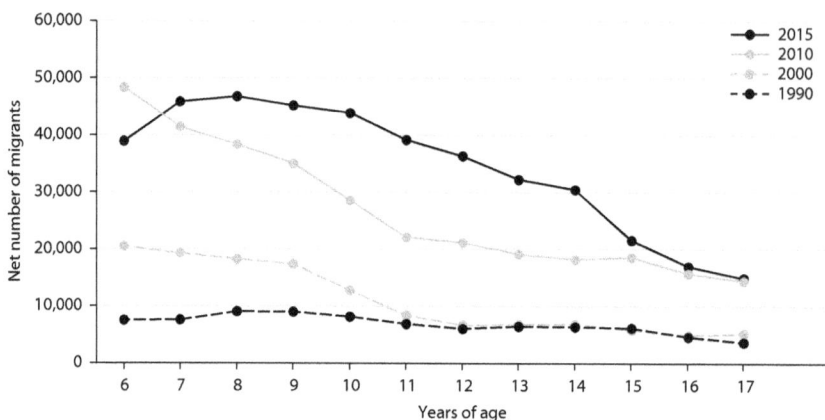

Figure 1. U.S.-born population, ages six to seventeen years, residing in Mexico, 1990–2015.

Source: Our estimates are based on census samples (INEGI 1990, 2000, 2010) and the *2015 Intercensal Survey* (INEGI 2015).

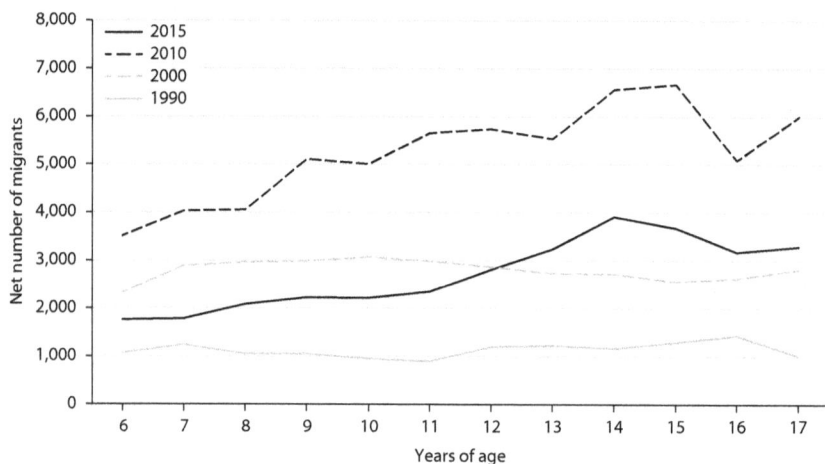

Figure 2. Mexican-born population, ages six to seventeen years, residing in the United States five years prior to the Mexican census or *Intercensal Survey*, 1990–2015.

Note: Because the children in the age group zero to five years were not asked for their place of residence five years prior to the census date, there is no information before the age of six for the Mexican-born children.

Source: Our estimates are based on census samples (INEGI 1990, 2000, 2010) and the *2015 Intercensal Survey* (INEGI 2015).

their dual citizenship, they have the option of going back to the United States to continue their studies.[3] However it may be, the data over time suggest that this is a population with intense cross-border mobility even in the early stages of life and that such mobility could interweave with educational decisions and experiences.

In contrast, Mexican-born minors who return to the country are more dispersed among different age groups. In younger age groups (ages six to twelve), the number is low while the number of adolescents aged sixteen and seventeen is considerable, especially in 2015. In the same year, one out of five young returnees were sixteen or seventeen years old. This may be an indicator of a different purpose of migration: returning to Mexico may not depend only on a family's strategies but also on the autonomous decisions of young people who have already left school, joined the work-force, and eventually became parents and formed a family of their own. We should not lose sight of the fact that, in Mexico, the transition to adult-hood at early ages is still frequent. According to the *2014 National Demographic Dynamics Survey* (INEGI 2014), before turning eighteen about half of the women in Mexico will have dropped out of school, 21 percent will have married, and 16 percent will have had their first child (Pérez Amador and Giorguli 2018). These are all possible reasons for the difference in age distribution between the two groups of child migrants according to their place of birth. However, these differences may also be reflective of the distinct social structures into which the children were born and thus may have existed since the children were born. As they stand, these musings remain hypotheses to be analyzed in the future.

The censuses also revealed interesting trends regarding the places of residence and geographic distribution of international child migrants in Mexico. While Mexico writ large is becoming increasingly urbanized, in the case of the children and adolescents who have moved from the United States to Mexico, the percentage of people living in urban settings have remained constant over the past twenty-five years and have actually begun to decrease, most noticeably within the Mexican-born group.[4] By the end of 2015, one in four migrants between the ages of six and seventeen years, regardless of their place of birth, lived in a rural community.[5]

The fact that most of these children migrate from urban environments in the United States but persistently return to rural communities in

Mexico (and data show that this number is growing) suggests that many child migrants experience starkly different life and school experiences between the two countries. In some cases children and adolescents migrate to their parents' communities of origin, and many of these communities are located in rural areas with less access to services and educational opportunities, in comparison not only to the United States but to Mexico in general. However, the majority of migrant youth live in urban areas that are not necessarily their parents' places of origin—that is, they live in different cities than those in which their parents were born (Masferrer and Roberts 2012). In any case the population-distribution data on the size of the place of residence suggest that child migrants have heterogeneous experiences and point to differences in access to social support networks, to social capital, and to educational opportunities that depend on the level of urbanization of the Mexican communities in which they settle or on their proximity to urban centers.

Finally, table 3 shows that, as with the broader patterns of general emigration, the distribution of regions to where school-age children return has changed. The data also suggest different settlement patterns according to a child's place of birth and age. In 2015, 62.5 percent of U.S.-born children under the age of six were living mostly in the northern states of Mexico. However, the concentration of child migrants in northern Mexico diminishes when we look at U.S.- and Mexican-born child migrants between the ages of six and seventeen. While the north continues to serve as a principal destination for the U.S.-born children, only 42.3 percent settled there in 2015, with a high concentration living in border states (Giorguli and Gutiérrez 2012). In fact, the data at the municipal level from the *2015 Intercensal Survey* show that the eleven municipalities with the highest number of child migrants are located in border states: Baja California, Chihuahua, Tamaulipas and Sonora. Two cities, Tijuana and Ciudad Juárez, are home to 15 percent of all child migrants nationwide and are located on the border: in Tijuana there were just under fifty thousand child migrants and in Ciudad Juárez there were more than forty thousand.

Northern Mexico, the traditional destination for return migration, became less significant for children ages six to seventeen coming from the United States. In contrast, states in central Mexico gained status as a destination region. Although these states received only 10 percent of the

Table 3 Sociodemographic characteristics of U.S.-to-Mexico migrants, ages zero to seventeen, by birthplace and residence five years prior to the Mexican census or *Intercensal Survey*, 1990–2015

| | 1990 | | | 2000 | | | 2010 | | | 2015 | |
| | U.S. born | | Mexican born, residing in the U.S. five years prior | U.S. born | | Mexican born, residing in the U.S. five years prior | U.S. born | | Mexican born, residing in the U.S. five years prior | U.S. born | |
	0 to 5 years	6 to 17 years		0 to 5 years	6 to 17 years		0 to 5 years	6 to 17 years		0 to 5 years	6 to 17 years
	52,910	81,430	13,580	127,997	132,595	33,538	249,292	320,851	62,981	138,246	412,246
Women (%)	49.7	51.1	50.6	48.5	49.4	51.4	49.0	49.6	51.9	48.6	49.9
Urban (more than 2,500) (%)	81.5	78.9	82.3	78.5	80.9	78.5	75.4	76.1	76.2	82.7	74.9
Age groups (%)											
0 to 5 years	100.0	-	-	100.0	-	-	100.0	-	-	100.0	-
6 to 11 years	-	59.0	46.1	-	72.7	51.3	-	66.6	43.4	-	63.0
12 to 15 years	-	30.7	35.9	-	19.7	32.4	-	24.0	38.9	-	29.2
16 to 17 years	-	10.2	18.0	-	7.6	16.2	-	9.4	17.6	-	7.7
Total	100.0	100.0	100.0	100.0	100.0	100.0	100.0	100.0	100.0	100.0	100.0
Region of origin											
North[1]	62.2	50.5	30.6	53.0	50.4	28.7	48.5	45.2	30.4	62.5	42.3
Traditional[2]	29.6	41.3	54.1	31.6	35.3	47.9	28.5	31.7	36.1	23.1	31.7

Table 3 (continued)

	1990				2000				2010				2015		
	U.S. born		Mexican born, residing in the U.S. five years prior		Mexican born, residing in the U.S. five years prior		U.S. born		Mexican born, residing in the U.S. five years prior		U.S. born		Mexican born, residing in the U.S. five years prior		U.S. born
	0 to 5 years	6 to 17 years	0 to 5 years	6 to 17 years	0 to 5 years	6 to 17 years	0 to 5 years	6 to 17 years	0 to 5 years	6 to 17 years	0 to 5 years	6 to 17 years	0 to 5 years	6 to 17 years	6 to 17 years
Center[3]	5.6	5.9		11.9		10.3	9.8	15.7		12.9	14.5	17.8		8.6	15.8
Southeast[4]	2.6	2.3		3.4		5.0	4.4	7.7		10.1	8.7	15.8		5.8	10.2
Total	100.0	100.0		100.0		100.0	100.0	100.0		100.0	100.0	100.0		100.0	100.0

SOURCE: Our estimates are based on census samples (INEGI 1990, 2000, 2010) and the 2015 *Intercensal Survey* (INEGI 2015).

NOTE: The U.S.-born population is divided into two age groups, to make them comparable with the Mexican-born population. Information relating to the place of residence five years prior to the census date is not captured for the age group zero to five years.

[1] This region includes the Mexican states of Baja California, Baja California Sur, Chihuahua, Coahuila, Nuevo León, Sonora, Tamaulipas, and Sinaloa.

[2] This region includes the Mexican states of Aguascalientes, Colima, Durango, Guanajuato, Jalisco, Michoacán, Nayarit, San Luis Potosí, and Zacatecas.

[3] This region includes the Mexican states of Morelos, Querétaro, Tlaxcala, Puebla, Hidalgo, State of Mexico, and Mexico City.

[4] This region includes the Mexican states of Campeche, Chiapas, Guerrero, Oaxaca, Quintana Roo, Tabasco, Veracruz, and Yucatán.

U.S.-born and 14 percent of the Mexican-born child migrants, there has been a significant increase among this age group in the southeast region over the twenty-five years of study. This change partially reflects the fact that states in central and southeast Mexico have notably increased their participation in the migration flows to the United States and are rapidly transforming into emerging zones of migration (Durand and Massey 2003; Durand 2016). However, there is a certain disconnect between the places in Mexico where school-age minors return (in most cases they arrive in Mexico with their parents) and the places with better work and educational opportunities such as the metropolitan areas in the center of the country or, in the case of more dynamic labor markets, the tourist centers in the south and southeast regions.

Last, as a final point about the geographic perspective of child migration from the United States to Mexico, we refer to figure 3, which displays the proportion of child migrants across municipalities in Mexico in 2015 (without denoting age or place of birth). This figure allows us to observe the presence of minors throughout Mexico who were born or have lived in the United States. Notably, very few municipalities in the country reported zero cases of child migrants. When we look closer, the data suggest a greater presence of migrant children in border states, where they represent between 3 percent and 9 percent of the total population of minors. The migratory route of these children also emerges, and we see their noteworthy presence in the western part of the country, which has a long tradition of migration. Given the size of the population in large metropolises, the relative presence of child migrants to the total population of children is lower so the significance of their increased settlement is not reflected on this figure.

CHANGES AND CONTINUITIES IN THE 0.5 GENERATION HOUSEHOLDS

The sociodemographic profile of children and adolescents who migrate from the United States to Mexico leads to three main conclusions. First, despite being associated with the mobility of adults, child migration has its own particularities in terms of sociodemographic profiles and geographic distribution, and these are also related to age and place of birth.

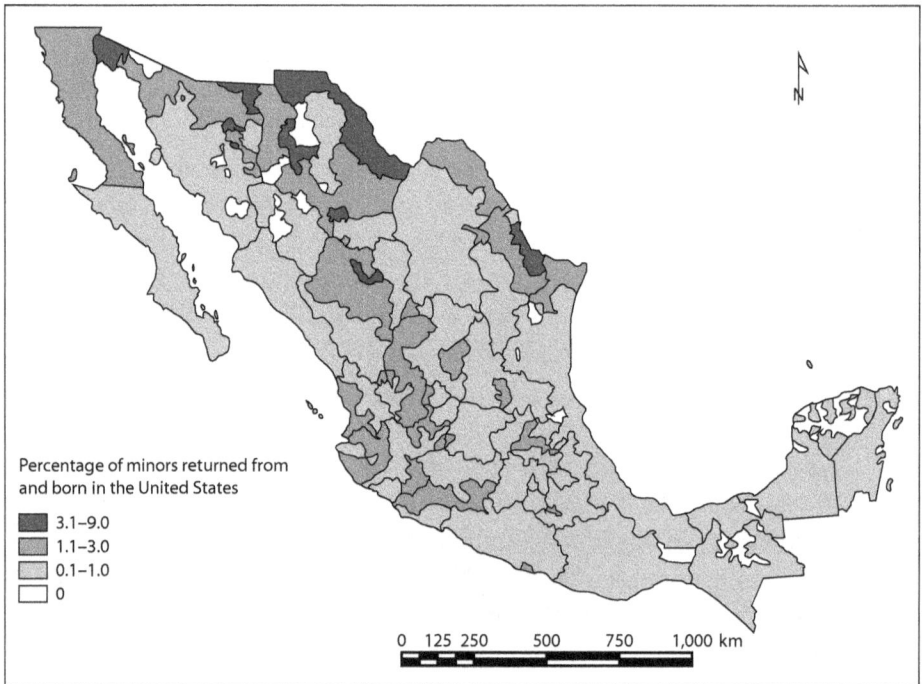

Figure 3. Percentage of U.S.-to-Mexico child migrants (U.S. born or Mexican born) of the total population, ages zero to seventeen years, by municipality, 2015.

Source: Our estimates are based on the *2015 Intercensal Survey* (INEGI 2015).

Second, these children's migration experiences are heterogeneous, as they are contingent on their geographic location in Mexico as well as their presence in either rural or urban localities. And, third, the integration process into destination communities may be different between U.S.-born and Mexican-born populations, as individuals in the first group arrive to the country at a younger age, while in the second group there is a significant presence of adolescents. For adolescents migration could be related to other intrinsic decisions such as leaving school, becoming a parent, or entering the workforce. In any case, these decisions, including that of changing their place of residence to Mexico, would still need supervision and authorization from an adult, most commonly from a parent.

The interviews we conducted with migrant youth and their families capture the heterogeneity of family arrangements, which include configurations such as the absence of one or both parents, coresidence with extended family (mainly with grandparents), contact with parents who continue to live in or have returned to the United States, and the reproduction of transnational parenting practices (Mummert 2012), among others. We show how the family plays a very important mediating role in the incorporation of children and adolescents into the social environment, especially into the school environment, upon return to Mexico.

The census data permit us to make a rough approximation of the family situation of school-age children and adolescents who move to Mexico from the United States and of the mobility of other members in their household (Aguilar Zepeda 2014). Despite the challenges often brought about by international migration and the myriad residential arrangements that unfold throughout the migratory process, most of the child migrants' mobility predominantly coordinated with that of their parents (see table 4). In most cases around 80 percent of both U.S.-born and Mexican-born minors aged six to seventeen are reported in the census or survey as the children of the head of household. To reiterate, among the U.S.-born children aged six and under, the status of son or daughter prevails in the household-position category, although it is less frequent compared to the other groups.[6] The next most relevant category is that of "grandchild of the head of the household." Let's focus on 2015. This group includes 14.9 percent of the U.S.-born migrants ages six to seventeen and 12.5 percent of the Mexican-born child migrants in the same age group. This confirms, once again, the importance of grandparents living in the communities of origin and their role as participants in the migratory strategies of Mexican families who are or were residing in the United States. Notably, nearly one in four U.S.-born children ages six and under lives in a household headed by a grandparent.

School-age migrants are most likely to live in nuclear households, although to a lesser degree than the national average in Mexico. Nuclear households represent more than 70 percent of all child migrants between the ages of six and seventeen, born in Mexico or in the United States. The next largest group of child migrants live in extended households best characterized as "vertically extended families" and include three generations living together. Again we see a distinctive profile regarding type of household for migrants between the age of zero to five: in 2015 one in three

Table 4 *Household characteristics of U.S.-to-Mexico migrants, ages zero to seventeen, by birthplace and residence five years prior to the Mexican census or Intercensal Survey, 1990–2015*

	1990			2000			2010			2015		
	U.S. born		Mexican born, living in the U.S. five years prior*	U.S. born		Mexican born, living in the U.S. five years prior*	U.S. born		Mexican born, living in the U.S. five years prior*	U.S. born		Mexican born, living in the U.S. five years prior*
	0 to 5 years	6 to 17 years		0 to 5 years	6 to 17 years		0 to 5 years	6 to 17 years		0 to 5 years	6 to 17 years	
Household position (%)												
Son/daughter	79.4	87.4	85.2	69.2	80.4	80.0	68.0	79.0	79.1	73.9	81.9	82.6
Grandchild	17.6	8.5	6.7	27.8	15.3	11.1	28.1	16.8	13.7	23.1	14.9	12.5
Other Relationship	1.8	3.0	6.7	2.2	3.0	5.6	3.8	4.0	7.1	2.9	3.1	4.6
Not related	1.3	1.1	1.3	0.9	1.2	3.3	0.2	0.2	0.1	0.1	0.2	0.2
Total	100.0	100.0	100.0	100.0	100.0	100.0	100.0	100.0	100.0	100.0	100.0	100.0
Type of household (%)												
Nuclear[1]	68.9	76.8	77.9	60.9	70.3	69.5	59.6	69.3	70.0	64.8	72.0	70.6
Extended[2]	26.9	19.5	19.1	37.5	28.1	28.1	38.7	29.2	29.1	33.6	26.9	28.1
Composite[3]	4.1	3.5	2.8	1.5	1.5	2.2	1.7	1.4	0.7	1.6	1.1	1.3
Other[4]	0.1	0.2	0.2	0.1	0.1	0.2	0.0	0.1	0.1	0.0	0.1	0.0
Total	100.0	100.0	100.0	100.0	100.0	100.0	100.0	100.0	100.0	100.0	100.0	100.0

SOURCE: Our estimates are based on census samples (INEGI 1990, 2000, 2010) and the *2015 Intercensal Survey* (INEGI 2015).

NOTE: The U.S.-born population is divided into two age groups, to make them comparable with the Mexican-born population. In the case of the Mexican-born population, information relating to the place of residence five years prior to the census date is not captured for the age group of zero to five years.

[1] The nuclear household consists of the father, mother, and children or only one parent with one or more children; a couple living together without children also constitutes a nuclear household.

[2] The extended household goes beyond the nuclear family to include other relatives (uncles, cousins, brothers, in-laws, etc.).

[3] The composite household includes other people unrelated to the head of the household.

[4] Other households consist of other types of family arrangements.

children in this category lived in extended households. This correlates with the previously presented data that show a large percentage of grandparents in the role of head of household.

Household composition and structure play a mediating role in the children's process of integration into the Mexican community to which they arrive, including their enrollment in and acclimation to schools. With regard to schooling, household characteristics determine the migrant child's learning environment and how their school performance is monitored. Educational research suggests that a child's home setting, and particularly whether or not they live with their parents, is one of the main factors associated with school attendance (Mier y Terán and Rabell 2003; Giorguli 2011).

As expected, we observed differences by age among child migrants regarding whether or not they lived with their parents. Most of the children lived with both parents; however, this percentage decreased as age increased, regardless of whether the children were born in the United States or Mexico (see table 5). At twelve to fifteen years old, one in four children lived only with their mother. As age increased, so did the number of adolescents who did not live with either of their parents. Particularly, at the ages of sixteen and seventeen, about one in five migrants born in Mexico lived in households where neither parent was present. More research is needed to corroborate the reasons for this percentage and to understand whether such a high number could be attributed to early emancipation or to family separation due to migration. However, this data point is indicative of the differences in the trajectories between U.S.-born and Mexican-born migrant adolescents and can be interpreted as a possible indicator of how the migration process is linked to these youths' transition to work life and leaving their parents' home.

The data source does not permit us to determine if the absence of one or both parents is the result of the family being separated by migration (e.g., one parent staying in the United States), the dissolution of the parents' relationship (e.g., a divorce or breakup), or another reason, such as the death of one or both parents, an older adolescents' departure from the home, and so on. Despite the limitation of this source, what the numbers do indicate is myriad possible connections between family trajectories and migration from the United States to Mexico.

Table 5   Distribution of the U.S.-to-Mexico migrant population, ages zero to seventeen, by birthplace and residence five years prior to the census or *Intercensal Survey* and by coresidence with parents, 2015

Age	Coresidence with parents	U.S. born (%)	Mexican born, residing in the United States five years prior (%)
0 to 5 years	Both parents	71.1	N.A.
	Mother only	21.3	N.A.
	Father only	1.8	N.A.
	None	5.7	N.A.
	Total	100.0	N.A.
6 to 11 years	Both parents	66.1	71.0
	Mother only	24.8	21.2
	Father only	2.4	1.9
	None	6.6	6.0
	Total	100.0	100.0
12 to 15 years	Both parents	62.6	63.9
	Mother only	25.6	24.9
	Father only	3.6	3.0
	None	8.2	8.2
	Total	100.0	100.0
16 to 17 years	Both parents	58.3	50.6
	Mother only	23.9	26.4
	Father only	4.0	4.8
	None	13.8	18.3
	Total	100.0	100.0

SOURCE: Our estimates are based on census samples (INEGI 1990, 2000, 2010) and the *2015 Intercensal Survey* (INEGI 2015).

NOTE: In the case of the Mexican-born population, information relating to the place of residence five years prior to the census date is not captured for the age group of zero to five years.

CONCLUSIONS

One of the greatest changes in migratory patterns from 2005 to 2015 is the prevalence of a constant return flow from the United States to Mexico, consisting of both return migrants and U.S.-born migrants. This is the largest migratory flow from north to south ever recorded in the current international context (Giorguli, García, and Masferrer 2016) and is contributing to the discourse depicting Mexico as a country of immigration. According to the most recent data, in 2015 about one million foreign-born individuals were living in Mexico. Of these the majority (n = 739,000 people) were U.S. citizens and accounted for 73 percent of the foreign-born population.

Two findings stand out from the data on this population. First, the majority (more than half a million) are minors and are concentrated in the age groups of fifteen years and younger—that is, early childhood through the first years of adolescence.[7] Second, around 200,000 of the total of 739,000 U.S. citizens (27 percent) arrived in Mexico during the past five years (Giorguli, García, and Masferrer 2016). Importantly, the majority of these individuals also have dual citizenship in the United States and Mexico. This population consists of two groups of young people: those who have recently entered the country within the past five years and, constituting the majority, those who have resided in Mexico for longer than five years. Again the socialization processes of both groups and their integration into the Mexican school system are different depending on how old they were when they arrived in the country. Regardless of the date of arrival, the data clearly show that this population consists of children and adolescents with full rights in both countries and the ability to freely cross the border for education, work, and family reasons. As the United States and Mexico share this population of youth, their experiences must be brought to the attention of both countries' governments and become the focus of public policies.

In addition to the migration flow of U.S. citizens coming to Mexico is that of the Mexican-born minors returning to Mexico after living in United States for varied amounts of time. The number of Mexican youths returning was largest between 2005 and 2010, particularly during the years of the Great Expulsion, which occurred due to the economic crisis of 2008 and because of the increased deportations during the Obama presidency.

The sociodemographic profile of the first- and second-generation Mexican population in the United States combined with the pattern of returnees to Mexico and the mobility possibilities of individuals with dual citizenship suggest that, for the foreseeable future, we will observe continuous migratory mobility of children and adolescents from the United States to Mexico. If the trend that we observed between 2005 and 2015 continues, this contingent of the population will mostly be made up of children born in the United States to Mexican parents. Douglas Massey, Jorge Durand, and Karen Pren (2016) have accurately pointed out that, in recent years, one of the main patterns of Mexicans' international mobility consists of those authorized to move between the two countries, whether by a residence permit, the acquisition of U.S. citizenship, or the possession of a temporary work visa.

What the available data from Mexico suggest is that children's mobility to Mexico is an important part—a third part—of immigration from the north, and this translates into considerably varied experiences depending on many circumstances, including those with dual citizenship status; those who do not have papers or who have slim possibilities, despite their expectations, of returning to the United States (Ramírez 2013); those who return with their parents or those who live with other relatives; those who arrive at their parents' communities of origin, where they may have family networks but possibly fewer educational opportunities; and those who stay in border towns or in large metropolitan areas. Certainly, this population's mobility to Mexico, and its subsequent needs regarding services and access to the education system, is an issue that will require further study and consideration as scholars look at new migration patterns between the two countries in the coming decades.

The demographic information presented in this chapter situates our focal participants, who represent five Mexican states, in a broader context to illustrate the diversity of their experiences and to articulate the need for creating a typology of child migrants who have moved from the United States to Mexico based on factors such as place of birth and age that can then be used for analysis. We present this typology in the following chapter.

3 The Heterogeneity of the Migratory Experience

The theoretical journey that has guided our understanding of child migration from the United States to Mexico over several decades has unfolded in tandem with a second goal: to develop a typology that illustrates the diversity of the migratory experiences of international child migrants in Mexico. Our research has shown that, while all migrant children, to varying extents, experience geographic dislocation, fragmented socialization, transitions from one school system to another, and a sense of belonging to the 0.5 generation, these phenomena affect children in different ways. As our study progressed, and we gathered more information about the children's migratory and educational experiences, the variability of their characteristics emerged. For example, with regard to migrant children's geographic dislocation and fragmented socialization process, we encountered children who had migrated only once in their lives (from the United States to Mexico) and others who had migrated twice (from Mexico to the United States and back again). These children experienced geographic dislocation differently from those who had migrated from one country to another three, four, or more times. As far as the transnational education of the children who live in Mexico, or who were living in Mexico at the time of the survey, we found a fundamental difference between those who had attended schools in the United States and those who had never enrolled in U.S. schools because they came to Mexico before they were of school age.

Migrant children's sense of belonging to the 0.5 generation varied significantly depending on their country of birth. As we previously explained, children born in the United States to Mexican parents were considered members of the second generation while they resided in the United States. Once they arrived in Mexico, they became members of the 0.5 generation, but, because of their dual citizenship, they continuously have the option of returning to the United States. If they were to do so, they would again become members of the second generation because they would be considered children of immigrants in the United States.[1] Children who were born in and later returned to Mexico belonged to the 1.5 generation while living in the United States; however, once residing in Mexico, they became members of the 0.5 generation. These children are less likely than those with dual citizenship to remigrate back to the United States during their childhood. Both cases of migrant children belong to the 0.5 generation but join through discernably different legal and subjective conditions. They differ from each other mainly by their legal status: some of the migrant children are free to legally move about Mexico and the United States, while others are limited in their binational mobility. Furthermore, one of the most striking traits is that the binational children, or those with dual citizenship, often envisage living their adult life in the United States. For children with single nationality or citizenship, these future plans remain uncertain. To develop a typology of migrant children and their experiences, we began by classifying the children according to the variables associated with the theoretical framework of country of birth, school experience, and geographic dislocation (see table 6).

In this section we present several cases of migrant children and explain how the typology captures their experiences. First, we begin with Lulú, who was born in Arkansas. She spent most of her childhood and early teens in San Diego, California, where she studied through seventh grade. She was thirteen when she arrived in Tlaltizapán, Morelos, in 2013, and she was living with her parents and her three sisters at the time of data collection. Lulú's maternal grandmother continues to live in California, along with several of her cousins, aunts, and uncles. After two and a half years in Morelos, Lulú's dominant language is still English, although her

Table 6   A preliminary typology of child migrants from the United States to Mexico

Country of birth and nationality	A1: Children born in the United States
	A2: Children born in Mexico
Influence of schooling in the United States	B1: Transnational students with previous school experience in the United States
	B2: Nontransnational students without previous school experience in the United States
Geographic dislocation	C1: Children with atypical migratory fragmentation and dislocation (three or more border crossings)
	C2: Children with typical migratory fragmentation and dislocation (two or fewer border crossings)

SOURCE: Our elaboration is based on the databases of Universidad de Monterrey (2015).

abilities to speak, read, and write in Spanish have improved considerably, thanks to her mother's immense efforts in supporting her complex language development. Lulú is a girl who belongs to the 0.5 generation, and, if circumstances are propitious, she may decide to return to Southern California and finish high school in San Diego or in another city where she has relatives with whom she could live. According to our initial typology, Lulú is classified as (A1) born in the United States, (B1) with transnational schooling experiences in the United States, and (C2) having had typical migratory dislocation and fragmentation.

Abel falls into a different category of child migrants. He was born in Zacatecas and was taken to the United States when he was nine months old. Abel lived in various locations throughout the United States until his parents settled in Saint Louis, Missouri, when he was five years old. There he attended school for eight years, from preschool to seventh grade. He had not yet turned thirteen when he arrived in Chihuahua. In 2005, at the age of fifteen, he moved to Jerez, Zacatecas. In Mexico Abel first lived with an aunt for two years; when we met him, he was living with a cousin's family while his father and younger sister continued to reside in Saint Louis. Abel, just like Lulú, had better spoken and written communicative skills in English. He was gradually acquiring the skills of written Spanish while studying at the local junior high school in Jerez.[2] Abel wanted to return to

Saint Louis, the city he called home at the time we met him, but he knew it would be very difficult to reach this goal. Without us having to ask, Abel shared that he lacked legal authorization to enter and reside in the United States. Scholars refer to the social and physical immobility that Abel was experiencing due to his lack of documentation to live legally in the United States as the "immobility effect" (Hernández-León 2008); however, instead of negotiating these limitations within the United States, Abel was feeling this effect in Mexico.[3] According to our typology, Abel is classified as a migrant with single nationality (A2), with school experience in the United States (B1), and with typical migratory fragmentation (C2).

Itzcalli is a child migrant who differs from Abel and Lulú in that she was never enrolled in a school in the United States. We met Itzcalli in April 2010 when she was six years old. She knew she had been born in the United States, but she could not remember where. When she was three years old, her mother took her to live with her grandmother in Izúcar de Matamoros, Puebla. At the time of study, Itzcalli was living separately from her parents because her mother had returned to the United States and, as she shared, "struggled to cross the border." Itzcalli falls into the categories of (A1), (B2), and (C2): she was born in the United States and had typical migratory experiences but had not attended school in the United States

We met Laurie and her brother Julio in September 2010. At that time they were thirteen and fifteen years old, respectively, and they were enrolled in a junior high school in Los Ramones, Nuevo León. Every year the two children joined their parents and siblings and migrated to Minnesota, where they completed part of their schooling during the months of April through June and August through October. They have never lived apart from their parents. These international migrant adolescents were born in the United States (A1) and were educated in schools in the state of Minnesota (B1); however, because they have been involved in seasonal circular migration since they were born, they experienced a unique type of geographic dislocation and fragmentation in the socialization process in that they have crossed the border many times (C1).

Paty was eleven years old and enrolled in the sixth grade when we met her in Villanueva, Zacatecas, in November 2005. Paty was born in Villanueva (A2), and, when she was five, her mother decided to migrate to Los Angeles, where some of her siblings (Paty's maternal aunts and uncles)

were living at that time. At the age of seven, her maternal grandparents took her by bus to Los Angeles. Paty told us that she thought she was going on vacation, but, to her surprise, they enrolled her in an elementary school, which she attended for two years (B1). When she was nine, once again her grandparents went to pick her up and brought her back to Villanueva (C2). A few months later her mother also returned to Villanueva "because she was already tired of the north." At the time of our interview in 2005, Paty was living with her mother at her maternal grandparents' house, but she did not rule out the possibility of returning to Los Angeles. If that was to happen—and we do not know if it did—then Paty could be classified as (C1), because, if she returned to Villanueva again, she would have migrated three or four times.

All these children, just like all the other 1,486 international child migrants that we surveyed between 2004 and 2013, have three characteristics in common. First, they were living in Mexico at the time of our survey or interview; second, they lived part of their lives in the United States; and, third, they were enrolled in a Mexican school when we met them. These characteristics make them international child migrants—or adolescents—studying in Mexican schools. However, as these vignettes show, these children's migratory experiences differ substantially, especially regarding the most crucial aspects of migration (e.g., place of birth, schooling experience, and geographic dislocation).

In this chapter we explain the usefulness of our proposed typology by depicting the heterogenous migratory experiences of school-age child migrants ages six to seventeen. We explain each category of the typology, beginning with our observations regarding how the children's country of birth influences their experience. Then we continue by analyzing the importance of schooling in the United States and conclude with discussing migrant children's geographic dislocation (i.e., the number of times they migrated from one country to the other).

COUNTRY OF BIRTH AND NATIONALITY

In the case of Mexico and the United States, children's country of birth determines their nationality because in these countries geographic territory is equated with sovereignty. The countries share the legal principle that if a child is born on the nation's territory, then they shall acquire the nationality of that country either by virtue of birth in the territory of a nation-state or by jus soli. Similarly, in both countries the parents' nationality determines the nationality of their children regardless of their place of birth. Both of these legal ways of determining nationality and citizenship coexist. Therefore, a child born in the United States to Mexican parents is both a U.S. citizen, according to U.S. law, and a Mexican "by birth," according to the Mexican Nationality Law, which has been in operation since January 1998.[4] Before this law was enacted, when Mexican citizens acquired another nationality, they forfeited their Mexican citizenship.

When we first surveyed 14,473 children and adolescents enrolled in 173 elementary and junior high schools in the state of Nuevo León in December 2004, we found 336 children who had migrated from the United States to Mexico (see table 7).[5] Since the sample is representative of the students enrolled in all schools throughout Nuevo León (with a margin of error of 8 percent), it was estimated that between 16,150 and 17,850 children between the ages of six to sixteen were international migrants and were enrolled in the state's elementary and junior high schools.[6] Slightly less than half of these children had been born in the United States (47 percent). According to our estimates, the Nuevo León school system was home to about 8,000 students with dual citizenship. Among them the largest group was born in Texas (over 80 percent), but we also found children born in Kentucky, Minnesota, Massachusetts, and Washington, states that are considered new destinations for Mexican migration in the United States (Zúñiga and Hernández-León 2005a).

In December 2005 we conducted the survey in Zacatecas with 11,258 students enrolled in 218 schools. In this sample we found 372 international child migrants from the United States.[7] Based on this data, the estimate for the entire school system of Zacatecas indicated that 7,600 to 8,400 international child migrants between the ages of six and sixteen were enrolled in the state's elementary or junior high schools. Approximately 64 percent of these children had been born in the United States—that is, approximately 5,000 children with dual citizenship were enrolled in schools in Zacatecas. Most of these children had been born in California, Texas, and Illinois, but in Zacatecas we also found cases of chil-

Table 7   U.S.-to-Mexico child migrants' country of birth by Mexican state

State and date of survey*	Total number of students	Total number of international child migrants	Estimated number of international child migrants enrolled in elementary and junior high schools	U.S.-born child migrants with respect to the total number of international child migrants (%)
Nuevo León (2004)	14,473	336	Between 16,150 and 17,850	47
Zacatecas (2005)	11,258	372	Between 7,600 and 8,400	64
Puebla (2009)	18,829	208	Between 11,400 and 12,600	75
Jalisco (2010)	11,479	486	Between 60,800 and 67,200	56

SOURCE: Our elaboration is based on the databases of Universidad de Monterrey (2015).
*Only states where the survey was conducted are included.

dren born in Alaska, Iowa, and Oregon, as well as in seventeen other states.

It was not until 2009, four years later, that we were able to continue our study in Puebla. There we surveyed 18,829 students enrolled in 214 schools. These data were collected within the economic context of the Great Recession of 2007–9, and at that time we were already seeing the preliminary impact that the financial crisis in the United States had on the lives of Mexican migrants. However, the quantitative findings from these surveys were not very different from what we had found in previous studies. There were 208 international child migrants enrolled in elementary and junior high schools in Puebla.[8] The results from this sample permitted us to estimate that between 11,400 and 12,600 international migrant children and adolescents were enrolled in schools in the state of Puebla and that most of them were located in the Mixtec and the Atlixco–Izúcar de Matamoros regions (Zúñiga, Hamann, and Sánchez García 2016). In Puebla the percentage of U.S.-born children increased compared to data collected in other states, reaching three-quarters (75 percent) of the total sample of transnational students. Based on these data, it was estimated that around 9,000 children with dual citizenship were enrolled in elementary and junior high schools in Puebla. These child migrants were mostly from New York and California.

In November and December 2010, we administered the survey in two hundred elementary and junior high schools in the state of Jalisco. The questionnaire was answered by 11,479 children and adolescents, among which we identified 486 international migrants from the United States.[9] Of these child migrants 56 percent had been born in the United States, a percentage notably lower than what we observed in Puebla the previous year. Of these very few were born in Texas. The majority of children with dual citizenship in the schools in Jalisco were from California, while the rest had been born in twenty-six different states such as Ohio, Idaho, New Jersey, Virginia, and Utah. Based on this sample, we estimated that between 60,800 and 67,200 international child migrants were enrolled in Jalisco's elementary and junior high schools in 2010 and that around 36,000 had dual citizenship in the United States and Mexico.

In September 2013 we were able to conduct the survey in only four schools (two elementary and two junior high schools) in the state of Morelos. While this sample size is too small to be representative of the state's entire school system, we can gleam some information about child migrants in this state. The questionnaire was answered by 1,383 children, of which 84 had migrated from the United States to Mexico. In this dataset 46 percent of the international migrants were born in the United States. Surprisingly, the children born in the United States had birth certificates issued by ten different states, without any one state standing out as the majority: California, North Carolina, Illinois, Minnesota, New York, Tennessee, Texas, Utah, Virginia, and Washington. This dispersion of migratory destinations is likely because the migration flow from Morelos to the United States is more recent than that from the states of Nuevo León, Zacatecas, and Jalisco. Because migrant networks in Morelos are less developed than in the aforementioned states, migrants may be carving out their own niches and, as such, creating a more diversified migrant flow.

In summary we propose the first element of classification in the typology of child migrants in Mexico: Mexican-born child migrants who have only Mexican nationality and U.S.-born child migrants who have dual citizenship. Both groups are of similar proportions, although in some states the number of U.S.-born children exceeds that of Mexican-born children. The Mexican censuses and surveys include only the recent experience (five years prior to the date of the census or survey) of Mexican-born migrant youth and provide the number of those born in the United States without specifying the year of their arrival. Our survey data helps illuminate the prevalence of child migrants with dual citizenship and the rapid growth of this group over the past ten years. Next we continue to develop the typology of child migrants in Mexico by including the importance of schooling in the United States as the second variable and category of analysis.

SCHOOLING EXPERIENCE IN THE UNITED STATES

While all the international child migrants that we surveyed or interviewed were enrolled in Mexican schools, some had previous schooling experience in the United States and others did not because they arrived in Mexico before they were old enough to enroll. Taking this experience into consideration, child migrants can be categorized according to those who are transnational students (i.e., they transitioned from one school system to another) and those who are not (i.e., their schooling has taken place only in Mexico). Because of their experiences in U.S. schools, transnational students have a unique repertoire of content knowledge as well as semiotic, linguistic, cognitive, and metacognitive skills distinct from those child migrants who have attended school only in Mexico. While in U.S. schools, child migrants accumulate binational knowledge, a valuable learning resource for school and for life. Mexican schools, then, have the opportunity to either recognize or ignore these valuable skills and dispositions.

International child migrants who arrived in Mexico before reaching school age and who are currently attending Mexican schools are not considered transnational students. In our samples all the children in this category (i.e., *not* transnational) were born in the United States. Coincidently, all the child migrants in our samples who were born in Mexico had attended at least one school year in the United States, making them transnational students. However, it is not necessarily the case that all Mexican-born child migrants are transnational students. For example, children could be born in Mexico, have migrated to the United States at age two, and returned at age three. In that case they would be natives of Mexico but would not have enrolled in school in the United States. However, our surveys did not render any children who met these criteria. For this reason our typology delineates only the following categories (when combining criteria A and B): (1) transnational students who were born in the United States; (2) transnational students who were born in Mexico; and (3) migrants who have lived in the United States but have attended schools only in Mexico and thus have mononational schooling experiences. In this latter category, referred to as "mononational students" from here on, all of our survey participants have dual citizenship because they were born in the United States. In this section we present our data on child migrants in Mexico configured according to these categories.

In the state of Nuevo León in 2004, 73 percent of the child migrants were transnational students (of these, 53 percent were Mexican born and 20 percent were born in the United States), and the remaining 27 percent were mononational students because they were born in the United States but had no previous school experience there (see table 8). This distribution in Zacatecas in 2005 was as follows: 61 percent were transnational students (36 percent born in Mexico and 25 percent born in the United States), and 39 percent were mononational students without previous schooling experience there.

In Puebla the distribution of child migrants across these categories was different. Slightly more than half of these children were transnational students, and this group was divided almost equally between Mexican-born and U.S.-born children. The other half were mononational students. Accounting for 47 percent, the percentage of mononational migrant children in Puebla was significantly higher than other states. In other words, half of the international child migrants enrolled in Puebla's schools arrived in Mexico at an early age and had no prior schooling experiences in the United States. It became clear that families were using an important migration strategy that was, in turn, shaping the children's experiences. Take, for example, the case of Itzcalli. Itzcalli's mother took her and her younger brother to Izúcar de Matamoros, Puebla, to live with their grandmother and then returned to the United States, where Itzcalli's father was living. During our interview with Itzcalli, she implied that her parents

Table 8   Percentage distribution of U.S.-to-Mexico child migrants enrolled in elementary and junior high schools

	Born in Mexico		Born in the United States		
State (year)	With previous school experience in the United States (%)	Without previous school experience in the United States (%)	With previous school experience in the United States (%)	Without previous school experience in the United States (%)	Total (%)
Nuevo León (2004)	53	–	20	27	100
Zacatecas (2005)	36	–	25	39	100
Puebla (2009)	27	–	26	47	100
Jalisco (2010)	44	–	31	25	100

SOURCE: Our elaboration is based on the databases of Universidad de Monterrey (2015).

were afraid of being deported and having to abandon their children in the United States. This fear led them to take preventive measures, such as bringing their U.S.-born children to a safe place (their grandmother's house in Izúcar de Matamoros).

This preventive strategy may be associated with the high percentage of U.S.-born children who arrived in Puebla before school age and is likely being used in other Mexican states with more recent and regional migration flows.[10] According to our 2010 survey data, the distribution of child migrants in Jalisco is similar to that of the children in Nuevo León: 75 percent were transnational students, of which 44 percent were born in Mexico, 31 percent were born in the United States, and a quarter were mononational students because they arrived in Mexico before reaching school age (see table 8).

If we consider the case of Puebla as an exception to the rule, we are in a position to affirm that, generally speaking, international child migrants in Mexico are also transnational students. Our synthesis of national demographic data corroborates and affirms that the presence of U.S.-born children who arrive in Mexico before school age is not atypical. And, according to the survey data from Nuevo León and Jalisco, approximately a quarter of the international child migrants being educated in Mexican schools have no previous school experience in the United States and, based on our sample participants, have the right to dual citizenship.[11]

As the compilation and analysis of our data progressed, we realized that school experience in one or several institutions in the United States was the determining factor that rendered differences among international child migrants. However, over time and with more detailed interview data, we gradually found that the importance of educational experiences varied remarkably depending on the number of years the children attended schools in the United States. As expected, we observed that certain skills, knowledge, and competencies acquired by the children who had been enrolled in U.S. schools for short periods were visibly less advanced than those acquired by children who had spent more time in U.S. schools. We also found that the longer they had been enrolled in schools in the United States, the more likely it was that child self-identified as "Mexican-Americans," regardless of their country of birth (Hamann and Zúñiga 2011).

As we developed the typology, it became clear that it was not enough to simply combine criteria A (country of birth) and B (previous school experience in the United States) to encompass the diversity of children's trajectories. Before long we realized that criterion B needed to be more specific and include a way to measure the importance of U.S school experiences in the children's lives. Schooling is as important as the country of birth because schooling in one country or the other has lasting effects on the children's linguistic, cognitive, affective, and cultural development.

THE IMPORTANCE OF SCHOOLING IN THE UNITED STATES

Migrant children's U.S. school experience is important to our study precisely because these children are living in Mexico: having attended school in the United States undoubtedly influences their experiences in Mexican schools. The most obvious effect that schooling in the United States had on the migrant children was their dominant language. Understandably, as a result of prolonged schooling in the United States, the children's dominant language across all domains (speaking, reading, and writing) is

English. Over time we became more aware that children who spent lengthy amounts of time in U.S. schools faced more complex challenges when they enrolled in Mexican schools and that the cognitive and symbolic fractures they experience in their learning are starker. Last but not least, children who arrive in Mexico after having attended schools in the United States for a significant number of years, as it is the case of Abel and Lulú, must overcome greater obstacles to integrate into Mexican society and its institutions.

Based on these findings, we decided to broaden the original dichotomy of criterion B (schooling) in our typology. The most straightforward way to measure the degree of importance of school experience in the United States in the migrant children's trajectory was to count the number of years they had attended school in that country. Thus, we identified five types of international child migrants by combining criteria A and B and then by breaking these criteria down into two categories based on how many years they had been enrolled in U.S. schools.

Type 1: U.S.-born children with dual citizenship, transnational students with short U.S school experience (one to three years of schooling)

Type 2: U.S.-born children with dual citizenship, transnational students with extensive U.S school experience (four or more years of schooling)

Type 3: U.S.-born children with dual citizenship, mononational students (never enrolled in schools in the United States, thus zero years of schooling in the United States)

Type 4: Mexican-born children, transnational students with short U.S school experience (one to three years of schooling)

Type 5: Mexican-born children, transnational students with extensive U.S school experience (four or more years of schooling).[12]

In the five states where we conducted the survey, we found a significant percentage of child migrants who had arrived in Mexico before their fifth birthday and therefore had never been enrolled in schools in the United States (type 3). As we explained, this percentage is remarkably high in Puebla but quite low in Nuevo León (see table 9).

When we look specifically at the child migrants who arrived in Mexico with previous schooling in the United States (i.e., types 1, 2, 4, and 5), the

Table 9   Percentage distribution of U.S.-to-Mexico child migrants, by country of birth and length of school experience in the United States

	Born in Mexico			Born in the United States		
State (year)	*Shorter experience in U.S. schools (1 to 3 years) Type 4 (%)*	*Extensive experience in U.S. schools (4 or more years) Type 5 (%)*	*Without previous experience in U.S. schools Type 3 (%)*	*Shorter experience in U.S. schools (1 to 3 years) Type 1 (%)*	*Extensive experience in U.S. schools (4 or more years) Type 2 (%)*	*Total (%)*
Nuevo León (2004)	45	10	22	13	10	100
Zacatecas (2005)	38	7	29	17	9	100
Puebla (2009)	14	16	42	15	13	100
Jalisco (2010)	27	13	30	15	15	100

SOURCE: Our elaboration is based on the databases of Universidad de Monterrey (2015).

group of children classified as type 4 represents the greatest proportion, followed by the group of child migrants classified as type 1 (see table 9). This means that most of the international child migrants enrolled in Mexican schools do not have long trajectories in U.S. schools—that is, they attended school for one, two, or three years, and, in many cases, this includes one or two years of preschool. Among the children with shorter U.S. school experience, those born in Mexico stand out numerically.

A representative example of child migrants classified as type 1 is that of Marioly, who was born in the United States but did not remember in which city or state. She lived in the United States until the age of six and attended two years of preschool and the first year of elementary school before moving to Lagos de Moreno. When she answered the survey, she was nine years old and enrolled in fourth grade. In the questionnaire she stated that she had learned English well.

Now let's look at the case of Orlando to illustrate the group of children classified as type 4. Orlando was enrolled in one of the junior high schools in Morelos, where we conducted the survey. He was born in Cuernavaca, and in 2013 he was twelve years old. He returned to Mexico when he was six, after having attended one year of preschool and the first year of elementary school in San Francisco, California. He had migrated to the United States when he was two years old, along with his parents and siblings, and he returned to Mexico with all his family members. As expected, Orlando did not experience any communication problems with his classmates and teachers upon entering second grade at the elementary school in Cuernavaca, although he did recall having difficulties in reading and writing in Spanish when he first arrived. In any case, for Orlando, the transition from one school system to the other did not include major fractures. Both these cases represent types of international child migrants that together constitute between 40 percent and 50 percent of child migrants in each state except for Puebla.

Next we present the characteristics of the child migrants with extended schooling experience in the United States (i.e., type 2 and type 5). In the states of Nuevo León and Zacatecas, these two groups of children represented between one-fifth and one-sixth of the total number of child migrants identified in the surveys; in Puebla and Jalisco, the proportion is higher, approaching one-third of migrant children surveyed (see table 9).[13] These children face greater difficulties in adapting to Mexican schools: their school transitions are more complex, their social integration into Mexico includes greater challenges, and, while their cognitive, linguistic, and social skills become a valuable resource for learning and adult life, many of the children in these categories face humiliation upon their enrollment in Mexican schools.

As we conclude this section, it is important to explore in more detail the uniqueness of child migrants in Puebla. These children embody contrastive experiences. On one hand, we found the highest percentage of children who arrived in the state of Puebla at a very young age without having attended school in the United States. But, on the other hand, we also found a high percentage of child migrants who moved to Puebla after having studied a considerable number of years in the United States (five to nine years). Schooling in the United States has left a significative imprint on these children, which is why, in Puebla, a high percentage of the children self-reported their dominant language to be English. In other words, Puebla continues to be sui generis: on one side, half of the child migrants (all born in the United States) had no prior U.S. schooling experience when they arrived in Puebla, and the other half (children who had been enrolled in schools in the United States) had been enrolled in U.S. schools for an extended period, much longer than observed in the other states.

Data from Puebla and Jalisco were collected in 2009 and 2010, and, as we were collecting data during this time, we were wondering if the migration patterns between Mexico and the United States had changed (Giorguli and Gutiérrez 2011a). Migration patterns show that the return of migrants from the United States to Mexico has increased, including the return of entire families that had resided in the United States for relatively long periods (Hernández-León and Zúñiga 2016). This would explain why there are more children arriving in Mexican schools after having been enrolled in schools in the United States for extensive amounts of time. The small sample collected from Morelos also sheds light on these shifting migration patterns.

We collected data from eighty-four international child migrants and adolescents enrolled in schools in the Mexican state of Morelos. In this group twenty-three children arrived in Morelos at a very young age, before beginning their schooling. Among the remaining sixty-one children, eight of them were first, second, or third graders, so they were not taken into consideration for classification purposes. According to the criteria for this typology, these children would not have had extensive experiences in U.S. schools because they have been enrolled in school for only three years or less. Of the remaining fifty-three children, 20 percent had attended schools in the United States for five, six, seven, eight, or even nine years. This represents a higher percentage than what was found in other states.

FRAGMENTATED MIGRATORY EXPERIENCES

To better understand how the fractures, dislocations, and fragmentations that international migrant children experience are operationalized, it was important to incorporate and further delineate the aforementioned variables (i.e., country of birth and experience in U.S. schools) in the typology. Of course, these factors are dependent on the children's migratory experience, and thus a necessary variable for classifying children and for comprehending their migratory trajectory was the number of times they moved from one country to the other. This mobility has a significant impact on children's lives and often has lifelong implications. As we take into account the criterion of geographic dislocation, the typology becomes even more complex: it now includes country of birth, previous school experience in the United States, the importance of that experience for the child migrants residing in Mexico, and the degree of fragmentation of the migratory trajectory. To best capture children's geographic dislocation and fragmentation, we divide this criterion into two categories: typical fragmentation (one or two changes of country) and atypical fragmentation (three or more changes of country).

In the municipalities located in the northern part of the state of Nuevo León, we encountered children whose answer to the question "How many years have you attended school in the United States?" was "Every year, because every year I go back and forth." Certainly, these children and adolescents attended every school year both in U.S. and Mexican schools. They represent a truly exceptional case of migrant children found in regions with long migratory traditions, where practically every individual engaged in the process of circular and seasonal migration has dual citizenship. They represent the extreme case of migratory fragmentation and have extensive schooling experience in the United States. For example, by 2010 Julio had moved between Mexico and the United States fifteen times, and his schooling had reflected the cyclical nature of his migration patterns: he alternated between U.S. and Mexican schools within each school year (Panait and Zúñiga 2016).

The migratory and educational trajectories of Julio and his sister Laurie represent a nomadic lifestyle that very few international child migrants have experienced. On the continuum of our typology, these children epitomize the extreme. It should be noted that the vast majority of the children surveyed have migratory trajectories that include no more than one or two migratory movements across the border (see table 10). This, however, does not mean that we should neglect the migrant children whose trajectories are more fragmented, because their migratory experiences may help us better understand the fractures associated with child migration. We found this type of constant, circular migration mainly in Nuevo León, a state that shares a border with the United States. As we described earlier, the northern municipalities of this state are mostly rural, and people there

Table 10   Percentage distribution of U.S.-to-Mexico child migrants, by fragmentation of the migratory trajectories and country of birth

	Born in Mexico		Born in the United States		
State (year)	Typical fragmentation (1 or 2 migrations) (%)	Atypical fragmentation (3 or more migrations) (%)	Typical fragmentation (1 or 2 migrations) (%)	Atypical fragmentation (3 or more migrations) (%)	Total (%)
Nuevo León (2004)	49	2	44	5	100
Zacatecas (2005)	41	2	56	1	100
Puebla (2009)	33	1	65	1	100
Jalisco (2010)	48	2	49	1	100

SOURCE: Our elaboration is based on the databases of Universidad de Monterrey (2015).

have long been involved in circular and seasonal migratory patterns that involve all family members (Zúñiga and Reyes 2006). The percentage of children with highly fragmented trajectories enrolled in Mexican schools is concentrated in the northern municipalities of Nuevo León. This category of migrant children is atypical throughout the rest of the country.

Why should we be interested in this exceptional type of child migrant? Because these children represent the extreme of the continuum and therefore experience the highest degree of linguistic, symbolic, cognitive, spatial, and educational fragmentations. Learning more about these children's situations permits us to comprehend what the other child migrants may be experiencing to a lesser degree. Children who have experienced atypical migratory fragmentations during their childhood, essentially, define fragmented socialization. Children who have changed countries only once or twice also experience these fragmentations, but less drastically. And U.S.-born children who arrive in Mexico at an early age experience these changes with much less intensity. In fact, in these cases fractures may be nearly nonexistent because these children did not transition from one school system to the other.

Last, our data indicate that the age of arrival in Mexico is significant to children's international migration experiences. Indeed, all these children have crossed national borders and are international migrants. However, the age when they *became* international migrants is of great importance, as we have been emphasizing throughout this book. Migrating from one country to the other during early childhood does not entail many ruptures and discrepancies in a child's socialization. The fragmentation of socialization is reduced because, at a very early age, children have not yet accumulated meaningful experiences in the country where they spent their early years, cultivated lasting emotional ties outside of their families, or started the schooling process. On the contrary, children who migrate after early childhood (between the ages of three and fifteen) will inevitably experience breaches in their socialization process and will be forced to develop mediation and negotiation skills within new contexts. The more advanced the socialization in one country, the more complex a child's integration or reintegration process becomes in the other country. This affects and alters all the characteristics of child migrants, including their linguistic, affective, symbolic, cognitive, moral, and scholarly characteristics.

The category of migrant children that is not included in this book is that of young adults pertaining to the 1.5 generation who were born in Mexico, moved to the United States at an early age, were fully socialized in that country, and later returned to Mexico (either voluntarily or by deportation) when they were of legal age.[14] These youth undergo a complex resocialization process from the moment they move to their birth country, a country from which they will not be deported but where they feel like foreigners and are often treated as foreigners by the people with whom they socialize (Anderson and Solis 2014; Olvera and Muela 2016; Hirai and Sandoval 2016; Loredo 2016).

CONCLUSIONS

All international child migrants have experienced a degree of geographic dislocation similar to those who participate in circulatory migration between the United States and Mexico. These migration experiences cause fragmentations in the socialization process and expose children to competing symbolic social worlds. All these children belong to the 0.5 generation of immigrants, and many of them were schooled in the United States. However, the realities of child migration are not homogeneous among all international child migrants living in Mexico. A few of the child migrants have experienced numerous geographic dislocations, especially considering their young age, while the majority have crossed the border once (e.g., from the United States to Mexico) or twice (e.g., from Mexico to the United States and back to Mexico). Likewise, children experience fragmentations in the socialization process in myriad ways. Many arrive in Mexico after having lived a considerable number of years (considering their age) in the United States, while others move to Mexico at a very young age. The fragmentations experienced by the children in the first group are more abrupt and visible than those experienced by the children in the latter group.

Closely associated with migrant children's geographic movement is their transnational schooling experience. Children who were enrolled in schools in the United States for many years and then matriculate in Mexican schools will be more affected by their transnational schooling experience than those enrolled in U.S. schools for a short time. Our data showed a significant percentage of children who had never been enrolled in U.S. schools before moving to Mexico. In our samples these children were all born in the United States, moved to Mexico at an early age, and began their schooling in Mexico. Finally, the sense of belonging to the 0.5 generation of immigrants may also vary among the child migrants. Children with dual citizenship pertain to this generation, but, if they were to return to the United States, they could once again become members of the second generation. On the contrary, children with only Mexican citizenship are less likely to circulate between the two countries.

While all these children are international migrants living in Mexico, and all have various features and traits in common, the extreme cases of transnational children show how contrasting their experiences can be. For example, we found children who had attended school mostly in the United States and are bilingual and culturally binational but who possess only Mexican citizenship. We also found children who had completed their entire education in both school systems by spending half of the year in U.S. schools and the other half in Mexican schools. These children experience the highest degree of fragmentation during their socialization process. And, last, we found children with dual citizenship whose connection to the U.S. society is limited only to their birth certificate, as they arrived in Mexico before turning one year old and have never visited the United States since then. We incorporated all these variations in the children's migratory and educational trajectories, including the exceptional cases, in the typology proposed in this chapter.

Thus far, we have drawn on several data sources to comprehensively present the experiences of child migrants in Mexico. In chapter 2 we analyzed national data sources to depict the broad context of child migrants who have arrived in Mexico after being born or residing in the United States. In this chapter we elaborated a detailed typology of international child migrants who have arrived in Mexico since the beginning of the twenty-first century and complemented each category with qualitative examples of migrant children's experiences. In the next chapter, we discuss in greater detail the geographic itineraries of the school-age minors (from all five focal states) that we interviewed as a way to integrate more information about and to further nuance these children's migratory experiences.

4 The Geographic Itineraries of Migrant Children

The United States of America is a federation composed of fifty states, including Hawaii and Alaska. Since the early 1990s, international child migrants have been forging a fascinating geography that reflects new patterns of Mexican migration to the United States that is dispersed throughout nearly all fifty states (Zúñiga and Hernández-León 2005a). These children are the principal characters in these countries' current migration story, and their transnational experiences shed light on possible future migratory scenarios. In 2015–16, the *Current Population Survey* (U.S. Census Bureau 2016) indicated that nearly 14 million second-generation children under the age of eighteen were living in the United States; all these children were born in the United States and at least one of their parents was a Mexican migrant. For an accurate count of Mexican migrant children, we must add the 1.3 million children born in Mexico living in the United States during the same time span to this number. This compiled population of more than 15 million minors is entitled to Mexican citizenship by birth. Those born in the United States, and some of the Mexican-born migrant children, have U.S. citizenship or may acquire it when they reach adulthood. Most of these children will be free to move, reside, work, and live in both countries. The size of this population indicates that Mexican migration to the United

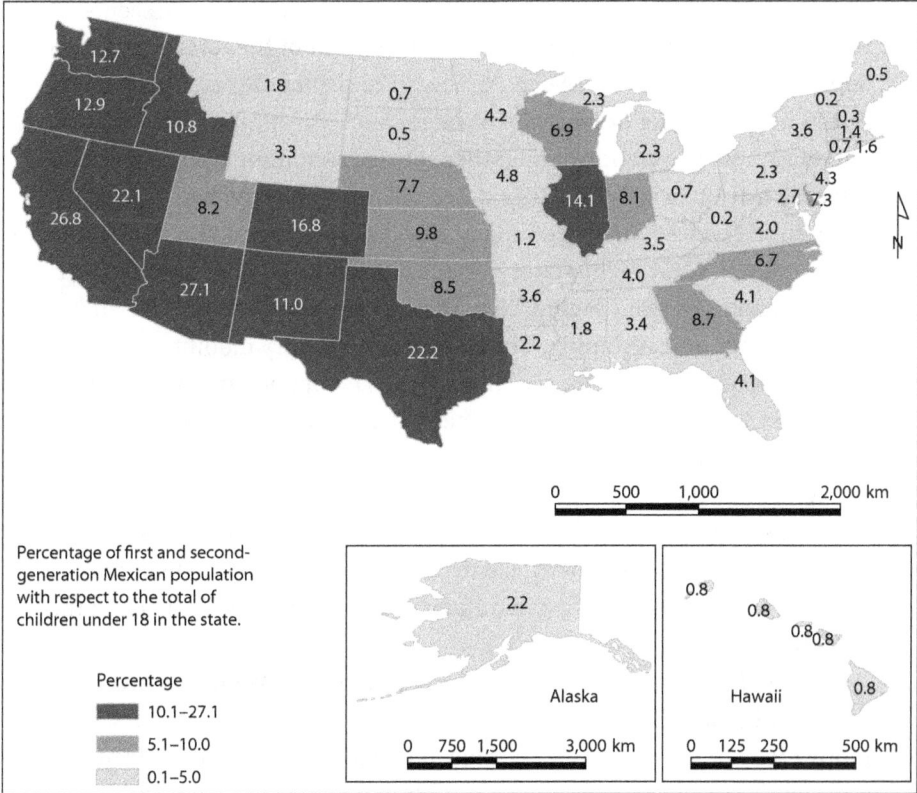

Figure 4. Percentage of Mexican-origin child migrants (first and second generation) living in the United States with respect to the total population, ages zero to seventeen, by state, 2015-16.

Source: Our estimates are based on the *Current Population Survey* (U.S. Census Bureau 2016).

States is, indeed, a familial phenomenon. Given the proximity between the countries, this data allows us to anticipate that if migration from the United States to Mexico were to increase again, it would continue to include first- and second-generation children of Mexican origin.

Minors of Mexican origin, whether they were born in Mexico or are children of Mexican migrants (i.e., the second generation), have a migratory presence of varying proportion in each U.S. state. Figure 4 depicts the geographic dispersion of Mexican-originating children and captures the importance of this group with respect to the total population of minors in certain states. For example, in 2015–16 children and adolescents of Mexican origin represented more than 20 percent of the total population under eighteen years of age in Arizona, California, Texas, and Nevada (listed in descending order by percentage).[1]

Our sample population of migrant children, stemming from 2004, represented forty-two out of the fifty states. All these children had experience living in the United States and many were born or attended school in the United States. Only eight states are not represented in our sample data: South Dakota, Hawaii, Maine, New Hampshire, Rhode Island, Vermont, West Virginia, and Wyoming. The children's migratory mobility is a result of a confluence of strategies, resources, risks, and opportunities. Migration is, in essence, a geographic movement that makes it possible to seize employment, education, and social opportunities while minimizing risks due to deportation or insecurity, employing coping strategies to deal with situations (e.g., divorce, death, homesickness, friction, and illness), and leveraging available resources, particularly the solidarity and support of relatives and friends who live in different regions in both Mexico and the United States.

In this chapter our purpose is strictly descriptive. While we present a cartography of children's migratory itineraries, we do not discuss their motivations or try to explain their movements. Here we focus only on the geographic mobility of school-aged children (ages six to seventeen) at the state level in both Mexico and the United States. In chapter 5 we explain the most significant migratory movements in which the children have participated: international migration from the United States to Mexico.

Our data has shown that child migration transpires quite differently in each Mexican state. To capture the distinct migratory attributes of Nuevo León, Zacatecas, Puebla, Jalisco, and Morelos, we present each state's survey data independently. Looking at each state individually is necessary for two reasons. First, the surveys were carried out on different dates. Second, each state has distinct characteristics that should be properly described and analyzed to highlight their uniqueness. Unlike any other issue, the geographic itineraries of migrant children have turned out to be a markedly regional phenomenon. That is to say, the geographic mobility of the child migrants in Nuevo León differs significantly from that observed in the other Mexican states, just as the other four states differ starkly from one another. Some of the characteristics of each state have already been documented in the literature on migration from Mexico to the United States; for example, Regina Cortina and Mónica Gendreau (2004) and Robert Smith (2006) studied the migration from Puebla to New York, and Miguel González Quiroga (1993) analyzed the strong historical links between Texas and Nuevo León. However, the geographic itineraries of the children presented in this chapter reveal different characteristics of international spatial mobility to which, until now, specialists have paid less attention and which cannot be gleaned from population censuses and administrative records.

Our descriptions and analyses of the children's geographic mobility at the state level are organized as follows. First, we present the migratory itineraries of the child migrants who began their journey in the United States. It is well known that, for decades, the majority of the Mexican population residing in the United States has been concentrated in the state of California (Zúñiga and Hernández-León 2017; Durand, Massey, and Capoferro 2005). Hence, our analysis begins by presenting the migratory itineraries of children born in California. In the case of Nuevo León, we focus on the international child migrants born in Texas, as this particular population was considerably important in our dataset. For similar reasons in the section about Puebla we include the children who were either born in New York or born in Puebla and later migrated to New York. Second, we describe the migratory itineraries of children born in Mexico, particularly in the focal Mexican states (Nuevo León, Zacatecas, etc.). At some point during their childhood, these children migrated to the United States and later returned to the state in which they were born. Some of these children made round-trip migrations, while others passed through intermediate destinations before returning to their birthplace. Next we direct our attention to the geographic movements of children born in any of the other forty-one U.S. states, excluding California or Texas (in the case of Nuevo León) and New York (in the case of Puebla).

We end each section by describing and analyzing the migratory itineraries of children born in Mexican states that were different from where they were living at the time of the survey. These children's migration stories are especially interesting because their arrival in Mexico is not a return to the state where they were born but to a different one, therefore combining the phenomenon of international migration with that of internal migration mediated by international migration.

The information children were asked about the places where they had lived was not always available, especially when the children were very young at the time of the survey or interview. Many of them did not remember or did not know the state in which they had been born or in which they had resided in the United States. While the portrait of geographic mobility presented here is incomplete, it does provide a sufficiently clear outline of the geographic patterns that characterize this international migrant children's mobility. This chapter is an initial description that captures both the persistence of traditional destinations (i.e., California and Texas) and the emergence of new destinations within the Mexican-U.S. migration experience.

As a final point of distinction, we discern the migrant children who arrived in the most significant urban communities in each of the focal Mexican states from the children who arrived in rural or less urbanized municipalities. For practical purposes we selected the following metropolitan areas in each focal state: Monterrey, Nuevo León; the principal cities in Zacatecas; the city of Puebla, Puebla; and Guadalajara, Jalisco. In Morelos we distinguish between the children who were in Cuernavaca and those in Zacatepec because the schools in which we conducted the survey are located in these cities. By making these distinctions, we can provide a more detailed answer to the question: "Where in Mexico do child migrants arrive?" We identify not only the state in which they arrived but also the specific regions to where they migrated when they moved from the United States to Mexico.

NUEVO LEÓN: CHILDREN COMING FROM TEXAS AND RETURNING TO MONTERREY

Nearly half (48.5 percent) of the international child migrants enrolled in Nuevo León's elementary and junior high schools in December 2004 were living in Texas at some point in their lives (see table 11).[2] Most of these children had been living in Houston, Dallas, San Antonio, Laredo, and other cities and counties in the Texas valley. Among them the majority had birth certificates issued in Texas. In fact, in the schools in Nuevo León, the

Table 11   Percentage distribution of child migrants' itineraries from the United States to Nuevo León, 2004 (n = 208)

		Destination		
Beginning of trajectory (birthplace)	*Intermediate destinations*	*Monterrey metropolitan area (%)*	*Other municipalities in Nuevo León (%)*	*Total (%)*
Texas	–	14.0	13.0	27.0
Texas	Other U.S. states	0.5	2.0	2.5
California	–	1.0	3.0	4.0
California	Other U.S. states	–	0.5	0.5
Nuevo León	Texas	15.0	4.0	19.0
Nuevo León	Other U.S. states	8.0	8.0	16.0
Other U.S. states		4.0	5.0	9.0
Other U.S. states	Other U.S. states*	0.5	2.5	3.0
Other Mexican states**	Texas	13.0	3.0	16.0
Other Mexican states	Other U.S. states (California included)	2.0	1.0	3.0
Total		58.0	42.0	100.0

SOURCE: Our elaboration is based on the databases of Universidad de Monterrey (2015).

*The other U.S. states include Colorado, Florida, Minnesota, Oklahoma, North Dakota, South Carolina, Alabama, Illinois, Ohio, Washington, Kansas, Louisiana, Michigan, Nebraska, Georgia, Indiana, Tennessee, Oregon, Kentucky, New York, and Massachusetts.

**The other Mexican states include Coahuila, Mexico City, Michoacán, San Luis Potosí, Tamaulipas, Jalisco, and Veracruz.

students born in Texas outnumbered those born in the Mexican states of Zacatecas, Jalisco, Chihuahua, Guanajuato, and Michoacán. The only group of students who outnumbered the Texas-born children were those from Coahuila, San Luis Potosí, Tamaulipas, and Mexico City. In Nuevo León we found students from many states of Mexico, but they were significantly fewer than those born in Texas.

Generally speaking, the Texas-born children followed a migratory itinerary from Texas to Nuevo León with no intermediate destinations. If we also take into consideration the children who were born in Nuevo León, migrated to Texas, and later returned to Nuevo León, the migratory space within which these children move is composed of only two states that, throughout history, have had close commercial, financial, cultural, and family ties and have formed a unique, cross-border space within which families, goods, and money have circulated since the mid-nineteenth century (González Quiroga 1993; Hernández-León 2008). These children—the Texas-born and the Mexican-born whose only destination in the United States was Texas—move within a relatively familiar territory, not only because people from Nuevo León are very familiar with many parts of Texas but also because their cousins, aunts and uncles, siblings, and other close relatives live in this state. An interesting characteristic of children coming from Texas is that about half were living in the Monterrey metropolitan area, while the other half moved to one of the other municipalities in the state. However, the Mexican-born children who followed the Nuevo León to Texas to Nuevo León itinerary returned mainly to the nonmetropolitan municipalities and lived in more rural areas. Equally interesting is the observation that the Texas-born children rarely passed through intermediate destinations before settling in Nuevo León.

The geographic mobility of the other half of Nuevo León's international child migrants looks completely different. First, those who were born in California and later came to Nuevo León are an exception and constitute only 4.5 percent of child migrants in this state. Among them the majority moved from California directly to Nuevo León. Then there are those born in other U.S. states—in twenty-one different states, not counting Texas and California. These children, unlike the Californians, are not, strictly speaking, exceptions because they represent more than 10 percent of the sample. Some of these children passed through intermediate destinations before arriving in Nuevo León. In most cases the intermediate destination was only one state, but we found a dozen cases of children who had passed through two or three different states in the United States before reaching their destination in Nuevo León.

These are the children who experience the most acute type of dislocation brought about by international migration. Such was the case of Mariana, who was fifteen years old when we interviewed her at a school located in Cerralvo, Nuevo León. She was born in Rio Grande, Texas, and later moved to South Carolina, where she began her schooling and was enrolled from preschool through third grade. From there she continued her studies in Georgia until the seventh grade. Later she moved to Nuevo León and resumed her schooling in the second year of junior high (equivalent to the eighth grade in the United States). Mariana, like all the children of agricultural laborers we met in Nuevo León, had always been accompanied by her parents throughout her migratory journey. During the interviews these children generally stated that such a nomadic life comes at a personal and emotional cost and has an impact on school performance.

To finish the description of the itineraries of children from Nuevo León, it is important to point out that we also found children in Nuevo León who were born in Coahuila, Mexico City, Michoacán, San Luis Potosí, Tamaulipas, Jalisco, and Veracruz. They had migrated mainly to Texas (though a small proportion had migrated to other U.S. states) and later returned to Mexico; however, they did return to Nuevo León as opposed to their native states. These children's itinerary represents almost a fifth of the total number of the trajectories in the sample. This suggests that Nuevo León and, specifically, the Monterrey metropolitan area is a return destination for Mexican migrants originating from other regions of Mexico. This finding is not surprising. Studies conducted forty years ago (Alvírez 1973) or twenty years ago (Zúñiga 1993; Zúñiga and Sánchez 2010) had already suggested that the city of Monterrey and its surrounding municipalities attracted Mexicans originating from different Mexican states who had lived in the United States.

Almost all the migrant children from Veracruz, Jalisco, San Luis Potosí, Mexico City, Michoacán, Tamaulipas, and Coahuila are originally from medium and large cities in their respective states, such as Guadalajara, Torreon, Ciudad Victoria, Nuevo Laredo, Tuxpan, Minatitlan, Morelia, Uruapan, and, of course, Mexico City. They are international child migrants of urban origin, who, after having lived a part of their lives mainly in Texas, returned to Mexico and settled in one of the urban municipalities within the Monterrey metropolitan area. These children's routes consist primarily of international migration movements. However, second to this we observe a type of return migration, which can be understood as a complete circuit of urban-to-urban internal migration. The percentage of migrant children from Nuevo León who arrived in the Monterrey metropolitan area is greater than that of the children who arrived in nonmetropolitan munici- palities. This is not the case in Zacatecas, Puebla, or Jalisco.

ZACATECAS: THE CALIFORNIA-BORN CHILDREN AND THEIR ARRIVAL IN RURAL TOWNS

Almost half of the migrant children studied in Zacatecas were born, lived in, or passed through California (see table 12). This figure was calculated by adding together the following groups: children who were born in California and from there moved to Zacatecas (29 percent); children who were born in California, passed through intermediate destinations in other U.S. states, and after that arrived in Zacatecas (3.5 percent); children who were born in Zacatecas, migrated to California, and later returned to Zacatecas (11 per- cent); and those who were born in other U.S. states, moved to California, and then came to Zacatecas (1.5 percent). However, this figure is not com- plete until we also include the children who were born in Mexican states other than Zacatecas, migrated to California, and then arrived in Zacatecas (2 percent). In one way or another, nearly half (47 percent) of the child migrants in Zacatecas have had a Californian experience.

The children born in Zacatecas had been geographically dispersed to an extraordinary extent. In addition to California, the children from Zacatecas migrated to Alabama, Arizona, New Mexico, Colorado, Illinois, Missouri, Nevada, New York, Oklahoma, Georgia, Indiana, Kansas, Louisiana, and Massachusetts. Children born in Zacatecas who then migrated to new destinations scattered across the United States numerically and propor- tionally outnumbered those who migrated to California and later returned to Zacatecas. Based on the data presented so far, child migrants in Zacatecas seemed to have followed two main, yet contrasting, routes. The first route begins in California and goes to Zacatecas, while the second starts in Zacatecas, disperses across fifteen U.S. states (including California), and returns to Zacatecas. The first route is prevalent among the children born in California, while the second is predominant among the children born in Zacatecas. The former group represents a third of the sample (29 percent), while the latter constitute a fifth of the sample (i.e.,

Table 12   Percentage distribution of child migrants' itineraries from the United States to Zacatecas, 2005 (n = 241)

		Destination		
		Cities in	Rural towns	
Beginning of		*Cities in*	*in Zacatecas*	
trajectory	*Intermediate*	*Zacatecas**	*in Zacatecas*	
(birthplace)	*destination*	*(%)*	*(%)*	*Total (%)*
California	–	10.0	19.0	29.0
California	Other U.S. states**	0.5	3.0	3.5
Zacatecas	California	4.0	7.0	11.0
Zacatecas	Other U.S. states	7.0	13.0	20.0
Other U.S states	–	7.0	16.0	23.0
Other U.S. states	California	0.5	1.0	1.5
Other U.S. states	Other U.S. states	1.0	2.0	3.0
Other Mexican states***	California	1.0	1.0	2.0
Other Mexican states	Other U.S. states	2.0	5.0	7.0
Total		33.0	67.0	100.0

SOURCE: Our elaboration is based on the databases of Universidad de Monterrey (2015).

*Cities in Zacatecas include Fresnillo, Guadalupe, Jalpa, Jerez, Juchipila, Valparaíso, Villanueva, and Zacatecas.

**The other U.S. states include Arizona, New Mexico, Kansas, Nevada, Georgia, Illinois, Iowa, Ohio, Texas, Colorado, Mississippi, New York, Oklahoma, Wisconsin, Washington, Alaska, Oregon, South Carolina, Tennessee, Maryland, Indiana, Louisiana, Massachusetts, and Utah.

***The other Mexican states include Aguascalientes, Baja California, Coahuila, Jalisco, Nuevo León, Tabasco, State of Mexico, Durango, and San Luis Potosí.

Zacatecas to U.S. states other than California to Zacatecas represented 20 percent). The group of Zacatecas-born children are considered participants in the new geographic diaspora of Mexican migration that began in the late 1980s and early 1990s across the United States.

The children of this new migratory dispersion are, in fact, more numerous than those who have experienced traditional migration patterns. If we add together those who began their itinerary in Zacatecas (their birth state) and then dispersed across the United States with the children who were born in U.S. states other than California (the traditional migratory destination), the geographic representation of child migration in Zacatecas looks quite different. The state of California most definitely represents the central point on the map, but no less important is the migrant children's geographic dispersion across the United States. As we pointed out previously, 20 percent of the migrant children were born in Zacatecas and migrated to fifteen different states other than California, but, at the same time, almost 26 percent of the children were born in states as remote as Utah, Alaska, Maryland, and Wisconsin. The migratory map of Zacatecas confirms the coexistence of what Jorge Durand (2002) defines as "patterns of concentration" and dispersion, and our 2005 survey data from the schools in Zacatecas complements this finding: both children born in Zacatecas and children born in the United States participate in this dispersion. Very few of these children passed through California, the traditional migratory destination.

Nuevo León is a return destination for international migrants who are originally from other Mexican states. This does not appear to be the case in Zacatecas, where only 9 percent of the child migrants enrolled in the state's elementary and junior high schools were born in a state other than Zacatecas. This small percentage of children are from Aguascalientes, Baja California, Coahuila, Jalisco, Nuevo León, Tabasco, State of Mexico, Durango, and San Luis Potosí. With the exception of Aguascalientes, these states do not border Zacatecas. This also contrasts with Nuevo León, where the children in this category were born mostly in neighboring states.

In the total sample of elementary and junior high school students in Zacatecas (n = 11,258), we found children born in twenty-three states throughout Mexico, from Yucatán to Baja California. If we compare the number of children born in those Mexican states with the those born in California, we observe that, in the schools of Zacatecas, there were more children born in California than in the Mexican states of Chihuahua, Coahuila, Guanajuato, and Nuevo León. The California-born children were much more numerous than those born in Tabasco, Tamaulipas, or Nayarit. Collectively, only the children born in the Mexican states of Aguascalientes, Durango, the State of Mexico, Jalisco, and San Luis Potosí numerically surpassed those born in California.

Most of the international child migrants in Zacatecas arrived predominantly in rural regions. Those born in the United States came mainly to rural locations; likewise, those born in Zacatecas returned mainly to small or medium-sized towns, such as Chupaderos (in the municipality of General Francisco R. Murguía), El Barreal (in the municipality of Jalpa), Cerrito de Dolores (in the municipality of Pinos), or San Antonio del Cerrito (in the municipality of Sombrerete). The children who were born in other Mexican states, migrated to the United States, and then later arrived in Zacatecas followed a different itinerary. A proportionally greater number of these children settled in the state's major cities, such as Zacatecas, Fresnillo, and Jerez. This difference is likely associated with the fact that these children (9 percent of the total sample) were natives of major cities such as Guadalajara, Aguascalientes, or the metropolitan area of Mexico City. Once again we observe that the international migration of children born in states other than the destination state combines with an internal, urban-urban migration trajectory. Only very few children's geographic itinerary included intermediate destinations. In total, there were eight children who passed through Colorado, California, or Kansas on their way to Zacatecas.

PUEBLA: GEOGRAPHIC DISPERSION AND CHILDREN WHO ARRIVE IN SMALL TOWNS

Among the international child migrants residing in Puebla in 2009, only about 40 percent followed the traditional migratory routes of New York to Puebla, California to Puebla, Puebla to California to Puebla, Puebla to New York to Puebla. The percentage of children who followed these routes was relatively similar: not one of these routes was more prominent than the others (see table 13). With these findings, it is difficult to claim that the main destination of migrants from Puebla is New York or that return migrants generally come to Puebla from New York. In fact, the group of California-born or Puebla-born children who returned to Puebla from California has the same relative weight as that of the children who were born in or arrived from New York. On the other hand, nearly 60 percent of the migrant children were born in or came from states other than New

Table 13   Percentage distribution of child migrants' itineraries from the United States to Puebla, 2009 (n = 140)

Beginning of trajectory (birthplace)	Intermediate destinations	Destinations		Total (%)
		Puebla metropolitan area (%)	Other municipalities in Puebla (%)	
California	–	2	8	10
New York	–	1	13	14
Puebla	California	3	6	9
Puebla	New York	2	6	8
Puebla	Other U.S. states	5	14	19
Other U.S. states*	–	4	30	34
Other U.S. states	Other U.S. states	–	5	5
Other Mexican states**	Other U.S. states	–	1	1
Total		17	83	100

SOURCE: Our elaboration is based on the databases of Universidad de Monterrey (2015).

*The other U.S. states include Florida, Indiana, Arizona, New Jersey, Georgia, Michigan, Minnesota, North Carolina, South Carolina, Oregon, Nevada, Colorado, Massachusetts, Texas, Washington, Maryland, New Mexico, Illinois, and Utah.

**The other Mexican states include Mexico City.

York and California. These results suggest that, toward the end of the first decade of the twenty-first century, migrants from Puebla were already fully participating in the dynamic dispersion of destinations across the United States.

The child migrants who arrived in Puebla in 2009 had either been born in or had lived in nineteen different states throughout the United States, not including New York and California. Not one state stands out among this sample of migrant children. For many states, like Georgia, Nevada, and South Carolina, only one child indicated it as their birthplace. Likewise, in North Carolina and Texas, we found only isolated cases of Puebla-born children who had been enrolled in schools. However, when all these cases are combined under the category of "other destinations," they become the majority of this sample. These other destinations include more traditional migratory destination states, such as Illinois, Arizona, New Mexico, and Texas; however, our data show that these states are not significant destinations or starting points for the children from Puebla. In our sample data from Puebla there was only one child born in Illinois compared to four born in Minnesota and eight in Washington. If we direct our attention exclusively to the children born in Puebla, we observe that the percentage of minors who migrated to California or New York is not larger than that of children who migrated to U.S. states other than California and New York. Uniquely, what characterizes the children born in Puebla is their geographic dispersion across the United States.

In the Puebla sample, highly fragmented migratory trajectories, which include several intermediate destinations before arriving in or returning to Puebla, are truly exceptional. We found only seven cases with geographic itineraries such as New York to Minnesota to Puebla or Texas to Illinois to Maryland to Puebla. The typical itineraries of migrant children in Puebla can be categorized as (1) "one-way trip" (such as a U.S. state to Puebla) or (2) "round-trip" (such as Puebla to a U.S. state to Puebla). The one-way trips represent about 60 percent of the total, while the round trips amount to about 35 percent.

Is the state of Puebla a destination for international migrants from other Mexican states? Our data indicate that this is not the case. In Puebla only 1 percent of the children born in Mexico originate from a Mexican state other than Puebla, and all of them were from Mexico City. Child migrants who arrive from the United States go not to the metropolitan area of the city of Puebla but to rural locations throughout the state. Notably, most were identified in the Mixtec region of Puebla and in the Izúcar region from Matamoros to Atlixco. Migrant children arrive in towns such as Acapetlahuacan (in the municipality of Atlixco), Lomas de San Francisco (in the municipality of Tepexi de Rodríguez), Huachinantla (in the municipality of Jolalpan), and San Miguel Boquerón or Tlamatzingo (both in the municipality of Acatlán). Only 13 percent of child migrants arrived in the city of Puebla and surrounding municipalities (e.g., Cholula, Juan C. Bonilla, and Tepeaca). The rest went to towns or to the centers of thirty-four different municipalities, including Tecamachalco, Zihateutla, Cuautempan, Izúcar de Matamoros, Acatlán, Ajalpan, Tlapanalá, Cañada de Morelos, Tulcingo, and Tepanco.

JALISCO: THE CALIFORNIA-BORN CHILDREN RESIDING
IN NONMETROPOLITAN MUNICIPALITIES

The geographic trajectories of child migrants in Jalisco are similar in many respects to those of the children in Zacatecas. Almost one out of every three children in both states started their migratory journey in California because they were born there. Coincidentally, in both states one out of every five children were born in either Jalisco or Zacatecas and lived and studied in California (compare tables 12 and 14). In the Jalisco dataset, when we add together the number of California-born children and the children who had migratory experience in California, the sum represents nearly half of the sample (i.e., California to Jalisco and Jalisco to California to Jalisco and California to other U.S. states to Jalisco add up to 49 percent). Thus, in 2010 the typical itineraries of Jalisco's child migrants were California to Jalisco and Jalisco to California to Jalisco. In contrast, children residing in Jalisco who were living at some point in the United States other than California represented only 34 percent of the sample. The migratory routes seem to have only two terminals—one located in California and the other in Jalisco. The child migrants in Jalisco who were born in and lived in other U.S. states represent a widely dispersed subpopulation: they have been in twenty-four different U.S. states besides California. These children were born in or resided in states such as Arkansas, Florida, Minnesota, Michigan, Idaho, Virginia, and Nebraska.

Migratory routes with multiple stops are not common among Jalisco's child migrants. Through the children's responses to our questionnaires, we identified only twelve children who had followed trajectories that included two or more intermediate destinations. Examples of these itineraries are California to Colorado to Jalisco; Illinois to California to Jalisco; and Tennessee to Missouri to Georgia to Jalisco. This latter itinerary is that of Marcela, who was only ten years old when she responded to the questionnaire in an elementary school in Zapopan. She was born in Nashville, Tennessee, and then studied two years of preschool and the first year of elementary school in Missouri. From there she moved to Georgia and attended the second year of elementary school. At eight years old, she moved to Zapopan and enrolled in the elementary school, where we met. International child migrants born in other Mexican states, whose return

Table 14 *Percentage distribution of child migrants' itineraries from the United States to Jalisco, 2010 (n = 296)*

| | | Destinations | | |
| | | | | |
Beginning of trajectory (birthplace)	*Intermediate destinations*	*Guadalajara metropolitan area (%)*	*Other municipalities in Jalisco (%)*	*Total (%)*
California	–	11	14	25
California	Other U.S. states*	1	2	3
Jalisco	California	7	14	21
Jalisco	New York	6	6	12
Other U.S. states*		9	19	28
Other U.S. states*	Other U.S. states*	3	3	6
Other Mexican states**	California	1	---	1
Other Mexican states**	Other U.S. states*	1	3	4
Total		39	61	100

SOURCE: Our elaboration is based on the databases of Universidad de Monterrey (2015).

*The other U.S. states include Arizona, Massachusetts, Arkansas, Colorado, Florida, Georgia, Illinois, Ohio, Oregon, Minnesota, Michigan, Oklahoma, Indiana, Washington, Idaho, Nebraska, Kansas, Louisiana, Missouri, Tennessee, Texas, Wisconsin, Virginia, and Utah.

**The other Mexican states include Baja California, Michoacán, Sinaloa, and Tamaulipas.

destination was Jalisco, do not represent a significant proportion of this dataset. In other words, the child migrants who arrived in Jalisco were born either in Jalisco or in the United States.

Let us take a moment to focus on the U.S.-born children and make the same comparisons that we made for the other focal Mexican states. As might be expected, internal migrant children from practically every state in Mexico, including Mexico City, were enrolled in Jalisco's schools, with the exception of Campeche. When comparing this group with that of the U.S.-born children, we found that the second group was significantly larger. In the elementary schools of Jalisco, there were more children born in the United States than children born in Colima, Mexico City, Michoacán, Sinaloa, Baja California, or Zacatecas. In the sample the children from

Colima represented the largest group of internal migrants. Importantly, the number of U.S.-born children was notably higher than the number of children from Colima.

Finally, one more characteristic of Jalisco's migrant children should be emphasized to complete the geographic description of child migrants in this state. Where do they go once they are in Jalisco? The data show that their predominant destinations are not within the Guadalajara metropolitan area (e.g., Zapopan, Tlaquepaque, Tlajomulco, Tonalá, El Salto, Juanacatlán, Ixtlahuacàn, and Guadalajara City) but in other regions of the state. Even if we added together the child migrants residing in Puerto Vallarta, Autlán, Ocotlán, Tepatitlán, Lagos de Moreno, and other medium-sized cities throughout the state, the distribution does not change significantly: six out of ten children born in the United States were residing in rural or semiurban towns and villages in Jalisco.

MORELOS: A GEOGRAPHIC CONUNDRUM

The routes of the child migrants from Morelos represent a series of sui generis geographic itineraries. It appears as if these children were from, migrated to, and returned from any location within the United States. Of course, this and other observations should be taken only as preliminary findings because the Morelos sample is not representative of the state's entire school system. The survey data gathered from four schools in Morelos suggests that the geographic dispersion of the migrant children residing in this state does not include any predominant routes or preferential geographic poles. On the contrary, it is a constellation of geographic points that includes twenty-four different U.S. states (despite the fact that this sample is much smaller than that collected in other Mexican states) and four Mexican states, all of which are located far away from Morelos.

The geographic itinerary that includes California either as a place of origin or as an intermediate destination represents less than 40 percent of the sample (see table 15). This proportion reflects the fact that the migratory itineraries of the child migrants from Morelos are heterogeneous, and, as such, we are not able to identify a principal migratory route. This geographic diversity is a conundrum that cannot be solved with our cur-

Table 15   Percentage distribution of child migrants' itineraries from the United States to Morelos, 2013 (n = 68)

Beginning of trajectory (birthplace)	Intermediate destinations	Destinations		
		Cuernavaca (%)	Zacatepec (%)	Total (%)
California	–	10	5	15
California	Other U.S. states*	3	1	4
Morelos	California	7	1	8
Morelos	Other U.S. states	26	–	26
Other U.S. states*	–	22	7	29
Other U.S. states*	Other U.S. states*	7		7
Other Mexican states**	California	10	–	10
Other Mexican states**	Other U.S. states*	1	–	1
Total		86	14	100

SOURCE: Our elaboration is based on the databases of Universidad de Monterrey (2015).

*The other U.S. states include Arizona, Massachusetts, Arkansas, Colorado, Florida, Georgia, Illinois, Ohio, Oregon, Minnesota, Michigan, Oklahoma, Indiana, Washington, Idaho, Nebraska, Kansas, Louisiana, Missouri, Tennessee, Texas, Wisconsin, Virginia, and Utah.

**The other Mexican states include Baja California, Michoacán, Sinaloa, and Tamaulipas.

rent data. Besides myriad departing points and intermediate destinations, we should also highlight the presence of child migrants who were born not in Morelos but in the Mexican states of Baja California, Michoacán, Sinaloa, and Tamaulipas. These children migrated to the United States and later arrived in Cuernavaca or Zacatepec, which were the locations of the schools in which we conducted the survey. The percentage of children who followed these routes (other states of Mexico to the United States to Morelos) is higher than what we found in Zacatecas, Puebla, and Jalisco.

This fact adds even more to the geographic conundrum and raises the question: Under what circumstances does Morelos become a receiving state for return migrants who are not originally from this state? We do not know. The provisional table 15 was created based on a sample, which is not representative, of the students enrolled in the elementary and junior high schools in the state. In any case what we can affirm is that, in these four schools, the myriad destinations and the heterogeneity of migratory itineraries are more predominant than what we observed in other regions of Mexico.

CONCLUSIONS

In this chapter we analyzed the geographic itineraries of migrant children by using the states in which the children were born, lived, and arrived in as a unit of analysis. This allowed us to identify prevalent, emergent, and exceptional geographic migration sequences in each of the focal states. The dominant migratory itineraries vary from state to state, although Zacatecas and Jalisco presented interesting similarities. Emerging sequences arose from the dispersion of origins and destinations in the United States that has covered almost the entirety of the country. We also highlighted exceptions in our analyses, which included mainly trajectories with multiple stops before reaching the destination in Mexico. With the exception of Morelos, in all the other focal states, the principal migratory sequences include, at some point, the states of California, Texas, and New York. On the other hand, *thirty-nine* additional U.S. states are present in the emergent migratory sequences, some as points of departure (because the children were born there) and others as intermediate destinations lived in before arriving in Mexico.

The routes drawn by the children's geographic trajectories in each of the states exhibit distinguishable characteristics. With the exception of Jalisco and Zacatecas, which show similarities, each state has its unique route. The child migrants in Nuevo León are strongly connected to the state of Texas, whereas the state of California does not typically appear in their trajectories. In contrast, in Jalisco and Zacatecas, California is the prevalent geographic point. The children from Puebla are divided between the New Yorkers and the Californians, while the international child migrants from the four schools in Morelos drew unexpected routes due to their extensive geographic dispersion.

In all cases, regardless of the year in which the survey was conducted and of the Mexican region where it was carried out, the geographic dispersion of a significant percentage of these children was constant throughout our study, since the very beginning in Nuevo León in 2004 until the last survey in Morelos in 2013. This is not a minor finding. To understand what international child migrants have been experiencing prior to their arrival in Mexico, it is of paramount importance to know the regions in which they were born or lived in the United States. This information cannot be obtained from other sources, such as the Mexican census or the *2015 Intercensal Survey*. In the United States, there are states with a long tradition of receiving Mexican-originating migrants. In these states numerous institutional initiatives and organizations service, in one way or another, the needs of Mexican migrants. On the contrary, there are regions in the United States with little or no experience in receiving Mexican migrants, and in these regions schools, churches, hospitals, workplaces, stores, sports clubs, neighborhoods, recreation centers, and many other spaces for social interaction do not provide (or did not provide until recently) any support to facilitate the integration of Mexican migrants into local communities.

The geographic map illustrates all the places where the migrant children have been, and it captures the spatial materialization of what we called "displaceability." This chapter shows that there are children who were born in Morelos, moved to Indiana, and later returned to Morelos. Other children were born in Alaska and arrived in Zacatecas at a young age. Additionally, there are children who were born in Tamaulipas, migrated to Florida, and later settled in Cuernavaca. In the next chapter, we analyze how these children explain the last leg of their trip: their arrival in Mexico after having been born or lived in the United States. We complement the geographic migratory itineraries presented here with the child migrants' narrated accounts of their experiences arriving or returning to Mexico. Their stories recount their versions of the conditions of their arrival in Mexico and of the circumstances that led to their migration to their parents' and relatives' country of origin.

5 Children of the Great Expulsion on Their Way to Mexico

Despite having been a sending country of migrants to the United States for more than a century, as of 2005 Mexico has become a receiving country for migrants from the United States. Most of the migrants who arrive in Mexico are Mexican adults who, after having resided in the United States for several years, return to the country accompanied by all or some of their family members, including their U.S.-born children. As we have explained, these children are the sons and daughters of the Great Migration (1990–2005) and of the Great Expulsion (2005 onward). This chapter presents the data that we have collected about these children's arrival to Mexico and their participation in the Great Expulsion.

Here, drawing on qualitative interview data and open-ended survey responses, we present the children's firsthand experiences and center—and respect—their perspectives on the migration experience. Because they too are international migrants, just like their parents and adult siblings, these children have firsthand knowledge of the meaning of migration. Agnes Heller defines the type of knowledge these children bring about migration as "everyday knowledge," asserting that it consists of two types of content—the first related to "knowing what" and the second to "knowing how." In the logic of practical life, both types of content are indissolubly linked. In fact, "knowing what" serves the "knowing how" and therefore "knowing what" cannot exist autonomously or fulfill a contemplative purpose (1977, 317–19). Migrant children have gained both types of knowledge from the Great Expulsion, of which they are participants

Two variables, age when migrating and knowledge accumulated during the migratory experience, are constitutive to these children's lives. We underline these dimensions because, for decades, the literature on international migration has been inherently adult-centric (Orellana et al. 2001; Orellana 2001; Quiroz 2001; Parreñas Salazar 2005; Ní Laoire, Tyrrel, and Carpena Méndez 2012). The adult-centrism of migration research, as Madeleine Dobson (2009) points out, depicts children as mere objects or "suitcases" carried by the adult migrants. Dobson uses the luggage metaphor to invite scholars to "unpack children in migration studies."[1]

To answer this call, we intend to "unpack" the migrant children in this chapter, and to do so we use different semantic and syntactic approaches. We now focus on listening to what child migrants have to say about migrating from the United States to Mexico, a pivotal event in their lives. We listen to them because they are migrants and have been directly involved in the Great Expulsion and also because, as Marjorie Orellana explains in her most recent book, "Listening to youth perspectives is important not just to teach kids, socialize them, or prepare them for the future—though it may inform all those goals. It is also important to learn from young people, about what's possible, and how we might learn to see differently" (2016, 48).

Furthermore, we listen to these children because the decisions that adults make in relation to migration are often motivated by parents' and grandparents' desires to offer their children or grandchildren the best possible life opportunities. As Deborah Boehm puts it, "Even if children are not the primary focus of migration research, they are certainly at the center of migration processes. Throughout my fieldwork, transnational Mexicans have indicated that a primary motivation for migrating is their children" (2008, 786). Consistent with this methodological approach, our data consists of stories and explanations provided directly by the child migrants.[2]

Throughout this chapter we present two types of narratives. The first stems from the 191 interviews that we have been conducting with migrant

children from 2004 until the time of writing. The conversational style of
the open-ended interviews permitted us to capture succinct life stories in
which the decision-making process regarding migration from the United
States to Mexico had a particular relevance.[3] Children generally know why
they or their parents, their siblings, or even just a part of their family
moved from one country to the other. We found only a few children who
were unaware of the circumstances that had brought them to Mexico. The
children's narratives, of course, do not contain the entire story of their
"return" (and neither do the adults'); however, it is *their* stories and perspectives that we seek to capture here.

The second type of narrative included in this chapter is not conversational nor is it part of the children's life stories. It is rather a short explanation that sheds light on the circumstances or conditions surrounding their
migration from the United States to Mexico. For this we draw from 638
short answers that children ages nine to sixteen (fourth through ninth
grade) wrote on the open-ended questions included in the surveys conducted at the schools. The international child migrants who were surveyed freely responded to the following question: Why have you returned
to Mexico? The children wrote their short responses independently and
without any guidance from the researchers. These written explanations
were generally short and sometimes limited to a single word. It should be
emphasized that the question was formulated in the first person (i.e., the
subject of who returned to Mexico was the child). We quickly learned that
the verb we used in this question, "returned," was not the most appropriate verb for this question as many of the children had not *returned to* but
rather *arrived in* Mexico for the first time. In their responses some of the
children surveyed pointed this mistake out to us.

In summary the empirical data that we present in this chapter consists
of both short stories and short explanations generated by children about
their experience migrating to Mexico. We begin by presenting some of the
children's stories and then continue with a compilation of the written
responses from the surveys. We first coded the interviews according to the
types of events that preceded and led to migration from the United States
to Mexico. We then selected focal stories from each category that were
representative of and that effectively illustrated the common phenomenon
that many migrant children experienced. For the children's short explana-

tions about their return to Mexico, we conducted an interpretive thematic analysis. These findings are presented after the children's narratives and in accordance with the resulting themes. The themes are arranged in order of relative proportion; that is to say, the theme that occurred most frequently across the children's written responses is presented first, followed by the others in order of prevalence. After presenting this data, we return to discuss the central research question: What have we learned about migration from the migrant children?

BACK IN MEXICO: STORIES OF CHILDREN BORN IN MEXICO

Felipe: "They Had Already Started to Take Everything Away from Them"

When we conducted the interviews in Atlixco, Puebla, in February 2010, the consequences of the Great Recession (2007–9) were taking their toll on the lives of Mexican migrants in the United States. Felipe was ten years old when we talked with him about his life in Dallas, Texas. He was taken there when he was eight months old, and he returned to Atlixco, his hometown, when he was eight years old.

In Dallas he lived with his parents and his four brothers. His three older brothers were born in Atlixco, while the youngest, who, at the time of the interview had just turned seven, was the only sibling born in the United States. Felipe understood to be true what he must have heard from his parents, aunts, uncles, or older brothers: that they were going to take things away from those who were not born in the United States. He did not give us more details and we do not know if, perhaps, his parents lost their house due to default on mortgage payments, or if his relatives, who were also living in Dallas, faced financial problems. The only thing that Felipe made clear is that this threat was the reason why his parents decided to return to Atlixco. The entire family returned except for his older brother, who continued to reside undocumented in Dallas at the time of study.

It is likely that Felipe knew of his family's decision to return well in advance. At some point during the interview, he revealed an additional factor in his family's decision to leave Dallas: Felipe alluded to the idea that there was a deportation order against his father or that his risk of receiving such an order was imminent. Whatever the reason, at his young age Felipe was aware of the fact that those without papers faced the risk of being deported.

Gaby: The Experience of Deportation

Gaby arrived in Chicago when she was four years old, returned to her hometown of Monterrey, Nuevo León, when she was nearly fourteen, and participated in an interview with us in December 2004. As she shared the chronology of her migration story, we learned that her father had worked as a bank employee in Monterrey in the early 1990s and was a victim of the financial crisis that affected Mexico during that time. "He lost his job," Gaby explained, and for that reason he chose to migrate to Chicago in early 1995. The family members migrated gradually until the entire family settled, first in a basement, then in a small apartment, and finally in a house. They had entered the United States with tourist visas. Gaby's narrative about her life in Chicago—at school, in the neighborhood, at the stores—stood out for its descriptive beauty and was accompanied by enthusiasm and energy until, all of a sudden, she revealed the reason why all her family was back in Monterrey.

Gaby's story is perhaps the most detailed narrative that we have collected since 2004. We include excerpts of her words here to capture the valuable information that she has shared:

> And my father worked at the airport, in a warehouse where merchandise arrived, and he had to pack it, wrap it in plastic, or, I don't know what, and he also put them on the plane, he accommodated everything. . . . My father was caught by immigration. I think that everything was already planned because they didn't take everybody [into custody]. My father says there was a list and they detained those who were on that list and took them away. . . . And they searched the whole car because one of my mother's friends went there to get the car and brought it back to her, and it was a mess. . . .

> It was August 26th. We had just started school. I was at home because I was taking care of my brother because my mother got off work at 6:30, and she came home around 7:00, so I didn't know. Then my mom's friend asked me if I could lend her the keys to my dad's car because he had left it. I don't

know, I don't remember what she told me then, but I gave her the keys and she went for the car and brought it home.

Later, my mother arrived, and the lady told her what had happened. After a while, my dad called and told her that he was in a courthouse, I don't know, that immigration had caught him, but we shouldn't worry, everything was fine. At that point, we contacted the Mexican consulate because the news story about this raid was being covered on TV, and there were phone numbers that you could call, so we were calling, and we were also trying to find out in which detention center he was being held in the meantime. . . .

And they also spoke with my mother, the wives of those men who [were being held]. They would call my mom because my father couldn't get in touch with us from the jail where he was [being held] because the call wouldn't go through, but the others somehow managed to get the call through to their homes, so, whenever those men called their wives, my father would ask them if they could please contact us so that we could tell him we were okay, so he wouldn't worry, and that his calls wouldn't go through. . . .

And from there on, we started to put everything in order, and we sold the house. We also had a truck that we had to return and go back again and sell everything, and that was it. . . . And after a month . . . [my father] asked for a hearing with the judge. Then they granted the hearing, and the judge told him that he was not going to be punished; all he had to do was leave the country.

Gaby lived in Chicago without documentation, as did her mother and her father. In fact, none of the members of her family had authorization to reside in the United States except for Gaby's younger brother, who had been born in Chicago. Interestingly, Gaby was determined to return to Chicago. So was Gaby's mother. We do not know if they succeeded. Paradoxically, the younger brother—a U.S. citizen by birth—was the only one who did not want to return to Chicago, as he was already starting to enjoy life in Monterrey.

Cindy: Redefining Life with Grandparents

Cindy's parents took her to Los Angeles when she was a baby. Since she was not authorized to reside in the United States, her parents decided that it was best for Cindy to return to Tepeaca, Puebla, to live with her paternal grandparents. She arrived at the Puebla City Airport when she was twelve, knowing that it would be difficult to return to Los Angeles. At the same time, Cindy was well aware of the legal conditions that would prevent her from having access to higher education in California once she reached the age of eighteen. Her parents were also undocumented migrants, while her fifteen-year-old sister and her eleven-year-old brother were U.S. citizens by birth.

Cindy returned to Mexico alone, but a few months later her father returned to Tepeaca, leaving his wife and two of his children in Los Angeles. We do not know whether the father was also taking precautions, in the same way he had done with Cindy (avoiding deportation), or simply wished to be close to his only undocumented daughter. Cindy did not clarify during the interview whether her father's decision was temporary or if he wanted to settle in Puebla. At the time of the interview in June 2010, crossing the border without documents was a costly and risky undertaking. Perhaps Cindy's father had chosen to return to Mexico to be with his daughter.

Cindy knew the value of her bilingualism but also that she would have to increase her proficiency in academic Spanish to be successful in junior high school: "I still don't have a good grasp on reading [in Spanish]." She identified herself as bicultural and had plans to study languages other than English and Spanish and pursue a career related to tourism. She knew very well that she could leverage the skills that she had acquired during her childhood to be successful in these areas. We asked Cindy, "How do you feel, Mexican or American?" and she answered, "I feel both."

David: "We're Better All Together in Puebla"

David's paternal family had found an attractive niche job in Michigan: they were working in a greenhouse. They had arrived in Michigan one by one: first David's uncle, then his two aunts, followed by several of his cousins and then his grandmother. After two years it was David's father's turn. Months later David, at nine years old, made the trip from Atlixco to Michigan. He did not tell us how he crossed the border, and we never asked for additional information about this topic. Knowing that children often entered the United States irregularly, it was not appropriate to bring up this subject or any other that might be traumatizing for them.

Sometimes the children themselves described such situations in great detail, but this was not the case for David.

The interesting thing about David's story is that only he and his father lived in Michigan. In fact, David studied for three years at a local school, from second through fourth grade. After that he and his father decided to return because the mother, who continued to live in Atlixco with David's two younger brothers, was not willing to take the risks associated with irregular migration: "We returned because my mother wanted to go there, to the United States, but then she was afraid she would get caught or something." David's father resumed his floriculture activities in Atlixco and had no intention of returning to Michigan. David returned to his school in Atlixco in the fifth grade and has good memories of his school experience in the United States. David returned to Atlixco knowing that his adventure in Michigan had been short-lived.

Beto: The Power of Parents' Love

Beto crossed the Tijuana–San Isidro border when he was two years old. His father was already living in Santa Ana, California, and he had planned everything so that his wife and son could live with him again. They departed from Ocuilan in the State of Mexico with the destination of Santa Ana, California. First, they paid a couple of U.S. women to take Beto across the border by pretending that he was their son and using false documents. A month later his mother arrived using the services of a Tijuana-based coyote. All of this happened between 2000 and 2001.

When Beto's father first arrived in California, he was supported by his extended family and mostly by his cousins. As the months went by, this support diminished, and he was soon forced to seek independent housing for his family of three. During the search he arrived at a low-cost hotel in Santa Ana, which ended up being a stroke of luck for Beto's father because he was able to offer his gardening services to the hotel managers. Subsequently, he demonstrated his abilities to help with maintenance tasks. In a short time, Beto's father became a valued employee by the owners, who frequently asked him to do work in their other hotels that were located throughout the United States. In fact, the room in which Beto and his parents lived at the hotel was part of his father's work benefits.

Beto lived in Santa Ana until he was fourteen years old. He made good friends at school, and, as one might expect, he spoke English as a native speaker, and he perceived himself as a boy from Southern California. This normality was suddenly disrupted by an unexpected event. Once, when Beto's mother was leaving the hotel, she was attacked and had her cell phone stollen. The mother reported the thieves, the police located them, and one was sent to prison. What Beto's mother did not know is that the thief belonged to a criminal organization whose members, in revenge, later showed up at the hotel and threatened Beto's parents: they were to leave Santa Ana or else Beto would be killed.

Within a few days they gathered all their belongings. They returned by land to a town in Morelos, where Beto's maternal grandmother was living. Beto didn't understand what was happening and wasn't given an explanation of why they had to make such a hasty decision. We know this story because we have talked with Beto's parents on several occasions. His mother has repeatedly justified the decision to return to Mexico by stating, "Nothing can be more valuable than our only son's life—not even a good life, house, job, or friends. We did not want to go back, and it was unfair that we were forced to leave everything because of that bad person, but when I think of my son and the happiness he has brought to us, I don't have second thoughts." They did not tell Beto the real reason for their return because they knew that he would do everything in his power to convince them to stay in the United States.

ARRIVING IN MEXICO: STORIES OF CHILDREN BORN IN THE UNITED STATES

Sandra: Legal Issues and Family Entanglements

In December 2004 we conducted an interview in which we documented one of the paths that lead children from the United States to Mexico. At that time we were just beginning to discover its importance in the migration experience. This was the path of "illegality" combined with family conflicts. Sandra was born in Santa Rita, Texas, and lived there for the first seven years of her life. She lived in a trailer and was constantly in the midst of family arrangements, adjustments and entanglements. Her mother "was selling clothes, packages of various products, and all that" because her father had been imprisoned for a reason that Sandra did not explain. We suppose that her father had been in prison for a long time because Sandra, who was eleven at that time, told us, "I have spent little time with my dad because he was locked up in prison. I only had three years with him." From what we understood from Sandra, her father was not deported because once he was released from prison, he continued to live and work in Texas. She explained, "He worked in those truckloads, I mean the cargo trucks that go to the stores over there. . . . In those things that make deliveries, that's what he was doing."

Things were not easy for Sandra's mother either. We learned during the interview that her mother had exceeded her maximum authorized period of stay in the United States. Sandra explained the situation as follows: "For a whole year, I did not live with her because they took her [border-crossing] card because it had expired, and they took it from her and locked her up for a year, and when she got out [of prison], I came here with her [to Escobedo, Nuevo León]."

Sandra arrived in Nuevo León when she was seven. Following Sandra's hasty narrative, it seems like her father made the decision to return to Nuevo León because his living conditions in Texas had become increasingly unsustainable. In fact, Sandra's explanation became even more complicated when she shared that, even before her mother went to prison, Sandra's paternal grandmother did not seem to have a good relationship with Sandra's mother. That conflict motivated her father to settle in Escobedo, get a job, and reunite with his wife, Sandra, and her brothers in the metropolitan area of Monterrey. Sandra explained, "My grandmother didn't love my mother, and my father said that he had found a job here and that we should come here [instead of where my grandparents live], and so then he brought us here." This first narrative sets the stage for learning about children's experiences migrating to Mexico for the first time. The children in this section, like Sandra, were born in the United States, lived in precarious conditions, suffered the consequences of their parents' "illegality," and witnessed family conflicts that precipitated their migration to Mexico.

As Sandra (a child who was eleven years old and had spent seven of those years in Texas) narrates her migration experience, the events are not in chronological order. Rather, they overlap with one another. The axes of her narrative are the periods of absence of her parents. First, Sandra describes a long period of absence that corresponds with her father's incarceration when she was one year old. Second, she shares a shorter period corresponding to her mother's absence that happened after her father had been released and was a delivery worker. We can assume that the paternal grandmother's animosity toward her daughter-in-law was felt throughout Sandra's life in Texas, but it became more relevant when explaining the reasons why her father decided to return with his family to a certain part of Mexico.

José Ángel: A Binational Child Preparing to Be Bilingual and Bicultural

José Ángel left no room for doubt: he is not a child who returned to Mexico but one who started to prepare for a life in which circular migration would become his modus vivendi and his opus operandi (i.e., "know what" and "know how"). José Ángel was born in Nebraska in the late 1990s. We interviewed him in Cerralvo, Nuevo León, in January 2005, only a few months after he arrived in Mexico. José Ángel spent his entire childhood in Nebraska, where his father continues to work, before beginning junior high school in Cerralvo in September 2004, when he was thirteen.

When asked why he moved from Nebraska to Cerralvo, José Ángel explained, "My dad thought I already knew English quite well, and he didn't want me to forget Spanish. And I came back to the junior high here." José Ángel was living in Cerralvo with his mother and his younger sister and brother. He speaks only English with his brother because they both know the language well and feel most comfortable conversing in English. Meanwhile, at the time of the interview, José Ángel's father and several of his relatives were still living and working in Nebraska. José Ángel talked to his father on the phone every night.

So what are José Ángel's plans? First, he intends to finish junior high school. After that, he is not sure whether to continue his schooling in Mexico or go back to school in the United States. Ultimately, he cannot make that kind of decision by himself. What he did know for sure is that he eventually wanted to work in the United States, "but [I would] come here every weekend." When we pointed out that moving between Nebraska and Nuevo León every weekend would be a bit difficult, José Ángel subsequently rectified, "or like every December."

José Ángel, as well as his parents and siblings, are able to reside legally in both Nuevo León and Nebraska. From this perspective it is clear that José Ángel was not "returning" to Nuevo León; instead, he was preparing to live successfully in both the United States and Mexico, two countries in which he has citizenship. Not acquiring conversational or reading and writing skills in Spanish would limit his integration into societal life in Cerralvo. These actions point to how José Ángel and his family use their bilingualism and biculturalism as a strategy to permit them to circulate between the United States and Mexico. José Ángel is binational but needed opportunities to develop his bilingualism and biculturalism, which are complex skills acquired over time. Thus, his "return" to Cerralvo is a preparatory phase for the nomadic life typical of people living in the northern part of Nuevo León.

What we learned from José Ángel's story is that there are migration trajectories wrongly classified as "return migration." These children, and sometimes even their parents (as in José Ángel's case), are not permanently returning to Mexico but rather are circulating in a singular and intriguing way. This has not been documented in the research about circular migration; instead, researchers have focused their attention on families' labor-related seasonal movements. Quite distinctly, José Ángel and his siblings are in Mexico to prepare for their return to their birth country—the United States. They will spend a period of their lives in Mexico to ensure that, as adults, they will not become or feel like linguistic and cultural foreigners in Mexico. They are currently in Mexico because they have already spent time in the United States; soon they will be living in the United States because they will have had an opportunity to spend time in Mexico. José Ángel's family is building their own biculturalism. This phenomenon was, for us, completely unknown.

Efrén: When Paternal Abandonment Leads to Mexico

Efrén was born in Los Angeles and lived in the United States for seven years, some of which he spent in Las Vegas. He arrived in the municipality of Villanueva, Zacatecas, at a *"ranchito* . . . [where] I saw many horses, animals, the river and everything" just before his eighth birthday. Efrén completed nearly all of his schooling, from second grade onward, in Mexico, first in the *ranchito* of Villanueva and later in Jerez, where we met him in 2006. At that time he was about to turn fifteen and was enrolled in ninth grade.

Efrén's family consisted of his mother, an older sister, a younger sister, and his maternal grandfather, who played a central role in the family's migratory story. Efrén's mother lived in the United States without authorization. However, Efrén's grandfather had "documents" that allowed him to reside and work in the United States, thanks to one of his third wife's children who "fixed" his situation (Efrén's mother is the daughter of his grandfather's first wife). The grandfather was widowed twice, and, based on Efrén's narration, we inferred that his third wife was a U.S. citizen and that her status somehow facilitated his grandfather's ability to obtain legal residency.

While Efrén was born in the United States, his two sisters were born in Mexico. The eldest had been born before the family migrated to Los Angeles, and the second was born in Villanueva eight months after they had returned to Zacatecas. In fact, Efrén recounted the story with a sense of humor. His mother arrived in Mexico without knowing that she was pregnant; had she known, she would have waited a little longer for her daughter to be born in the United States.

This intricate web of different legal statuses and family relationships melds with the reason for their return: Efrén's father abandoned them. Efrén explains it like this: "I was in Los Angeles. My father left us there, and so then my mother came here, and I no longer know my father." At another point during the interview he said, "I asked my mom if I should look for him [my father] when I go there [back to Los Angeles], and she said no because he abandoned us." Apparently, not only had the father abandoned them, but he had also disappeared: "Yes, I met my father, but we don't have, we no longer have a father. He separated from my mom and no longer speaks to her or anything, or to my aunts. So all I really have now is my grandfather."

Efrén arrived in Zacatecas when he was seven years old. He was about to complete ninth grade when we interviewed him. By then Efrén was already making plans with his grandfather to move to Las Vegas and enroll in high school, despite the fact that he had practically forgotten the English he had learned during his early years. Efrén did not *return* to Mexico. His family migrated to Mexico because they were abandoned by his father, who continued to live in the United States. Rather, Efrén *would return* to the United States, thanks to his dual citizenship and to the support of his maternal grandfather.

Andrés: What Happened with the Remittances?

For more than ten years, Andrés's father had been sending U.S. dollars to Villanueva, Zacatecas. During our interview with Andrés in November 2005, we found out that his father had planned to invest his money in his own ranch, so he asked his sister to buy heads of cattle and livestock equipment. At some point he discovered that his sister had been selling—not buying—animals and that the money earmarked for this investment had been used for other purposes. Thus, the ranch was not generating any profit; on the contrary, it was accumulating debt. Andrés, at age thirteen, concluded, "He sent them money, but that wasn't enough for them, and they sold the bull anyway." At least from Andrés's perspective, it seems that selling the bull was effectively the last straw. His entire family returned to Villanueva: his mother and father, his older sister (who was born in Idaho), Andrés, and his two younger brothers, the latter three all Chicago-born.

The mismanagement of the remittances that Andrés' father was sending was accompanied by another circumstance. His father was working in a paint factory located in the Chicago metropolitan area; there was less work to do at the factory, and, as a result, people were being laid off. It appears that Andres's father was, or was about to be, laid off, although Andrés does not explicitly state this. "They told me there were hardly any jobs available there. . . . They were being fired." The combination of these events, the risk of job loss in Chicago, and the mismanagement of their money by the family living in Mexico proved to be disastrous. It was necessary for their family to return to Mexico and to regain control of their ranch in Zacatecas. Andés explained, "We came by land, and we were seeing everything, and I said, 'No, Mexico gotta be like a desert.' That's how we imagined it there in the United States. And we came to see it, and it's better. It is a city [the municipal capital of Villanueva], but we thought it was a desert. My little brother used to say, in English, 'Let's go home.'"

Andrés's family is dispersed across various regions in the United States. His aunts, uncles, and cousins are living in Illinois, California, Idaho, and Massachusetts. During the interview he implied that he would return to the United States to study, work, and live, if his relatives offered him this option. Again Andrés and Efrén made it clear they were not return migrants, but rather young people preparing to move between Mexico and the United States.

Charlie: The Boy Stricken with Misfortune

Charlie was ten years old when we interviewed him in a small town near Villanueva, Zacatecas. He was enrolled in fourth grade and had spent the first eight years of his life in Storey, Nevada, where he attended one year of preschool and two years of elementary school. In Nevada Charlie lived with his parents and older siblings, a sister and two brothers, all born in the United States. In Zacatecas Charlie's father collected scraps to feed cattle. Why was Charlie in Villanueva instead of Nevada? Two years prior Charlie and his siblings got up in the morning as usual to get ready for school and found their mother dead in her room.

Charlie's account of what happened is laconic: "I live here with my father, Luis and Manuel" (while his older sister continues to live in the United States). "And your mom?" we asked during the interview. Charlie replied, "She died two years ago. There, on the other side [of the border]. When we got up, she was already dead. We came here." At this point Charlie struggled to continue. He only shared how they returned: "My uncle brought us. In a truck. I didn't want to come. And we came at night. And we arrived at night. I felt bad. I didn't know anyone. My dad told me to say hi to my grandfather, but I didn't know him." The mother's unforeseen death led to the father's return to Mexico with his sons, where they settled with Charlie's paternal grandparents. Suddenly, parenting conditions completely changed, and Charlie's paternal grandmother assumed the role of primary caregiver. To draw our interview with Charlie to an end, we decided to change the subject. When asked about his future, he told us that he wanted to be a police officer in the United States because the teachers from his school in Nevada had given him a police officer hat. However, there may be one major obstacle for Charlie as he pursues this goal: he admitted that, since arriving in Mexico, he had practically forgotten English.

Elías: Inevitable Migratory Circulation as a Member of a Sui Generis Family

Elías was fourteen years old when we interviewed him in Apozol, Zacatecas. He shared his story in chronological order and with vivid descriptions. Elías was born in Fresno, California, as were his younger brothers. From California he moved to Oregon, where he lived for four years. Despite the fact that Elías had already turned seven, he did not attend school in Oregon. In fact, his schooling began in Apozol, when the mother returned to Mexico to "fix her immigration status" to avoid a possible deportation order. This was the reason for Elías and his brothers' first migration to Mexico: their mother's legal status. His father stayed in Oregon, where he was working in a factory where they produced "something related to aircraft parts."

When Elías's mother went to the United States for the first time, she crossed the border using the services of a coyote. Elías could not specify the details because it had happened such a long time ago, before he was born. According to the story, his mother went to California to meet the man who would be Elías's father—a man he had not recognized as his father until one of his maternal cousins told him who his biological father was. Let's go one step at a time. In keeping with Elías's story, his mother crossed the border without authorization around 1990. Elías was born in 1991. Later the mother established a new relationship with a man, a U.S. citizen of Mexican origin, who fathered Elías's two younger brothers—the man whom Elías considered his true father until his cousin's revelation.

> When we were there [Oregon] with my dad, well, he's my stepfather, I was with him there. My real dad was here [Zacatecas]. As a child, I called him "uncle." When I was older, a cousin told me, "the mere truth: he is not your father," and I went crying to my mom, and she said, "It's not true." And then she said, "Yes, forgive me," and all that. And she told me that my dad left us when I was little.

Elías moved between Fresno, California, and Bend, Oregon, until he was seven years old. Then he came to Apozol. This first migration is explained, as we pointed out previously, by his mother's legal precautions. When he was eleven, he returned to the United States, along with his mother and siblings, to his stepfather's house. In Oregon he attended four years of school, from sixth through ninth grade. However, he did not finish ninth grade because his family had to return to Apozol. He explained the reason: "My grandma was going to have a surgery on her leg, [because] she could no longer move or do her chores." In summary Elías's first migration to Mexico was triggered by legal reasons and the second by family duties—the need to support his ailing grandmother, who was having difficulties getting around.

Elías did not really know his mother and stepfather's (whom he considered his father) plans for the near future. However, one thing was for sure: the whole family would return to Oregon. Meanwhile, Elías was repeating ninth grade in Apozol; he was convinced that he would not forget English and that life was better in the United States than in Mexico. The future of this family was in Oregon: his mother's immigration status had been resolved, all the children are U.S. citizens, they all loved their father, and, of course, the grandmother would not live forever. Elías and his family are not "returning" to Mexico but circulating from one country to the other, motivated, at least for the second occasion, by their love for their grandmother. Elías, in fact, imagines his adult life circulating between the two countries: he wants to live "there" but have a house "here."

Erasmo: A Nomad from Apozol

Erasmo was thirteen years old when we interviewed him in Apozol in November 2005. His nomadic life began when he was born. Part of the year—from April to October—he lives in California (we were unable to understand the name of the town due to issues with the audio recording) and the other part in Apozol. At the time of our interview, Erasmo had crossed the border with his parents and younger siblings thirteen times, and everything he shared with us indicated that he expected to maintain this kind of life for the near future: "I got used to it." The only family member of his who stays in California is his older brother because he was not born in the United States.

Erasmo's migratory experience is similar to that of the children from the municipalities of northern Nuevo León. However, we selected his story for two reasons: (1) Erasmus's father was not an agricultural worker but a factory worker, and his mother worked in a day care, and (2) Erasmo's case is illustrative of seasonal migration in remote regions that are geographically far from the Mexico–United States border.[4] In these cases the category of "return" is even less useful, as these children are not returning to Mexico or to the United States: they are migrants who experience the most extreme type of dislocation as they participate in international migration. These binational children, for whom the notions of immigration and emigration have no meaning, develop their bilingualism and biculturalism in a more fragmented way than what we already observed in cases like José Ángel.

According to Erasmo, his parents were not engaged in any gainful employment during the months they spent in Apozol. This leads us to believe that, for this family, November to March is actually a vacation time, and the income saved from their work in California allows this family (with the exception of the oldest son) to enjoy five "sabbatical" months each year.

Flor: Close to Her Mother or Close to Her Father?

Migration scholars have generally omitted the alienating working conditions suffered by Mexican workers in the United States in their research. We tend to give priority to the "objective" elements of the labor market: salaries, acquired skills, and access to benefits. Flor's story serves as a reminder that strenuous work routines in the United States can instigate migration to Mexico.

Flor's mother had been cleaning clothing stores for work in Portland, Oregon, ever since she divorced Flor's father. She worked double shifts and would typically work about seventy hours a week, including her commute time. Still, the money was not enough to pay for a babysitter who would have made her life easier when Flor and her older sister were little. We know all of this because we had the opportunity to talk, on multiple occasions, to Flor as well as with her older sister, Ruth, and their mother.

Flor's father still lives in Portland, where he owns a repair workshop. Being his own boss allowed him to take care of his daughters periodically and help his ex-wife. The years passed by until, eventually, the consequences of this intense lifestyle caught up with the family. When Ruth was in her teens and enrolled in high school, she began to hang out with young men who belonged to gangs and eventually started dating one of the gang members. During her senior year of high school, she became pregnant and eventually dropped out of school. As for Flor, she began to express her dissatisfaction with the fact that her mother was never around, claiming that she was closer to her father, who often picked her up from school and spent the afternoon with her at the repair shop.

In 2013, before Ruth's son was born, Flor's mother evaluated her situation. Things were not right, and it seemed like they could get even worse for her daughters if she did not make some changes in her life. That is when she decided to return with her daughters to Jiutepec, Morelos. Flor was aware of the implications of her mother's decision. Flor was ten years old when we met her at her elementary school. During the interview she told us, "My mom and my sister will always be with me, and you can't have everything. You have to make some sacrifices, but step by step, we can make it." Given the migratory status of Flor's mother, her decision of returning to Mexico was practically irreversible: it would be very difficult for her to go back to the United States. The months passed and eventually Ruth's son was born. Flor was present at the birth, and, while the baby's father was still in Portland, he was able to be virtually present by phone.

Flor's mother returned to Mexico to make up for the lost time with her daughters and to take care of her underage daughter as she began the adventure of motherhood. She hoped that, perhaps one day, she would win her daughters' trust back. Things did not quite turn out as the mother had planned. The differences between Flor and her mother gradually ballooned into major disputes, economic issues soon arose, the Mexican school where Flor was enrolled turned out to be a disappointment, and the support of their extended family in Morelos was scarce. In 2014 Flor decided to return to Portland to live with her father and to continue her schooling. In her migration story, Flor did not "return" to Mexico; in fact, she returned to the United States, where she continues to live. In one of our last telephone conversations, she told us, "I'm doing good over here, but I miss my mom, my sister, and my nephew. . . . School is good. I am getting Bs, like eighty in Mexico."

Nanys: "We Weren't a Family Anymore"

During each interview the children we asked which language they preferred to speak in: Nanys spoke in English for the entire interview. Nanys had spent fourteen years in the United States, living in California and Colorado. When we met her in February 2010 in Jolalpan, Puebla, she had been in Mexico for no more than month and was not very familiar with Spanish as the socially dominant language.

At the beginning of the interview, after she had shared essential information about her life in the United States, we asked her why her family had come to Mexico. Nanys came to the country accompanied by her parents and a younger brother, who had also been born in California and then moved to Aurora, Colorado, just like her. She answered the question as follows:

> Because my parents were, I don't know, they weren't okay with the lifestyle we were having there because we weren't really a family anymore because there was too much work. And then, we, huh, I don't know how to say it in English. *No convivíamos.* So we, like, but didn't see each other because we were at school, they were at work, we got home, we ate, so we weren't really a family anymore.

Nanys was enrolled in ninth grade at the time of the interview, which in Mexico is the cumulating year of *secundaria*. She explained in detail that her parents were trying to revalidate her studies and that they were considering two education options for her to enroll in high school. The first one was in Denver, Colorado, where her aunts, uncles, and paternal cousins were living. The second option was to go to Mexico City, where a maternal aunt was living. Both options to continue her high school studies were motivating and feasible for Nanys to fulfill one of her aspirations: to become a lawyer so she could help her fellow Mexican immigrants in the United States. The first option was considered more suitable because her level of written Spanish was limited. However, returning to Colorado for high school would directly contravene the family's decision to move to Puebla and live together as a family.

Mary: When Girls Get to Decide

The stories about migration from the United States to Mexico in which the children willfully decide to migrate are not common; however, we found such cases in Jalisco and Morelos. In this section we present Mary's story, which we consider to be illustrative of other, similar cases. In March 2011 we met Mary in Lagos de Moreno, Jalisco, when she was twelve years old. She and her younger sister were born and raised in the Chicago metropolitan area. Her parents had the opportunity to visit their families in Lagos de Moreno twice a year ever since Mary and Carlota, Mary's younger sister, were little. We inferred, based on the frequency of their visits to Lagos, that the parents were authorized to reside and work in the United States. These visits allowed Mary to become familiar with life in Lagos de Moreno and to bond with her two grandmothers and her aunts, uncles, and cousins in Mexico.

The frequent visits allowed Mary to compare life in Chicago with life in Lagos. The contrasts between the two ended up convincing her that she would rather live in Lagos de Moreno. As such, Mary did not return to Mexico; she decided to live in Mexico. On one hand, she witnessed her father's frequent job dissatisfaction in Chicago when he was working as a mechanic on car transmissions. "Every time he came home from work, like, well, he told me he was acting. I mean, he was angry about work, and, well, he was tired, bored." This was the first major contrast: in Lagos her father owned his own auto repair shop. Additionally, Mary's daily life in Chicago seemed like monotonous routine: waking up, getting ready to go to school, studying at school, going to the beauty salon where her mother worked, doing homework, coming home, having dinner, bathing, and watching TV. Going outside, according to Mary's testimonies, was something that was totally forbidden to her. Mary justified it by saying that "Mexicans are crazy . . . [and non-Mexicans], those too, well, all of them!" Mary's social life in Lagos was more pleasant, and there was more interaction in the streets, town squares, shops, schools, and cyber cafes—a second major contrast. Finally, the weather in Chicago during both winter and summer is very uncomfortable for Mary, while the climate of the Altos de Jalisco is enviable.

Thus, Mary openly expressed her decision to move to Lagos de Moreno. Her father agreed, and Carlota reluctantly agreed. However, Mary's mother continued to live and work in Chicago. Mary wants to go to college in Mexico, not in the United States. On three occasions we asked her if she had plans to return to Chicago, where her mother and maternal relatives were living. On all three occasions, her answer was no. We insisted and asked her to explain her reasoning behind this decision. Mary explained, "Because it is more beautiful here." Mary had a few ideas about how she could convince her mother to follow in her footsteps.

So in Jalisco we met a girl who, with her arguments, managed to convince a part of her family to move to Mexico. Two years later, in Morelos, we would meet three girls who suggested to their parents, who were undocumented in the United States, to move to Mexico after they had learned about their uncle's deportation. This is the case of Lulú's family, who we have described in chapters 1 and 3.

WHY HAVE YOU RETURNED TO MEXICO? AN OVERVIEW OF SHORT ANSWERS

In this section we summarize and classify the responses that the children wrote to open-ended questions included in the surveys administered in schools throughout Mexico. This dataset is relatively large and includes the responses to the question: "Why have you returned to Mexico?" As we pointed out previously, the respondents' answers were generally short: 3 percent wrote only one word, 78 percent wrote one sentence, and the remaining 19 percent wrote two or more sentences. In fact, we were surprised at the children's elliptical answers. The first thought that came to mind to explain such short answers was that children did not have sufficiently developed writing skills to produce more elaborated narratives. However, we soon dismissed this explanation because, in other sections of the questionnaire, in which they were asked to describe some of their life experiences in the United States, the children were more eloquent and detailed. Taking this into consideration, we came to a second conclusion: migrant children know precisely what circumstances led them from the United States to Mexico (or at least they think they do) and therefore do not feel the need to create stories but rather get straight to the point and indicate the condition, force, eventuality, friction, ethical duty, aspiration, or determining factor that caused this major bifurcation in their lives: moving from the United States to Mexico while they were still underage.

The children who answered this open-ended question have the following characteristics: 56 percent were born in Mexico and 44 percent in the United States; the majority (73 percent) were between twelve and sixteen years old and enrolled in sixth grade through ninth grade; and 48 percent were boys and 52 percent were girls. With regard to the Mexican states in which they were surveyed, 9 percent of the responses were obtained from the Nuevo León survey, 22 percent from the Zacatecas survey, 16 percent from the Puebla survey, 48 percent from the Jalisco survey, and the remaining 5 percent represent the answers from the Morelos survey.

Analyzing the 638 responses from 638 children who answered the question and organizing their explanations into thematic categories was a difficult task. We began by using standardized migration categories such as "voluntary return" versus "involuntary return" or "economic reasons," "family reasons," and "educational reasons," but we eventually concluded that this was distorting the content of the children's responses and the meaning behind their actions. Therefore, we opted for an inductive approach. First, we would ask ourselves what the respondent was trying to convey or what they were trying to tell us through that short answer. Very few of the children wrote two responses to this question. In those cases we chose the first answer that the respondent had written. The following section presents a list of the children's short responses arranged by the themes generated throughout our interpretive analysis.

Family Reunification in Mexico

A first explanation that children transmitted through their answers is as follows: we are here in Mexico because we want to be together and stay together as a family. If we stayed in the United States, we would grow up without a father or a mother or without some of our siblings, and, as a family, we are not willing to live divided by the border. This first explanation refers to the complex and restrictive legal conditions that prevent families from staying together in the United States. Undoubtedly, some families decide to remain separated, and other families opt to minimize the distance brought about by this separation, such as when parents or siblings, forced to return to Mexico, chose to settle in the border cities of northern Mexico to facilitate frequent contact with their relatives who live on the "other side of the border" (Masferrer and Roberts 2012). However, this is not the case with the children who responded to the survey in Nuevo León, Zacatecas, Puebla, Jalisco, or Morelos.

Our survey depicts *families who decided to reunite in Mexico*. At the very least, this includes the parents and the children who are still minors, if not all the family members. These responses included families in Mexico at the time of study due to deportation, risk of deportation, or fear of deportation. This group offers a clear picture of how international child migrants residing in Mexico are a constitutive part of the Great Expulsion (see the examples in part 1 of the appendix). According to table 16, the percentage of children who gave this explanation for their return to Mexico represents one-sixth of responses in Nuevo León, about one-fifth of the answers in Zacatecas, and about one-fourth of the explanations in Puebla, Jalisco, and Morelos.

Filial Duties

A second explanation of the migrant children's "return" stems from an ethical principle that establishes that *filial duties* carry more importance than individual well-being and stability. Children learn this concept when they become aware of the fact that they migrated to Mexico to be with their grandparents and act in solidarity to support one another, a value sacred to many families (see the examples in part 2 of the appendix). Families' decision to move to Mexico, especially within the political and legal contexts that obstruct and restrict circular migration for migrants without authorization (Sandoval and Zúñiga 2016), means that many parents and some children will no longer be able to return to the United States or that it will be very expensive and risky for them to do so. Still, families fulfill these filial duties when grandparents are sick or in need of support. Both adult and child migrants are willing to bear the costs of this responsibility. These undocumented migrants, who were what Rubén Hernández-León (2008) described as "trapped" in the United States because their migratory status, upon returning to fulfill their filial duties

Table 16 Percentage distribution of explanations of migration from the United States to Mexico

State (year)	Families' decision to reunite in Mexico (%)	Filial duties (%)	Living conditions in the United States unbearable, undesirable, or unacceptable or better conditions in Mexico (%)	Family dynamics modified by conflicts such as illness, death, separation, and abandonment (%)	Lack of job opportunities in the United States or better job opportunities in Mexico (%)	Circulation or preparation for circular migration (%)	Unclassified explanations (%)	Total (%)
Nuevo León (2004)	16	4	12	10	18	10	30	100
Zacatecas (2005)	19	17	15	11	5	8	25	100
Puebla (2009)	24	21	14	14	3	6	18	100
Jalisco (2010)	23	10	17	4	4	11	31	100
Morelos (2013)	27	11	11	14	5	7	25	100

SOURCE: Our elaboration is based on the databases of Universidad de Monterrey (2015).

will again be trapped, but in Mexico, since it is highly unlikely that they will be able to obtain authorization to return to the United States. According to the distribution shown in table 16, *filial duties* explain a considerable percentage of the reasons given for the children's "return" migration to Mexico. In Nuevo León this explanation appeared in one out of every twenty cases, while in Zacatecas and Puebla it was almost one in every five cases, and in Morelos and Jalisco about one-tenth of the responses were classified in this category.

Living Conditions

A third theme that emerged to explain the children and their families' return to Mexico was that the living conditions or lifestyles in the United States had become unbearable, undesirable, or unacceptable. At times children contrasted the expulsive conditions in the United States with the positive conditions that they find in Mexico, in Mexican society, or in the specific region or locality where they now live. In this category we also include the short responses that underlined the benefits of being in Mexico, even if the child's sentences did not explicitly establish a comparison. The undesirable conditions most frequently included in children's responses are lack of employment, precarious jobs, monotony, discrimination, nostalgia, fatigue, and lack of freedom. The explanations that emerged with this theme provide details of different types of expulsive forces that were distinct from, but still related to, restrictive legal frameworks (see the examples in part 3 of the appendix).

The legal landscape of migration fosters living conditions that become less and less bearable: inadequate housing, urban segregation, underperforming schools, dangerous neighborhoods, precarious employment, and legal vulnerability. These undesirable conditions contrast, in the eyes of children, with the favorable, or at least less difficult, conditions that they find in Mexico. As table 16 shows, between one-tenth and one-sixth of the migrant children's explanations fall into this category. Children from Zacatecas and Jalisco were more likely to give this explanation. As we know, most of the children in Zacatecas and Jalisco come from California, where the traditional labor markets for immigrants are more saturated than in other regions of the United States, the intraethnic competition for niche labor is fiercer, and legal measures and actions that exclude low-income families have become the norm (Light 2006).

Conflicting Family Situations

The fourth type of explanations for the children's "return" to Mexico is not related to economic, legal, or social conditions. Instead, it encompasses conflictive or sad events that altered their family dynamics. The children point out that illnesses, deaths, separation, and abandonment drastically changed family relationships, and that these changes led to new intra-family arrangements that translated into return migration to Mexico for all or some of the family members. For example, if a father dies or abandons his family, the mother is forced to return to Mexico in search of familial stability. If a mother becomes ill or dies, the maternal grandparents, who reside in Mexico, may take care of the young grandchildren. If a divorce takes place in the United States, adjustments are needed to ensure the welfare of the children, and a return to Mexico may be part of these adjustments. In short, when families are destabilized, they create new arrangements that often bring about return migration (see the examples in part 4 of the appendix). According to the distribution of the responses presented in table 16, these explanations constitute between 10 and 15 percent of the total responses, except in Jalisco, where this kind of family destabilization was less frequent.

Working Conditions

Generally speaking, migration from Mexico to the United States has been classified as a labor-driven phenomenon, and Mexican immigrants have been synonymous with working-age men (Batalova and Fix 2010). However, parents' work as a reason for children's migration to Mexico was significantly less frequent than the previous explanations, except in the case of Nuevo León. Still, these observations require some clarification and nuance. First, children's responses that indicated parental job dissatisfaction, the lack of job opportunities, or the 2008 economic crisis as a trigger for return migration are not included in this category but in the *undesirable living conditions in the United States* category. However, even if we had made a different decision when classifying the responses, the percentages would not have changed significantly. And we justify this taxonomic decision because when a ten-year-old girl says that her family returned to Mexico "because we had no money, and my dad got fired, and they took our house away from us," this points more to the unbearable living conditions in the United States than it does to the dynamics of the labor market. In short, in this fifth category we included only the work-related explanations that were not accompanied by other considerations—that is, responses that indicated lack of job opportunities in the United States or better job opportunities in Mexico (see the examples in part 5 of the appendix).

In total, these explanations do not exceed 5 percent of the responses, with the exception of Nuevo León, as shown in table 16. This exception leads to a second clarification: the case of Nuevo León is interesting because nearly 20 percent of these children's responses were classified in the work-related category. According to the children's assertions, they are return migrants who find it convenient to migrate to the Monterrey metropolitan area to obtain tangible employment benefits like ensuring retirement in Mexico, regaining a job, continuing a career, and starting a business. This finding is probably associated with the fact that in Nuevo León we found the highest percentage of children who were natives of other states of Mexico.[5]

If we add the short answers that invoked the family preparation for circular migration (typically children wrote, "Every year we come back and then return to the United States" or "We were there [the United States] just for saving money; my parents planned to return to Mexico"), the explanations described in the typology presented in this section represent about 70 to 80 percent of the migrant children's answers. This means that there were some answers that could not be classified in the aforementioned categories. These unclassifiable responses mainly fall into four groups. The first group consists of vague written responses that did not provide enough detail to classify them into one category or another. Examples of these answers are "my mom and dad brought me," "we came here with my mom and dad," "for my family." The second group of unclassifiable responses included when the respondent did not elaborate with an explanation, such as when children wrote, "because we wanted to," "because they decided so." The third group was those that indicate that the child was not aware or did not know the reasons of their families' return to Mexico. Many children responded with a simple "I don't know" or "I don't know why they brought me." The last group of unclassifiable answers included the responses of the children who assertively stated that they disagreed with their families' decision to migrate to Mexico. In some cases migrant children answered the question by writing, "they forced me" or something similar.

The numerical importance of the family-related explanations for why migrant children returned to Mexico is perhaps the most significant piece of information in this section. When adding together the percentage of explanations included in this category and across the subcategories, this reason accounted for 30 percent of responses in Nuevo León, 47 percent in Zacatecas, 60 percent in Puebla, 37 percent in Jalisco, and 52 percent in Morelos. When comparing our results with the convergent, mostly quantitative, research on families' migration to Mexico, we found that the findings coincided. We now briefly look at two of these quantitative studies.

Using the panel surveys from the *National Survey of Occupation and Employment*, from 2005 to 2012, José Luis Ordaz and Juan José Li Ng (2013) found that in 2005, 90.7 percent of the Mexican migrants returned to Mexico to reunite with their families. These percentages do not vary much in the subsequent years analyzed in this study: 91.7 percent in 2006–7; 88.9 percent in 2008–9; 89.7 percent in 2010–11; and 88.5 percent in 2012. In contrast, the percentage of those who indicated that they returned for work was close to 3 percent during the same time frame. In the same vein, a survey coordinated by Jaqueline Hagan, Rubén Hernández-León, and Jean-Luc Demonsant (2015) in Guanajuato found that 51 percent of the 204 migrants in the sample returned to Mexico for the family reasons, as opposed to only 9 percent who returned for "economic reasons." Regardless of the fact that the percentages are different, it is clear that when adult migrants are asked about their motives or reasons for their return to Mexico, the majority of responses revolve around their families.

We think that the content of the adults' responses regarding the motivation for migration from the United States to Mexico is reflected in the children's stories and explanations that we have synthesized and analyzed in this chapter. When adults select "family" on the surveys, they are harboring those events, frictions, strategies, moral duties, conflicts, and disappointments that the children explained with much greater precision. The evidence presented here shows that Orellana (2016) was indeed correct: by listening to the children, adults can learn to see phenomena differently.

CONCLUSIONS

The children's stories and explanations that we have synthesized, analyzed, and classified in this chapter highlight the fact that international migration is an eminently political act; it is the act of crossing national borders (Waldinger 2015). Of course, it is a political act that often has positive economic consequences, but the political act stands out in the eyes of children, not the economic factor. In the specific case of Mexico and the United States, the first political act materializes when Mexicans arrive on U.S. territory and become noncitizens. As such, their rights to reside in U.S. territory (i.e., defined time limits for their stay, settlement conditions, specific jobs, limitations in expressing political ideas and preferences, etc.) are restricted, and they are, by definition, subject to repatriation: they are deportable. In the case of the undocumented migrants, the notion of illegality is added to their status as foreigner, which then intensifies and systematizes their deportability. The entirety of their lives becomes wrapped in the cloak of "illegality" (Jones-Correa and Graauw 2013). The children's narratives, with their embedded political emphasis, become like a deposition about the ways that restrictive immigration policies operate in real people's lives.

In the era of restriction and recession that has been unfolding in countries with a long history of immigration, such as the United States, the political nature of migration is exacerbated, and deportability intensifies to maximum levels. The Great Expulsion of adult migrants from the United States, accompanied by their children (Hamilton, Masferrer, and Langer 2023), is a consequence planned and operated by the legal frameworks of expulsion and repatriation. The children explained that they are being removed from the United States and that they come to Mexico to meet their parents, to reunite with their families, to visit or support their grandparents (who cannot go to the United States), or to escape from the undesirable labor and social or cultural conditions that characterized their lives in the United States.

The children described the process of expulsion; they also reported that family reunification in Mexico is a defensive strategy and how the strengthening of family ties becomes a valuable resource. Returning to the country of origin (i.e., the country whose citizenship they possess and therefore the country in which they are not deportable) is a form of defense, generated through social capital used to push back against the restrictions to migrant families in the United States. Children show us the true face of the asymmetric political confrontation between the state and migrant families (Hernández-León and Zúñiga 2016) as a new iteration of what Néstor Rodríguez (1996) calls "the battle for the border." Children teach us that keeping the family together and enacting the ethical principles of filial responsibility are fundamental resources to minimize costs and risks in the midst of this war.

At the same time, we discovered that events that undermine family covenants (e.g., death, abandonment, conflict, and illness) evoke new strategies and agreements between the members of the migrant families, among which return migration is included. All is not rosy when it comes to family, as children attest. There are parents who abandon their children, couples who separate, grandparents who come into conflict with the children's parents, mothers who threaten to "turn us into the immigration authorities," and aunts and uncles who refuse to offer support. In short, children migrate from the United States to Mexico to maintain family ties or to reestablish or mend broken family ties.

However, their "return" to Mexico is not only a defensive strategy. The children also described another strategy, which is aspirational in nature. Many children of adult migrants have the right to both U.S. and Mexican citizenship: they are minors who have the right to reside in the country that deported their parents and siblings. The children explained how dual nationality is understood as a resource, for the children and for their families, that will be used in the future. However, this legal resource needs to be complemented with certain skills to maximize its value. Children with dual nationality who develop their bilingualism and biculturalism will be able to sustain a productive life in the United States while still belonging to the society to which their parents, and some of their siblings, will most likely remain confined. In the stories of the children born in the United States, this aspirational strategy differs substantially from the experiences of the "children of immigrants," or members of the second generation, for whom the destination society is the one they have to assimilate into by means of school education. In contrast, the narratives of the binational children who belong to the 0.5 generation reveal the way in which they are developing, through school education in Mexico, their own bilingualism and biculturalism.

Of course, the children taught us that their parents know that, for their binational children to be successful, it is important that they speak English as native speakers and learn to live in the United States so that, when they become adults, they will not feel like foreigners in that country. As such, the process of integrating socially and occupationally will be more favorable for them. However, the parents' vision does not entail a resignation of their Mexican affiliation: without ignoring the value of education in the United States, they also emphasize school education in Mexico so that their children do not feel like foreigners there either. These parents' aspirations are bold: they aim to ensure that their binational children become both bilingual and bicultural.

This is how children of the 0.5 generation, who were born in the United States, are preparing to circulate between the two countries. Through their stories they present a new type of migratory circulation, unprecedented in the history of migration between Mexico and the United States. Some of these children, at least at the time we met them, had plans to live and study in Mexico. However, they knew that they would always have the option of returning to the United States and using that resource to their benefit. Others, the majority, had plans to work in the United States. This aspiration is not hypothetical: they have everything they need to make it a reality. And their situation will be even more advantageous if they possess bilingual and bicultural skills, which can be acquired only if their schooling experience is also binational and bicultural. Thus, the equation is clear: they must develop their own biculturalism and bilingualism to optimize integration into the society and economy of the United States while seeking to maintain their full membership in the society from which their parents and grandparents originate.

The stories of children born in Mexico are completely different. If their experience in the United States allowed them to develop linguistic competencies in English and their sense of belonging to the U.S. society, then they most likely will make use of these resources in Mexico while, at the same time, improving their linguistic competencies in Spanish and their sense of belonging to Mexican society. These children may also be able to capitalize on their learning in the United States, should the legal conditions be favorable to them. By contrast, mononational children who did not have the chance to develop their bilingualism and biculturalism because their school experience in the United States was short will likely remember their life in that country mostly as an insignificant event. A bilingual person can easily switch from one language to the other (although one of the two languages will always be dominant). A bicultural person does not feel like a foreigner in either country. Some of the mononational migrant children managed to acquire these skills because they had longer school trajectories in the United States and because they are receiving an education in Mexican schools.

The children of the 0.5 generation are classified into two large groups: binational and mononational. However, the distinction of binational alone does not suffice. In Mexico there are binational children with and without transnational schooling. There are parents who have the means to offer them transnational schooling, and others who do not. And there are mononational children with and without transnational schooling. Their legal situation prevents them from moving freely between one country and the other, so, once they return to Mexico, the process of developing biculturalism and bilingualism may be truncated. In all cases school education is crucial in the lives of the international child migrants as well as for their integration into Mexican society and their entry into adult life.

6 International Child Migrants in Mexican Schools

This chapter is devoted to analyzing the integration or reintegration of international child migrants into Mexican schools. We direct our attention exclusively to those children who made the transition from U.S. schools to Mexican schools because their adjustments and fractures in socialization are more visible. The schooling experiences of child migrants who arrived in Mexico without having been enrolled in U.S. schools is not addressed in the chapter because we interviewed very few children in this situation.

Child migrants who were born in Mexico and who have previous schooling experience in the United States have generally experienced two transitions. First, they moved from a Mexican school to a U.S. school, and then they made a full roundtrip back to a Mexican school. Among the Mexican-born children, those who began their schooling in the United States represent a minority. Generally speaking, the U.S.-born migrant children have made only one transition: from a U.S. school to a Mexican school. Few are the children, regardless of their country of birth, who have made more than two transitions, and even fewer are those who attend school in both countries every school year. We include children from this latter group (those with the most fragmented educational trajectories) only to illustrate a certain type of fragmentation in socialization that, for obvious reasons, is more visible due to the children's trajectories.

In this chapter we describe, measure, and analyze the transitions and fractures in the schooling trajectories of the child migrants in Mexico. Henceforth, we discuss in detail the challenges that Mexican schools face in supporting these children, particularly regarding curriculum design and teacher training. Mexican schools, like the vast majority of schools in the world, have been conceived for mononational students who legally and symbolically belong to a single national society (Zúñiga and Hamann 2008). Since the nineteenth century, common schools have fulfilled a significant social and political function for the construction of nation-states: to make new generations join an abstract, although in many ways also concrete, community that is partially invented and partially real (Vázquez 1975; Fass 2007)—or, to put it differently, a community that begins to transform into reality while it is simultaneously being invented (Anderson 1991; Hobsbawm 1990; Gellner 1988). To achieve this schools teach and inculcate national history, national language, national geography, and a set of symbols and rituals that have certain national homogeneity. The purpose of this nationalization of content is so that children will begin to construct an understanding that a territory, a governing state, and a society are connected to compose a single entity called a nation. This complex process is happening in both Mexican and U.S. schools.

The transition between national school systems does not only entail navigating the delivery of academic content (i.e., learning objectives) or curriculum design (i.e., what is learned here, what is learned there; how is it taught here and how it is taught there). When child migrants move from schools in the United States to those in Mexico, they experience not only discrepancies or delays in terms of content and learning objectives but rather fragmentations that result from the chasm between the two school systems or the mutual ignorance among systems. Schools in the United States, especially those who serve migrant children, carry out assimilatory functions, most powerfully through the emphasis on the acquisition of U.S. English—a practice that is in line with the country's ideological stronghold of monolingualism.

This is why child migrants and the children of immigrants are often grouped under the category of "English Learners" in U.S. schools. A main goal of most U.S. schools is that migrant children acquire spoken and written English as soon as possible and perform "at grade level" so that they can be compared to their native-English-speaking peers (Ruiz 1984; Crawford 2004; Gándara 2002; Gándara and Contreras 2009; Panait and Zúñiga 2016). Language is a means and an end. It can be understood as a means because it is through the English language that students access the academic content, skills, and competencies required by the school curriculum. As such, in U.S. schools children labeled as "English Language Learners" are trapped in a type of waiting room for academic learning (Valdés, Capitelli, and Alvarez 2011). Once children enrolled in these groups achieve acceptable language proficiency (i.e., they understand, speak, read, and write), they can join the "regular" groups of children who are learning the academic curriculum directly and in English.

The acquisition of English is also considered an end because the ability to speak, understand, read, and write English is a substantive part of fully belonging to the local and national community. As they undergo the process of learning English, child migrants and children of immigrants in U.S. schools not only acquire the language but pledge an oath of allegiance, internalize political beliefs, develop loyalty, participate in patriotic liturgies, and, in some school contexts, may consider themselves as the heirs of the British pilgrims and are moved emotionally by the country's historical and geographic myths and stories. All this ideological and cultural material becomes instilled in migrant children through the English language.

When international child migrants arrive in Mexican schools, especially those who have only ever attended school in the United States, they do not know the Mexican national anthem or who Miguel Hidalgo is, they do not know the names of most of the Mexican states, they have not developed allegiance within Mexico as a nation-state, and, perhaps the most notorious and complex issue for many of these children, they do not have the necessary skills to read and write in Spanish.[1]

The empirical data and analysis in this chapter explicitly show how the two theoretical notions that we discussed in the first chapter operate: "fragmented socialization" and "transnational schooling." In short, the first refers to the challenges and contradictions that children experience when they move from one sphere of meaning into another. Throughout this process, child migrants engage in multiple negotiations to circumvent the tension between the two spheres. Transnational schooling, on the contrary, refers to the learning, competencies, and skills acquired by children who were educated in diverse and sometimes competing contexts. These are skills that will allow them, to varying degrees, to become bicultural individuals capable of moving between contrasting contexts while being able to interpret them successfully.

To describe, measure, and analyze the child migrants' integration or reintegration into the Mexican school context, we draw on different data sources. First, and for specific purposes, we use data from our state surveys and in-depth interviews—the same sources we used in previous chapters. Second, and for the first time in this book, we use data from interviews with teachers and principals, which were carried out at different times and locations. We interviewed a total of thirty-three teachers and principals during the 2004–5 school year; during that time these interviewees were working in schools in Nuevo León. During the following school year, we conducted eighteen interviews with teachers and principals in Zacatecas. In Puebla, during the 2009–10 school year, we conducted seventeen interviews. A year later we were able to interview only three teachers from Jalisco due to budget cuts. More recently, during the 2014–15 school year, we interviewed twelve teachers and principals assigned to elementary or junior high schools in Morelos. All together we have a total of eighty-three interviews with teachers and principals. The teachers we interviewed were not randomly selected; only those who agreed to be interviewed were included in our study. All the teachers interviewed were working in institutions in which students who had experience in U.S. schools were enrolled. Finally, the last data sources we consult in the final two sections of this chapter are the Mexican censuses (INEGI 2000, 2010).

TEACHERS AND PRINCIPALS

Invisibility

In October 2004 we visited a school located in the municipality of Santiago, Nuevo León, with the aim of pilot testing the questionnaire that we would eventually use for the formal survey. We chose this school without having any prior knowledge about the students enrolled. Upon our arrival, we introduced ourselves to the principal, showed her the letter of authorization that permitted us to administer the questionnaire, and briefed her on the objectives of our study. The principal was intrigued because, she assured us, in her school, there were no children who had been previously enrolled in schools in the United States. We explained that this circumstance would not be a problem for our study since the measurement exercise would still add value to our research, even if the results indicated that there were, in fact, no international migrant children in the school.[2] The principal was pleased to hear this, and she led us to a sixth-grade classroom and introduced us to the teacher.

Again we explained the purpose of our study to the teacher. Just like the principal, she asserted that there were no children with prior schooling in the United States in her class. There were twenty-six students enrolled in sixth grade. So we gave the teacher the same explanation that, even if there were no students in her group with previous schooling in the United States, the results would still add value to our research. We administered the questionnaire, and, to the teacher's surprise, we found a boy and a girl who had studied in the United States. The girl had just arrived in Mexico during the summer of 2004. When we finished administering all the questionnaires to the other groups, we asked for permission to interview the sixth-grade student. At the beginning of the conversation, we gave her the option of conducting the conversation in Spanish or English: she opted for English. The principal and the teacher could not hide their surprise: the student spoke English as a native speaker!

Why are international migrant children invisible in Mexican schools? First, by design, Mexican schools have been conceived to receive children who were born and who are living and being raised in Mexico. The way in which the students are viewed and classified from the pedagogical, curricular, and administrative perspectives excludes any international trajectories. Second, there is the absence of indicators that these children are, in fact, international migrants. The children who arrive from the United States have the same surnames as the children in Mexico, as would be expected since their parents are generally Mexican. Their last names are not Smith or Brubaker but Rodríguez, González, or Sánchez. In addition, their grooming and ways of dressing resemble those of the mononational children. And, most important, with few exceptions, these children are fluent in Mexican Spanish because it is the language to which they have been exposed to at home since birth; they have been using Mexican Spanish to communicate with their parents, aunts, uncles, and grandparents.[3]

What we observed while piloting the survey in Nuevo León turned out to be one of the substantial findings from the first phase of our studies about international child migrants' integration and reintegration into Mexican schools: they are invisible.[4] However, invisibility is not absolute or invariable; rather, it emerges in different forms. Out of the eighty-three teachers and principals interviewed, only eighteen admitted to not being aware of the presence of students with previous school experience in the United States and to having found out about their existence only from our survey. The remaining sixty-five teachers had some idea about these students' existence. Some of them (n = 32) had a vague idea: during the interview, they referred to the students as if they were all grouped under a general category (i.e., they were in the United States) but did not have more information about them, such as the number of years they spent in U.S. schools, the name of the states or cities where they had lived, the reasons why they were in Mexico, or the students' dominant language(s). Others, especially the English teachers (n = 13), not only knew about their existence but were also aware of their English proficiency level. Finally, we found a group of teachers (n = 21) who had clearly identified the children, knew their parents, and had relatively accurate information about their migratory movements. This latter group were all teachers who worked in schools located in small towns where migration is a common phenomenon. For these teachers, especially for those who knew the community well, it was practically impossible for their migrant students to be invisible.

The teachers to whom students with previous schooling in the United States were visible were working in towns in the state of Nuevo León, Zacatecas, Puebla, or Jalisco. In those small or mid-sized towns, participating in emigration to the United States is a generalized trait of the community, which is why the teachers in those towns were familiar with their students' migratory status. In schools located in municipalities and localities with a long-standing migration history and a high density of international migrants, the idea that child migrants could become invisible is completely ruled out. However, in other regions and cities, international child migrants are less visible or totally invisible unless the state educational programs formally acknowledge these students' presence.[5] To some teachers international migrant children are completely invisible. To others they are more or less visible, and still, to others, they are visible. The question that arises is what the teachers see or do not see. The interviews we conducted suggest that teachers either do not or cannot see the difference between migrant children and other students in their classes—that is, they do not have the necessary training to identify and, at the same time, appreciate the uniqueness of the children who studied in a different school system. In the next section, we synthesize and classify the visions and non-visions of the teachers interviewed.

Invisibility of Difference and Indifference to Difference

In all our conversations with teachers and principals, we addressed the characteristics of the children who had studied in the United States. We asked the interviewees to describe migrant children, to identify their most important educational needs, and to define pedagogical actions that should be implemented to meet these children's needs. Teachers frequently began their responses by delimiting the validity of their statements:

I feel very limited. I'm actually talking about three people [students]. (Interview, Los Ramones, Nuevo León, 2005)

I don't know exactly [how many there are]. They are quite many. (Interview, Los Ramones, Nuevo León, 2005)

As we are always changing grade levels, and since we have been in different schools as well, we have not been able to keep track [of these children]. (Interview, Linares, Nuevo León, 2005)

I'm only now realizing it. (Interview, Guadalupe, Nuevo León, 2005)

I barely know her. This girl wasn't here before. It's only been a week since she arrived. (Interview, San Nicolás, Nuevo León, 2005)

It was a surprise that I didn't know. He attended elementary school in the United States. (Interview, Escobedo, Nuevo León, 2005)

I've just found out because I also just arrived [to this school] myself. The only thing I knew was that [one of the migrant children] was a girl in my class, but apparently she spent time there [in the United States] for a while and then came back, and it seems that she's still here. I think she was in Texas, but I don't have any specific information, but I think it's been more or less two years [since she came back]. (Interview, city of Zacatecas, 2006)

Oh, well, only the parents are there [in the United States]. For example [the student's name] from third grade, I think he was there. [The interviewer points out that there was another international migrant student]. . . . In the other school where I worked, I had a student who had also been in the United States and came here during junior high school. (Interview, city of Zacatecas, 2006)

There are a few children, those who come from the United States or who attended a school year there and then came here; there are a few children. I can tell you right now about [the student's name], who is in the eighth-grade class, in group H. I was his teacher last year, during seventh grade . . . and I've just found out that he came from there [the United States]. I did not know that. Right now, when the teachers went to ask who had come here from the United States, I'm only just now realizing it. (Interview, Fresnillo, Zacatecas, 2006)

It's the first time I realized that I have a student, and I've just discovered that; it was not before. During my classes with him, well, he mentioned that he had been in the United States. I thought he had gone only for a visit, not that he had lived there. (Interview, Atlixco, Puebla, 2010)

Yes, I've had [this type of child]. About ten years ago, a girl arrived in my seventh-grade group. (Interview, Jiutepec, Morelos, 2015)

The truth is that I don't know how many years they lived there, or what kind of schooling they received. (Interview, Jiutepec, Morelos, 2015)

What we observed in our conversations with the teachers is that, due to the training they had received, the curricular and administrative pressures to which they are subjected, their nonexistent or limited knowledge about U.S. schools, and the nationalism inherent to their mission within the school system, they failed to see the uniqueness of transnational students. This nonvision prevents them from envisioning the pedagogical needs of a child who has made the transition from one school system to the other.

The "invisibility of difference" and the "indifference to difference" have been extensively analyzed by researchers interested in the functioning of the school systems in which intercultural pedagogies are a relevant part of the political-educational discourse and debate. These authors conclude that the political discourse around the equality of all human beings is transformed in schools into pedagogical blindness, and this prevents the clear identification of differences; in turn, what emerges is a phenomenon that they call "the indifference to difference" (Bressoux and Pansu 2003; Payet, Giuliani, and Laforgue 2008; Le Blanc 2009; Payet 2016). This indifference produces a way of seeing children and adolescents that inevitably leads to the preservation of established forms of educational injustice or to the creation of new forms of injustice (Dubet 2007). In other words, the more indifferent the educators are to the social, cultural, linguistic, religious, gender, and other differences of their students, the more institutionally ignored their singularities, and resulting pedagogical needs are. It is this ideological and pedagogical framework that breeds "social exclusion" in school environments and the failure to acknowledge authentic differences (Lenoir and Froelich 2016).[6] In the following sections, we synthesize and classify the ways in which the Mexican teachers manifest their indifference to the uniqueness and richness of child migrants' previous school experiences. All the interviewees, with a single exception, shared in one, two, three, or all four of the visions described in the following sections.[7]

"Child Migrants Are Children Just Like the Nonmigrant Children"

Many teachers and principals began their narratives about the students who had studied in the United States by emphasizing their psychological traits, indicating that these youths are distinguished from their peers not because of their backgrounds or school trajectories but by their internal dimensions that make them who they are. From this point of view, the children are distinguished not by having a history of migration or transnational schooling experiences but by their inherent personality traits.

By acting in this way, the Mexican teachers completely overlooked their migrant students' educational experiences, especially those teachers who resort to categorizing students within the dichotomy of normal and abnormal. By classifying students from U.S. schools simply as "normal," they become homogenized to the point where there is nothing that distinguishes them from the other students who have been educated exclusively in Mexican schools. The good intention that underlies these responses (the teachers seek to make it clear that the child migrants are not problematic) results in making invisible the students' complex transition to Mexican schools and ignoring the unique and rich attributes they bring because of this experience:

> Well, I have noticed that they are like very normal [kids]. I've never talked with them or anything, but it seems, you know, that they are happy here. (Interview, Los Ramones, Nuevo León, 2005)

> They are not any different from the kids here. (Interview, Monterrey, Nuevo León, 2005)

> [Is a different pedagogical strategy required?] No, a normal one [should do it]. It's not difficult for them to interact, [especially] the ones I have been in charge of. (Interview, Linares, Nuevo León, 2005)

> For me all the children are the same, and we treat them in the same way. (Interview, Guadalupe, Nuevo León, 2005)

> The child has all the features of a Mexican person, and if he tells us that he is a foreigner, that is not easy to notice. . . . He is a child just like the others. (Interview, Monterrey, Nuevo León, 2005)

> They speak like a typical Mexican, a typical high school student, nothing out of the ordinary. (Interview, Hualahuises, Nuevo León, 2005)

> I think there are many similarities in their way of being, even in their way of studying. They are very similar to other students. (Interview, Linares, Nuevo León, 2005)

> [Are there any differences compared with other students?] It is a biological thing. There are adolescents [classified as types] I, II, III, IV, and V. We deal with I and II types biologically; type III and the rest are sent to those specialized in psychology, but, strictly speaking, it is a matter of teenage rebellion and things like that, not a matter of binationals or anything like that. (Interview, Monterrey, Nuevo León, 2005)

> [Are there differences?] Not due to the fact that they have been affected by the fact that they were educated in another country before they came here. No, I haven't noticed anything like that or anything else that caught my attention, something relevant. (Interview, San Nicolás, Nuevo León, 2005)

> I've had to work with several [children] of different character. For example, in the case of the first [migrant] student I had in my class, I said, "Well, he must be like that because he's a boy." (Interview, Fresnillo, Zacatecas, 2006)

Her attitude within the group, for example, I think that one's way of being has nothing to do with [migration]. I think that her behavior is rather based on something internal, more than on anything else, not on her [previous] education, something that she sees, she is like that . . . because it's something inherent to her way of being. (Interview, Fresnillo, Zacatecas, 2006)

The child comes to school very relaxed. . . . He's not hyperactive. He's within the usual, average. He is normal. He is a normal kid who relates to any other boy or girl, with any of his peers. I have no complaints so far. (Interview, Fresnillo, Zacatecas, 2006)

He is a child who's normal. He doesn't seem different, because I would have detected [if anything was off with him] from the beginning. (Interview, Atlixco, Puebla, 2010)

[Student's name] was a very cheerful and happy girl. Here she adapted easily with her classmates, except for [another student's name], maybe because of her way of being. . . . It depends on each student's character and on their upbringing in their family. (Interview, Jiutepec, Morelos, 2015)

The problems of [the student's name] are hormonal, typical of adolescence, but. anyway, he seems to fit in quite well. (Interview, in Cuernavaca, Morelos, 2015)

According to the teachers, the international migrant children in their classes are "normal" because they do not present problems or cause issues in the day-to-day activities of school. Within the context of this reassuring "normality," many teachers told us that they, nevertheless, observed a common and distinguished psychological characteristic of child migrants: they are shy, self-conscious, inhibited, faint-hearted, and they keep to themselves. Dozens of interviews pointed to these characteristics and are represented in the following interview segments:

They are also more self-conscious. . . . At the beginning, they are a little shy when they first arrive. (Interview, Anáhuac, Nuevo León, 2005)

She is a very reserved girl, very kind. Her sisters were the same, you see. It's not because she's been there [in the United States], but because her family is like that. (Interview, Guadalupe, Nuevo León, 2005)

It's only [the student's name]. There's something in his attitude, like he's much more respectful or timid. I don't know what he's trying to say. . . . He's always been very calm, very serious. . . . I think that this child would benefit from psychological support, so that he could open up a little bit more. . . . He is submissive. (Interview, Monterrey, Nuevo León, 2005)

They hardly ever engage in conversations; they hardly ever speak. They are very good girls, especially the older one. She seems like a quiet and very nice girl. (Interview, Jerez, Zacatecas, 2006)

The girl is like this, she keeps to herself. She studies hard. She's very responsible, works very well, very neatly, but she's very reserved, very quiet. When I ask her something, it takes a while before she answers. First she turns to see everyone else as if waiting for their authorization to speak. And the girl speaks properly, she is focused, she gives clear answers to my questions, but it takes a long time, and maybe she doesn't wanna answer, or she just doesn't answer. In my opinion, that is what's wrong with her, but, no, it has nothing to do with whether she's been there or here, because it's something that's inherent to her way of being. (Interview, Fresnillo, Zacatecas, 2006)

They are somewhat shy. They are not acquainted with the others, although they are from here, because this is now the second [migrant] child who has come through [this school], and the first one was like very shy, but little by little they start mingling. He's naturally quiet, introverted. . . . The other two who are absent, one of them is more or less integrated; the other is a little shy. (Interview, Atlixco, Puebla, 2010)

I honestly believe that they are a little more [reserved]. As I told you, maybe it's because of the integration process, but they are more reserved. They are more reserved, but after one, two, three, four months, they are already well integrated and already showing their true colors, right? But it's true, at first, they are more reserved. (Interview, Acatlán, Puebla, 2010)

[The student's name] reached third grade, then went on to fourth [grade]. She was a very dedicated [and] calm girl. There was no problem. (Interview, Jiutepec, Morelos, 2015)

Paradoxically, very few teachers associated the transnational students' silence, reserve, or inhibition with language differences. We know from our interviews with the children that during migrant children's first months in Mexican schools they have difficulty understanding what they are being told at school by both their teachers and peers and expressing their ideas, even though they were exposed to Spanish in their homes. Only two teachers wondered if the child migrants' tranquility, introversion, or isolation were associated with the fact that they actually did not understand what they were being told or did not feel confident that they could adequately communicate in Spanish what they wanted to say.

"Child Migrants Are Distinguished by Their Language Problems"

Many teachers perceive the children's multiple languages as barriers; however, they do not point to language as a way to explain the international child migrants' "shyness" in Mexican schools. Instead, the language barrier is defined by the teachers as a learning deficit. The teachers' argument is not that these children have been schooled in English and therefore need a period of exposure to schooling in Spanish while being simultaneously recognized for their achievements in English. On the contrary: the teachers almost exclusively focus on the language deficits that the children have in both written and spoken Spanish. When the teachers affirm that the children "are performing poorly in Spanish," they do not follow with an explanation—which would seem logical—regarding the children's previous schooling experience; they focus their attention only on children's limitations and insufficiencies.

Mariano, whom we interviewed in Fresnillo in April 2005, is a fourth-grade teacher with twenty-eight years of experience. He explained that the language limitations that the child migrants may have in Spanish stem from their previous schooling in the United States, where they are not allowed to develop their language skills in Spanish:

> We have seen their work [and] how they perform ... those who speak Spanish very little, because there are places in the United States where they are prohibited from speaking Spanish in schools. According to our experience, there are children who write half in Spanish and half in English.

Ezequiel, a teacher who was working at an elementary school located in a rural town in the municipality of Zacatecas, explained the children's inability to read words as follows:

> As far as reading is concerned, I have paid much attention to this matter, because I think that if they go there [to the United States], they begin to learn the language, and then they come here. . . . When I ask her something, the girl sometimes struggles to read a word. One must pay attention to the

words that are most difficult for them, and in this case almost everything I have identified is the language.

Ezequiel, who gave a long and detailed interview, revealed himself to be a responsible teacher, willing to learn and committed to the learning of his students. However, he could not see the origin of his student's difficulties: she can read, but in English, and needs support in transitioning the skills she has in English literacy to Spanish literacy. This student has already acquired complex literacy skills that should be drawn on to successfully transition into reading and writing in Spanish.

Vicky, like ten other teachers, made a more elaborate hypothesis. Vicky works at an elementary school in Cuernavaca and graduated from the Escuela Normal del Estado del Morelos (Morelos State Teachers College). We interviewed her in May 2015, and she stated that the migrant children, at least those that she knew, were characterized by a general language problem that was emotional in nature and affected them when speaking and reading:

> There was [the student's name]. When this girl was in my group, she was struggling a lot to thread the words together into a whole. She would spend a lot of time processing the words. Throughout the entire school year, I would speak with her classmates and asked them to include her, to invite her, to help her, and they would say, "She doesn't understand us!" ... Her attitude is difficult; her disposition is problematic. [These problems are] related to her learning, but they also have to do with her home environment. I asked her mother to pay more attention to her because the girl has an emotional problem that affects her development. We forced her, and we found her a place where she could take her to therapy. When [the student's name] arrived, she did look very distracted, like, who am I, where am I? But in the end, although everyone would help the girl, she did not know how to copy the date and other information from the blackboard. We realized that it was a different type of behavior. It wasn't because she wasn't able to because, for example, she could copy word by word from a book. . . . I don't know if there was violence at home.

Sometimes the teachers' deficit perspectives about the students' literacy skills were not regarding only Spanish but also English. This happens when the teachers assume that the challenges children face when reading and writing in Spanish are also related to their low level of English acquisition. This type of discourse emerged only in interviews with monolingual teachers. Below are selected excerpts from the interview with Guadalupe, a junior high school teacher in Anáhuac, Nuevo León, in February 2005:

> Very bad. It's Spanglish, and they don't speak English well, judging by the few words I know, nor Spanish. I tell them, they are not even from here. Yes, they do stumble [over their words when speaking Spanish] and even more when they are writing. One is dictating [the words] to them, and in the dictations they omit letters, they don't write correctly, and this is besides their spelling. It's terrible, because when it comes to spelling, yes, everyone who comes from over there [has] very bad spelling!

In contrast, the English teachers we interviewed presented an entirely different picture. Such was the case of Martha, an English teacher at a Los Ramones, Nuevo León, high school who, in February 2005, very emphatically explained,

> They interact a lot with children, with students who speak Spanish. These kids in particular have difficulties when speaking Spanish and with the Spanish grammar, and, apart from that, they speak English perfectly, 100 percent spoken perfectly. They stand up for themselves. They don't mix up the words, as they say.

"Migrant Children Are Distinguished by Their Educational Delays"

The teachers and school principals carry out their educational work guided by a formal curriculum that determines the certain content that students must learn along with specific skills they must acquire within an established timeframe. This framework leads teachers to classify students into two categories: those who are advanced and those who are behind. The teachers do not resort to this practice naturally, nor is it a firm educational principle. Rather, the institutional mechanisms in which they carry out their work—programs, assessments, evaluations, reports, and so on—impose the criteria, pace, and indicators to which everyone (both teachers and students) is subject. The conditions in which they work "isolate teachers, silence their autonomy and push them towards standardization and homogenization" (González 2005, 3).[8]

Within this framework, when international child migrants arrive to Mexican schools, they are almost automatically classified as being behind. They are viewed as being behind in their reading and writing skills (in Spanish) but also as lagging in geography, history, mathematics, and civic education. Thus, in 2010 Juanita, a teacher with twenty years of experience who worked in a *telesecundaria* in Izúcar de Matamoros, Puebla, warned us,

> Look, I had two students who came from there [the United States], and in math they were doing more or less okay. What is really difficult for them are other subjects such as history, civic education. They have no idea. They ask what that has got to do with anything; they don't teach us that in the United States. They are lagging behind in these subjects, and they don't even know why we are talking about that hero or that date.[9]

Luz María, an elementary school teacher who was working at a school in Jerez in 2005, described it this way:

> Regarding the educational aspect, both [migrant students] are lagging behind, and I think that it is because they have studied in various schools, because when they come straight from the United States. . . . Especially in Spanish, we do have problems [with these students], because they arrive [in Mexico], and they speak Spanish very poorly . . . and they perform low in math, too. . . . I've even told these two girls that week I needed them to stay in math class [for extra support]. . . . I see it as really problematic, because, according to this, their educational level is high when they come here, but it's really not [true]. They are very different when they arrive. The truth, it's very different because they often have to lag behind in grade placement, due to what they learned there [in the United States] . . . because it's almost impossible to find a kid who possesses knowledge similar to [what is learned] here.

In short, according to the teachers, the children arriving from U.S. schools are not on track with the learning objectives or the curriculum of Mexican schools.

According to Alejandra, a math and chemistry teacher at a Monterrey high school whom we interviewed in 2005, child migrants are not only behind but also have no substantial content knowledge that can be considered essential for their academic performance in Mexico:

I don't know what the system is like there, but I do know that when [a student] arrives here, he is lagging behind a little, for example in history. He didn't know anything, and I already talked to the history teacher. I told him what he needed. . . . And the same with [the student's name]. He doesn't know Mexican history. He needs to be patient . . . that he would do very well in English, that maybe he might be a little behind in math, but they are supposed to come with more solid [knowledge] bases because supposedly there [in the United States] they advance at a slower pace than they're supposed to, where content is concerned. . . . In history, the situation seems tough for them, and the history teacher here is very strict; he's very demanding. . . . The truth is that here they don't give us any option—that is, they [the authorities] hand you the program, and you have to adjust to it. . . . Say, [the student] just has to adjust to the [teaching] pace and to the content and to the [knowledge] bases we have here, no matter what it takes—by force, shouting and yelling, leaping and sometimes going backward, sometimes running and sometimes moving at a slow pace.

Helena, a teacher whom we interviewed in Jiutepec in 2015, was more emphatic:

I am going to talk about a girl in particular. Last year, [the student's name] was doing so badly in math. Of course, she couldn't read, but she didn't know how to add or subtract, and she was ten years old. I don't know if they don't teach that to children that age. I don't know how the system works there.

Thus, as the teachers clearly pointed out, the child migrants are viewed as lagging behind the other children and must "catch up" with the rest of their peers as soon as possible, even if "by force, shouting and yelling." Their knowledge of the history, geography, and political system of the United States is irrelevant and ignored—and consequently despised—in Mexican schools.

"Migrant Children Have Not Adequately Developed Allegiance to the Homeland."

Teachers instill Mexican nationalism by using curricular content (i.e., national history and civic education) and highly codified school liturgies in which students routinely participate, such as the flag salute, singing the national anthem, and national festivities and celebrations. Using the teachers' language to describe this phenomenon, said curricula and ceremonies allow the new generations of Mexicans to know and appreciate "our roots."

These educational semantics make teachers suspect that the child migrants who arrive from U.S. schools lack allegiance to the homeland, and, consequently, they are not Mexican in the full sense of the term. Of the eighty-three teachers interviewed, fifty-seven addressed this topic directly. Some addressed the topic in detail and others did so circumstantially. Here we present six excerpts illustrative of this theme.

Juan Manuel, an elementary school teacher in a town in Atlixco, Puebla, whom we interviewed in 2010, described the teachers' mission in Mexico:

> Somehow, we, the teachers, try to make the children aware [of the fact] that they should stay here [in Mexico], where their roots are, where our customs are, where our traditions are, because this is what we hope they will understand, so that they can somehow truly see. I cannot say in any way that we don't love our Mexico. We definitely adore our country, but, yes, I hope the children can also reach that [level of] awareness.

Ofelia, the director of a *telesecundaria* located in a small town in the municipality of Fresnillo, who has twenty-four years of teaching experience and whom we interviewed in 2006, described the transition process that the child migrants undergo as follows:

> Their change is total. It's a change of identity, a cultural change, a change of feelings, and I think this is what the teacher's main mission is all about, to make them identify [with their roots], to touch the students' soul—that is, reach their hearts and tell them, "You are here with us now; you are still Mexican." That matter of identity, I think it's the first task [for the teachers]. You're Mexican because I'm Mexican. There is a [common] identity.

Felipe, an English teacher at a Nuevo León high school, seemed rather pessimistic about the civic education of children coming from U.S. schools. In the lengthy interview we had with him in 2005, he stated,

> I believe that, at least in these three cases, they have an identity which is different to the Mexican one in some respects. For example, due to their same

experience in the U.S. educational system, the authority figure of the teacher is not as strong as it is here, in Mexico. . . . I used to chat with them, with the people who are Mexican Americans, and they tell you, "I come here, and I don't feel Mexican. I feel like a *pocha* [a pejorative label to designate Spanglish speakers]." Yes, [it's] really intense. Here [in Mexico], they are the *pochos*, and there [in the United States], they are the Aztec Indians. . . . The civic issues, that is, they don't know any of them, flag-raising [ceremony] either. For them, the Independence of Mexico is something small, and for us it's a big deal. Their system of civic values is quite different.

Helena, a primary school teacher in Jiutepec, reached an even more pessimistic conclusion during the brief interview we had with her in 2015. She stated, "She [a ten-year-old student] said she was from the United States and wanted to return there, and she did say that with great pride." The pride with which Helena declared her U.S. citizenship represented for this teacher an insurmountable obstacle for instilling a love for Mexico in the migrant children.

In 2005 we interviewed Leonel, a teacher at a *telesecundaria* in a town in the municipality of Linares, Nuevo León. He was more emphatic:

In fact, at first when he arrived, he did seem a little reluctant, and we noticed that he would reject things that he was not used to. In fact, he didn't know the [Mexican] national anthem. The teacher who was the principal [at that time] and myself, as I was teaching his group, had to talk with him and make him see that he had to learn certain things that were part of his identity, such as [showing] respect for the flag, the national symbols, the national anthem. . . . Now he has even participated as the leader of the flag-salute ceremony, conducting the hymn, even as master of ceremonies at the weekly flag-salute [ceremony]. At first, [when he arrived] he had that attitude that was maybe a little rebellious, but I think [because] we talked to him and told him, "You know what? Look, this is how things are, this and that, here you have to abide by certain rules, certain norms. We have to do this and that for you to catch up with your classmates. Just as your classmates pay their respect to the flag, you must do so, too." . . . They have a different culture, different customs, and they come here [as if they were] know-it-alls. . . . The parents never forget their Mexican roots. Their children are those who change a little, those who were born there [in the United States], who were raised there [in the United States], some of them even say, "I'm not Mexican. I'm American," even if they were born to Mexican parents. I mean, if we as Mexicans let ourselves be influenced by the United States,

I don't want to imagine how the Mexican Americans who are on the other side [of the border] would be influenced.[10]

The sense of nationalism and fatalism of the teacher from Linares are not shared by all teachers. Dolores, a junior high school teacher in Jolalpan, Puebla, shared the same goals, but not the same means to achieve them. She painted an entirely different picture:

> So I think it's possible to create in them a love for Mexico. Yes, you can [do that], because, anyway, their inclinations, their enthusiasm for the Mexican things. I just tell them over and over again, the only thing is that the environment is different, and perhaps they had more comforts there [in the United States] and that is why they don't like it here [in Mexico]. But I believe that, with time, it can be achieved.

TEACHER AND ADMINISTRATOR TRAINING

Without exception all teachers and principals interviewed stated that they had not received any training while they were studying at their universities or even at the Universidad Pedagógica Nacional (National Pedagogical University), nor through any additional professional development courses or workshops. All but two teachers said they were not familiar with the schools in the United States. And the two teachers who were had seen only the school buildings without actually entering the schools. Most of the teachers we interviewed are monolingual, but many expressed the desire to acquire communication skills in English to help international child migrants. Some adopted certain prejudices about the education system and the teachers in the United States (e.g., permissive, slow, not based in pedagogy but in technology), while others clarified that they were not familiar with the academic programs and pedagogies in U.S. schools.

The teachers in Nuevo León and Zacatecas, whom we interviewed in 2005 and 2006, were unaware of the existence of any professional development program that specifically responded to the educational needs of child migrants who had arrived at their schools.[11] Some even questioned whether these programs were important or useful, arguing that the students who came from U.S. schools to Mexican schools were few and were not worthy of resources and institutional actions to attend to their needs. Several teachers from Puebla, Jalisco, and Morelos (interviewed in 2010, 2011, 2014, and 2015) knew of the existence of professional development programs but had not been invited to participate in them. All teachers, to varying degrees, wanted to be better trained and prepared to respond to the challenges specific to the integration and reintegration of child migrants into Mexican schools.

In sum these children are transnational students, while the Mexican teachers (as are most of the teachers in the United States) are mononational (Zúñiga and Hamann 2008). The teachers are located, professionally and personally, in a single national space because that is how they were trained. It was not until the middle of the first decade of the twenty-first century that things changed, and the teachers and principals were caught off guard when international child migrants began arriving in their classrooms. The Mexican teachers' visions and nonvisions about working with child migrants are a direct consequence of the lack of training for in-service teachers and the indifference of the educational policies in Mexico to the broader immigration context.

STUDENTS AND THEIR SCHOOL TRANSITIONS

Let's now turn our attention to the students. They make the transition from U.S. to Mexican schools once, twice, or even more times. These transitions make them transnational students, and, upon their arrival in Mexico, they become part of the 0.5 generation. According to the data we have analyzed, these transitions are characterized by discontinuities and fractures. In this section of the chapter, we analyze how these disruptions affect the children's learning progress when they are integrated into schools in Mexico.

Grade Repetition, Loss of Years in School, and Absenteeism

The most visible discontinuities throughout the child migrants' school trajectories are grade repetition, loss of years in school, and school absenteeism or dropouts. Grade repetition is when the child is forced to reenroll in the school grade that they have successfully completed in the other school system and for which they have received credit and is always the product of a decision made by the principals or curricular advisers. The loss of years in school is the result of incompatibility between school and migration calendars. Sometimes children arrive at their destination in Mexico and, for various reasons, are unable to enroll in the school designated to serve their residence area and lose an entire year of school. Finally, persistent absenteeism, or dropping out, is the type of discontinuity that has the most serious consequences on child migrants' schooling trajectories because the children stop attending school. International migration—which includes the international transit between schools—becomes a factor of school exclusion since the children interrupt their schooling either temporarily or permanently. We address each form of discontinuity and explain some of the underlying causes.

The data from the surveys conducted in elementary and junior high schools in four states of Mexico allow us to affirm the following: one-third of the child migrants enrolled in schools in Zacatecas in 2005 had repeated one, two, and or even three years of school. Of these students 64 percent repeated grades in Mexico, and the rest of them had repeated grades in U.S. schools. The percentages are almost identical in Puebla, with the only difference being that half of the child migrants from Puebla repeated grades in the United States, while only 36 percent of the child migrants in Zacatecas repeated grades in U.S. schools. In Jalisco and Morelos, the percentage of children who experienced repetition is lower: 26 percent in the first state, and 11 percent in the latter.[12] In Jalisco the child migrants repeated grades mainly in Mexico, while in Morelos they did so in the United States.[13]

To corroborate data on grade repetition, we compared the average age of the child migrants with that of the nonmigrant children, who had never been enrolled in U.S. schools, based on the grade in which they were enrolled at the time of the survey. The results of this comparison are revealing: in all cases the average age of the children who migrated from the United States to Mexico is higher than that of the nonmigrant children. For example, the average age of migrant students enrolled in the seventh grade in Zacatecas in 2005 was 12.98 years, versus 12.36 in the case of the nonmigrant children. The average age of migrant students enrolled in ninth grade in Puebla in 2010 was 14.70 years, compared to 14.37 for nonmigrant students. In Jalisco the average age of migrant students enrolled in fifth grade was 10.58 versus 10.34 for nonmigrant students.[14] Our data go up to ninth grade. The data from the *2015 Intercensal Survey* confirm this trend for a nationally representative sample and show that grade repetition increases, especially after the expected age for elementary school completion (that is, after twelve years of age), and continues to increase throughout adolescence.

Why do migrant children, among those interviewed, repeat grades they have already completed? The principals and teachers interviewed in Mexico justify this decision by arguing that the children are "lagging behind" (they do not have the knowledge required for the grade, or they have not acquired the competencies required, according to the school curriculum). Regardless of whether these justifications are valid and, in some cases, obvious (e.g., a child who arrives in Mexico with five years of previous schooling in the United States, including one year of preschool and four years of elementary school, does not know the history or geography of Mexico), the consequences for children are inevitable: they experience this decision not as a measure that will enable them to be more successful in school but as an institutional message that invalidates what they have previously learned.

The differences in the average age according to grade is also linked to the loss of years in school. Upon arrival at their destination, the children were unable to enroll in schools and, consequently, did not complete the grade they had started in the previous country. In Zacatecas we found that 23 percent of the students encountered this obstacle, most when they first arrived in Mexico. And this was the case for 15 percent of the migrant students surveyed in Puebla, 9 percent in Jalisco, and 10 percent in Morelos. For most of the migrant children, this happened to them in Mexican schools, although some were also held back in the United States. The survey question about this topic is impeccably clear. The students were asked, "Have you lost a school year because you could not enroll in school?" If the migrant students answered affirmatively, they were immediately asked to specify whether this had happened in Mexico or in the United States. About two-thirds of those surveyed—with variations according to state—answered that it had happened in Mexico.[15]

Dropping out of school is the most severe discontinuity that migrant children may experience in their educational trajectory. Some children come to Mexico from the United States and either do not enroll in schools in Mexico or, when they do enroll in elementary or junior high, drop out after a period of time. Currently, we have very few longitudinal studies to provide empirical data about the relationship between migration from the United States to Mexico and school dropout rates.[16] However, we do have information from a small sample of ten children from Morelos, whom we have been interviewing since 2013. The results are not encouraging. Five of the ten children dropped out of school: one during elementary school and four during junior high. Of the other five children (who experienced interruptions in their schooling over two to three years), four eventually returned to the United States and enrolled in schools there after spending two years without attending school in Mexico. A closer look at the ethnographic data collected about these migrant children's homes and families show that the Mexican schools were not able to provide conditions conducive to their integration, and, as a result, the children told their parents they wanted to stop going to school (Román González, Carrillo, and Hernández-León 2016; Román González 2017). Unfortunately, we lack sufficient longitudinal data about international child migrants in Mexico that could allow us to approximate the kind of impact that these interruptions have on their school trajectory. Findings from the national data set of school attendance and dropout rates in Mexico are paradoxical and combine different experiences (INEGI 2015). In fact, one of the differentiating factors included in this dataset is international experience, which is further delineated by child migrants' place of birth.

Fractures

A child's transition from a school in the United States to one in Mexico inevitably leads to disruptions in schooling that can be understood as fractures. Cognitive, emotional, linguistic, or social fractures emerge from the central phenomenon that U.S. and Mexican school systems are divorced from and ignore each other. This means that, from a child's perspective, what was learned, internalized, and acquired in one school system is not useful, viewed as less valuable, or not even recognized in the other system.

Essentially, the migrant children "land" in Mexican schools without a landing strip.

Our data show that children experience a greater disruption when they attend Mexican schools after having completed a significant portion of their schooling in the United States, and that, not surprising, the disruption is less when their schooling experience in the United States was short. Similarly, the fractures are more abrupt when the children started their schooling in the United States and arrived in a Mexican school without any previous experience in Mexico. On the contrary, children who started their schooling in Mexico, continued it in the United States, and then returned to Mexico experience less severe discontinuities.

Linguistic Fractures

When migrant children arrive in Mexican schools, they experience linguistic fractures to varying extents. All of them speak Mexican Spanish more or less fluently because it is the language they used at home while living in the United States. However, very often the language proficiency they have acquired in Spanish is not the linguistic resource they need for their successful development in school (Despagne and Jacobo 2016). They have acquired the latter skills, but in English and in accordant with the school curricula in the United States. That is why, when integrating or reintegrating into Mexican schools, they seem "shy"; in other words, they are "shy" because they do not understand what is being communicated to them. It is not that they do not understand Spanish, but that they are not familiar with the register used in Mexican schools. In some cases this leads children to incorrectly internalize the belief that they really do not understand Spanish.

In fact, according to the interviews we conducted with teachers and children, migrant children frequently suffer humiliation because of their pronunciation or the way that they construct sentences in Spanish. The testimony of Mariano, a sixth-grade teacher at a school in Valparaíso, Zacatecas, whom we interviewed in November 2005, is relevant to this point and synthesizes many other stories gathered through interviews with teachers:

> [The student's name] investigated different situations, about tornadoes, [because] he said that in the United States they were very common, so his

classmates laughed a lot because of the language he used. They didn't understand him. But he tried over and over again. Then the children were very impressed. One thing stuck with them. He said, "When a tornado comes, run or get into the *sotáno*," and, uh!, everybody burst into laughter, "the so-*táno*." But he went on with his presentation as though nothing had happened. So I really liked these children's attitude, that, despite all their limitations, they wanted to participate. That was a very cool experience. And, well, the experiences like this *traumating [sic]* are those when [they say,] "Well, I don't understand."[17]

The "very cool experience" that the teacher described was, in fact, a humiliating one for the child. Mariano described the event as something comical, while the focal student, whom we interviewed the same day, was convinced that his skills in Spanish were clearly insufficient. However, in this scenario, Mariano did not disapprove of the other students' mockery but celebrated it.

International child migrants, to varying degrees, face complex linguistic challenges in their transition from English literacy to Spanish literacy, a process they generally take on either alone or with the help of their families.[18] In doing so, they first face the challenge of establishing letter-sound correspondence, such as when Laurie, a thirteen-year-old student from Los Ramones, Nuevo León, wrote "elephante" instead of "elefante" in Spanish. In a 2011 interview, she explained, "The teacher scolded me because I did not write it well" (see Panait and Zúñiga 2016). Letter-sound correspondence requires the development of phonemic awareness that child migrants have not been able to develop in Spanish by the time of their enrollment in Mexican schools (Richek et al. 2001). Certainly, child migrants know the Latin alphabet, but they may not associate sounds with individual letters or letter combinations in Spanish (Panait 2011).[19] The children, who generally receive very little support in schools, face challenges with the symbolic representation of phonemes and the polyphony of graphemes.

Second, the children who have acquired print literacy in English face another challenge with written Spanish regarding the diacritical marks, or accents, which do not exist in English. The process of learning the written accent marks in Spanish causes much doubt and confusion, leading some migrant children to believe that these marks should not exist and that they only complicate the already difficult task of acquiring print literacy skills in Spanish (Panait 2011).

A third linguistic challenge is related to vocabulary and comprehension. When reading the textbooks used in Mexican schools, child migrants come across many words that they have never heard and, even less, have used in their daily lives. Most of their Spanish (or Indigenous language) vocabulary has been formed through domestic conversations with their parents, grandparents, uncles, and other members of the Spanish-speaking or Indigenous-languages-speaking communities in the United States. Child migrants experienced a linguistic process that Tatyana Kleyn (2022) calls "language learning, unlearning, and relearning." As a result, in school contexts, certain terms like *familiarizado, indagar, extranjero, comunicativa, timbres, modalidad, disputaron, guerreros, aumentar, desterrado, legendario,* or *invencible* are unfamiliar to them or difficult for them to understand (Panait and Zúñiga 2016). This directly affects their reading fluency and comprehension as well as their accuracy and fluency in word recognition—that is, migrant children not only do not know what those words mean but also do not know how to pronounce them. Often, as Catalina Panait (2011) has documented, when reading these words, they substitute other words that are similar in form or that are more familiar to them without even realizing that they are doing so. And Kleyn complemented these findings by observing what happens when child migrants face the challenges of writing in Spanish: "For transborder students who found themselves suddenly learning in all-Spanish schools, writing posed the most difficulties" (Kleyn 2022, 97).

For example, Panait (2011, 83) found that, when asked to read passages in Spanish, two migrant students (ages thirteen and fifteen) read *seguridores* instead of *seguidores, general* instead of *ganan, veces* instead of *vencer, español* instead of *España, azainas* instead of *hazañas, vivo* instead of *vivió,* and *aceptaban* instead of *acentuaban,* among others. As child migrants navigate the challenges of acquiring vocabulary and developing comprehension upon their arrival to Mexico, they may be discouraged because their reading fluency is notably lower than that of their peers. In turn this may lead them to believe that their developing reading ability in Spanish indicates that they are not intelligent. Due to the frustration they experience while reading, the children might reach the conclusion that they really "don't know" Spanish. Nanys, a ninth grader whom we interviewed in Jolalpan, Puebla, in February 2010, uses this situation to her advantage and explained how she translanguages (Orellana 2016) to not fall into that trap: "Well, for me it's harder because I understand Spanish, but sometimes, like in my head, I change the words into English to understand better, but sometimes, when I can't change the word into English, it's a little bit harder." But this was not the same for Ramiro, whom we interviewed in March 2010 at an elementary school in Izúcar de Matamoros, Puebla, after he had attended three years of school in California. A ten-year-old at that time, he told us,

> Right now, I'm not doing very well [in school] now. I've already failed like three subjects. [At the school in Santa Ana, California,] I would get straight As, and everything was going well. The truth is that here, I don't understand, well, almost anything, reading. I couldn't read that well, but there, yes, I could read everything well.

The fourth linguistic challenge that the migrant children face is related to more complex dimensions of written language such as grammar, syntax, and discourse structure, linguistic components that have been scarcely explored with this population until now and have emerged only in some of the interviews with the children. Studying cross-language transfers and feed-forward and feed-backward activation processes have been analyzed in U.S. schools during children's transition from Spanish to English but are still very much unknown regarding the transition process from English to Spanish (Schwartz, Kroll, and Diaz 2007).[20] It could be argued that all Mexican students face similar difficulties to those described in the previous paragraphs as they learn literacy skills in schools—that is, that these linguistic challenges are not exclusive to children who come from schools in the United States. This is correct; however, three substantial differences must be considered. First, child migrants do not experience linguistic challenges as difficulties inherent during the passage from oral language to written language, as what happens with all students who are learning to read and write, but because of their developing Spanish language. In fact, the message that they frequently receive from their teachers is that they are "deficient" in the Spanish language. Second, mononational students undertake the difficult task of learning the written language while using the dominant oral language as a resource (Terrail 2009), while transnational students have a more complex task: managing transitions between and drawing on two oral languages (spoken Spanish and English) and two written linguistic codes. Last, transnational students have a broader linguistic repertoire, which allows them to translanguage, make cross-linguistic transfers, and use loanwords, but it is classified as deficient, not as resourceful, in Mexican schools.

Curricular Fractures

We have already presented the teachers' accounts that describe how child migrants arrive in Mexican schools with little or no knowledge of the history and geography of Mexico and their limited training in Mexican civic education (denoted because they are unfamiliar with Mexican rituals, songs, and patriotic prose). These narratives suggest what we call "curricular fractures" because the students' prior knowledge acquired in U.S. schools is unrelated to Mexican curricula and is not considered valuable in Mexican schools. These curricular fractures are confirmed by the surveys conducted in Zacatecas, Puebla, Jalisco, and Morelos. We asked child migrants with previous schooling in the United States which subjects in the Mexican curriculum were most difficult for them. Their responses are worthy of consideration. Undoubtedly, the most difficult subject was mathematics: almost 40 percent of the responses indicated that mathematics was the most difficult subject. (This percentage was calculated with respect to the total responses to this question, not to the total number of children surveyed because children were able to indicate two, three, or more academic subjects on the questionnaire). Notably, the second most difficult subject was history (including civic education), which accounted for nearly a quarter of the responses.

When this variable is controlled for the number of years that have elapsed since the children arrived in Mexico, the order is reversed. For the children who recently arrived in Mexican schools (meaning that they had transitioned from the U.S. school to the Mexican school one or two years before the time of the survey), the most difficult subjects were history, civic education, and geography. As time passes, the difficulty of these subjects loses its importance, and mathematics becomes the most difficult subject.

However, even after several years, history and civic education continues to be particularly difficult for these children, surpassing Spanish and the natural sciences (i.e., physics, chemistry, biology) in terms of percentage.[21]

Social Fractures

In this section we use only two, relatively simple, indicators of social divisions and fractures. The first regards how nonmigrant children (those who do not have previous experience in U.S. schools) depict the child migrants. To answer the question "What are the students who have studied in the United States like?" respondents had to choose between three options: (a) just like me; (b) different from me; and (c) I do not know any. After answering the question, they explained why. If they chose the first option, they were stating that they did not identify any social divide between themselves and those who came from U.S. schools. This statement indicated the absence of social divisions. On the contrary, if they chose the second option, they identified divisions, separations, or distinctions important enough for them to group the child migrants into a different social category and therefore displaying a social fracture.

Out of the total number of nonmigrant students who answered this question in Zacatecas, Puebla, Jalisco, and Morelos (n = 29,580 students enrolled in fourth grade through ninth grade), 43 percent stated that they did not know any peers who had studied in the United States.[22] Since this group did not (consciously) know any child migrants, they could not articulate any differences or similarities, so we could not use their responses in this analysis. Therefore, we focus only on the answers of those who indicated that they knew international migrant students (n = 16,730 students across the four states). Before we present the results and analysis of this latter group, it is important to delineate the geographic differences that we found regarding nonmigrant students' lack of knowledge about migrant children in their schools. In Jalisco and Morelos, only a quarter of the children stated that they did not know any peers who had studied in schools in the United States; this percentage rises to 35 percent in Zacatecas. However, this proportion is much higher in the schools in Puebla, where two-thirds of those surveyed stated that they did not know any international migrant peers (64 percent).

These differences can be explained by two factors. The first is the migration density according to each of the states and to the regions within each state; the greater the migratory density, the greater the presence of international child migrants in schools. This is why in some regions of the state of Puebla where the migratory intensity is low, practically all children stated that they did not know any peers with previous schooling experience in the United States. The second factor is the date when the survey was conducted. The visibility and presence of the child migrants in schools is concomitant to the "return" of Mexicans from the United States to Mexico (Giorguli and Gutiérrez 2011b). It is probable that, for this reason, in Jalisco (where the survey was conducted in December 2010) and in Morelos (where the survey was conducted in September 2013) the percentage of children who *did not* know any classmates with previous schooling experience in the United States is notably lower, even lower than that observed in Zacatecas in 2005, a state characterized by high migratory density in nearly all regions.

The analysis of the responses and their distributed percentages according to the gender of participants shows that, generally speaking, there are more students who perceive child migrants as different from them, the proportion fluctuating between 49 percent and 71 percent, than those who see them as equals, except in two cases: the girls from Jalisco and Morelos (see table 17). In these cases the proportion of students who affirmed that the child migrants are just like them is slightly higher than the percentage who indicated that they were different from them.

Compared to the other states, nonmigrant children from Puebla privileged differences rather than similarities. The differentiating characteristics that nonmigrant children describe across the four states are mostly linguistic ("they speak differently," "they speak English," "sometimes they do not understand what the teacher explains," "they speak two languages," "they know more English than I do") or positive traits ("they are smarter," "they are more studious," "more focused," "they are better prepared," "they get better grades," and "they know more things"). The negative differentiating characteristics, in all states, are those related to the child migrants' claims of superiority: "they are very arrogant," "they are conceited," "boastful," and "they have a lot of money, and they are smug" or to behaviors considered inadmissible: "they are rebellious," "they discriminate against

Table 17   Percentage distribution of nonmigrant students' perceptions of migrant students from answers to the question: "What are the students who have studied in the United States like?"

State (year)	Gender	Just like me (%)	Different from me (%)	Number of students surveyed
Zacatecas	Girls	40	60	2,362
(2005)	Boys	38	62	2,358
Puebla	Girls	31	69	2,127
(2009)	Boys	29	71	2,146
Jalisco	Girls	51	49	3,449
(2010)	Boys	46	54	3,288
Morelos	Girls	51	49	578
(2013)	Boys	42	58	422

SOURCE: Our elaboration is based on the databases of Universidad de Monterrey (2015).

Mexicans," "they have a temper," and "they are contaminated by the U.S. culture." These negative differentiators occurred more frequently in Puebla. One of the children from Puebla synthesized it as follows: "We are Mexicans, and they are city folks." Finally, more information is necessary to adequately explain why girls (at least in Morelos and Jalisco) privileged similarities more than differences. While these percentage variations by gender are not very stark, they require further studying. The nonmigrant girls may be more inclusive than their male peers. In chapter 8 we provide data to support this hypothesis.

Let's now turn to the way in which the international child migrants perceive their peers who have never studied in U.S. schools. They answered the following question: "What are the students who have not studied in the United States like?" In this case the options were "just like me," "different from me," and "I do not know how to explain." If their answer emphasizes similarities between the two groups, we can infer that they do not consider themselves as belonging to a distinct category based on particular characteristics—that is, if they chose "just like me," it can be inferred that they consider that all the children or adolescents in the school belong to the same category. The opposite would occur if they considered the

mononational children as different from them. As in our previous explanation, their identification of other children works like a mirror: "different
from me" means, from the respondents' point of view, that they belong to
a distinct group of children who constitute a minority within the school.
The last option allowed the children to express their uncertainty.

The results in table 18 indicate that between 26 percent and 42 percent of international child migrants emphasize differences, and the percentage of children who chose similarities varies according to the state
and gender. Half of the girls in Zacatecas opted for similarities, while this
option was selected only by 23 percent and 28 percent of the girls and
boys in Puebla, respectively. What differences did they identify? Again the
linguistic characteristics are the most numerous: "they don't understand
English," "they speak more Spanish than English," "they speak differently,"
"I can teach them English," "at first, when I arrived in Mexico, I didn't
understand them," and "They speak a different language." However, they
also signal forms of differentiation that are noteworthy: "they are more
educated, and they are nice," "they curse and do disgusting things, well,
the boys [not the girls]," "they are Mexican, and I am American," "I have
known a different world," "they know less than I do," "they are so bad that
they go begging on the street," "because we have different rights," "they
don't know how to read or write," "they don't follow the same rules," "they
think very differently," "they don't like the United States because Mexico
and the United States are enemies," "very different, because they don't
respect me in the same as they do there [in the United States]," "I feel
alone," and "[here] they wear a uniform, and there [in the United States]
they don't."

Academic Achievement and Performance

Are international migrant children who have been arriving in Mexico
since the beginning of the twenty-first century successful in school? Do
they get good grades? Do they complete fewer or more years of school
than their peers who have not lived in the United States? Do they acquire
the reading, mathematical, scientific, and technical competencies established in the school curriculum of Mexico, according to each grade
and educational level? These questions about academic learning,

Table 18   Percentage distribution of migrant students' perceptions of nonmigrant students from answers to the question "What are the students who have not studied in the United States like?"

State (year)	Gender	Just like me (%)	Different from me (%)	I do not know how to explain (%)	Number of students surveyed
Zacatecas	Girls	50	27	23	92
(2005)	Boys	44	32	24	88
Puebla	Girls	23	34	43	35
(2009)	Boys	28	42	30	50
Jalisco	Girls	48	31	21	148
(2010)	Boys	42	26	32	139
Morelos	Girls	36	32	32	25
(2013)	Boys	33	29	38	24

SOURCE: Our elaboration is based on the databases of Universidad de Monterrey (2015).

achievement, performance, and school success cannot be answered with the data we have at our disposal. These are fields of study that must be studied both from a quantitative perspective, using the databases produced by the institutions that evaluate academic learning in Mexico, and through longitudinal studies to gain better comprehension of the child migrants' school itineraries from the moment they are integrated or reintegrated into Mexican schools.

Various scholarly attempts to answer these complex questions address the relationship between international migration and school performance and achievement while focusing on academic learning in municipalities and regions with a long migratory tradition (Jensen, Mejía Arauz, and Aguilar Zepeda 2017). These research efforts have provided valuable findings that we synthesize here. The impact of remittances received by families does not necessarily have a positive relationship with the children and adolescents' school achievement and performance. As Adam Sawyer (2014) states, "money is not enough." This ambivalent relationship between remittances and children's educational achievements arises from the fact that the impact is mediated by various intervening factors that do not necessarily align: mothers' level of education, quality of schools, plans that young people have to emigrate to the United States, and others, all prevent child migrants and those who stay in Mexico (while their parents are in the United States) from achieving longer schooling (Jensen, Giorguli, and Hernández 2013).

The impact of international migration and school performance measured by standardized tests, such as EXCALE (a Mexican national achievement exam), is not positive or negative. This indicates that the children's exposure to international migration does not necessarily decrease their performance or enhance it. Other contextual or ecological conditions (e.g., socioeconomic stratum, rural conditions, separation of family members due to migration to the United States, type of school, etc.) interfere and modify the associations between these variables. For this reason, in a recently published article, we argued that the findings about the relationship between international migration and literacy development, measured according to standardized tests, both confirmed and refuted our hypotheses (Jensen, Giorguli, and Hernández 2016). On one hand, family conditions and the migratory history of the community do not seem to relate to these test scores, nor does the certainty of the young people regarding their future emigration to the United States. However, paradoxically, an approaching date of emigration has a positive impact on test performance, especially in the case of the students belonging to lower socioeconomic strata. Last, attempts to identify the impacts of international migration on school achievement and academic performance show that the "culture of migration" (Kandel and Massey 2002; Zúñiga 1992) not only favors school dropouts but also discourages adolescents in their educational trajectory since they have their eyes set on migration to the United States and not on academic achievement (Giorguli and Serratos López 2009).

While these studies generally attempt to understand the impact of migration on children and adolescents' school education, they do not specifically address international child migrants' school achievement, success, or performance. The aforementioned authors measure exposure to migration utilizing one indicator: the proportion of international migrants within the family. This indicator is often linked to the separation of families (e.g., the father, mother, siblings are in the United States while the minors are studying in Mexico). These studies focus on minors who have never migrated to the United States but plan to as opposed to studying the children who have immigrated from the United States to Mexico.

One way to approximate the impact of migration from the United States to Mexico on school performance is to examine the average grades obtained by the children when they were enrolled in U.S. schools and compare them with the children's average grades attained in Mexican schools. We drew on the surveys of state school systems to conduct this exercise. The children were asked about their grades. Their answers do not necessarily reflect their actual grades, as we did not have access to the documents that would allow us to compare the grades that they declared with their grades on official transcripts. However, it would be appropriate to consider that a child who received mainly Cs and Ds in a U.S. school would report that his or her grades were "bad" or "regular" and that these students would have no reason to report that they got "excellent" grades.

Furthermore, the perception that a student has of their school success as measured by school grades is as objective as the grades reflected in school transcripts. And not only is it equally objective, but this perception of oneself as a student and learner has a more favorable or more pernicious effect on the school trajectory than the "real" grades. When children declare that they are getting "excellent" grades in schools in Mexico, most probably feel successful and plan on staying the same in the future. If children perceive that they are failing in school, permanence in school is at risk (Tedesco 2011).

With these considerations in mind, we compare the average grades in U.S. schools (declared by the children) with those obtained in the Mexican school they were enrolled in at the time of the survey. This comparative exercise reveals that only 44 percent of child migrants perceived that they have similar grades in both U.S. and Mexican schools. (For example, they had poor grades in the United States, and they continue to have poor grades in Mexico.) The remaining 56 percent perceive their grades differently. This latter percentage is divided between those who perceived their grades as improving and those who perceived their grades as worsening. Those who had perceptions of improvement (that is, they perceived that their grades in Mexican schools were higher than those obtained in the United States) account for 13 percent of the total. The remaining 43 percent declared that their grades in Mexican schools were worse than, not

Table 19   Percentage distribution and comparison of the average grades obtained in U.S. and Mexican schools by child migrants in fourth through ninth grade in Zacatecas, Puebla, Jalisco, and Morelos

Grades obtained in U.S. schools	*Grades obtained in Mexican schools*				
	Low (%)	Regular (%)	Good (%)	Excellent (%)	Number of students surveyed
Low	7	43	31	19	16
Regular	4	70	24	2	139
Good	2	44	47	7	275
Excellent	4	33	45	18	140

SOURCE: Our elaboration is based on the databases of Universidad de Monterrey (2015).

better or equal to, those they obtained in U.S. schools. In summary, proportionally, there are as many child migrants who perceive that they have similar grades as those who perceive that their grades dropped once they enrolled in Mexican schools.

The case of the children who declared that their grades in the United States were "excellent" deserves further delineation. Out of the total number of children surveyed, 140 responded that their grades were excellent in U.S. schools, but only 18 percent of them maintained excellent grades in Mexico, while 37 percent declared that their grades were low or that they had regular grades in Mexican schools (see table 19). Furthermore, most of the children who stated that their grades in the United States were "bad" improved their grades in Mexico. However, this group is numerically small (n = 16), so it does not permit us to draw a solid conclusion at this time.

The corollary of this comparison is that the students who arrived from the United States tend to undervalue themselves while enrolled in Mexican schools. This result is congruent with what we described and analyzed in the first sections of this chapter: the child migrants "land" in the Mexican schools without a landing strip (i.e., they experience ruptures, not transitions), and at the same time many teachers view the children who arrive from U.S. schools as students with deficits rather than as students with strengths.

Children's Academic Aspirations

The topic of academic aspirations offers us the opportunity to close this chapter on an encouraging note: attending U.S. schools produces a positive effect because it encourages children to pursue college education. Migrant children aspire to go on to university regardless of the opportunities they may or may not have to fulfill this goal. The data in table 20 is powerful. Pursuing a college education is consistently more important for children with previous school experience in the United States. Moreover, this aspiration occurs more frequently in children who were born in the United States, with or without prior schooling in that country. Additionally, the children's gender positively influences their aspirations. Girls, in all cases, expressed their goal of pursuing college education in a greater proportion when compared to boys. When the three variables are combined— that is, in the subgroup composed of girls born in the United States with previous schooling in the United States—the highest level of academic aspiration is observed: 80 percent of these children expressed their desire to go to college compared to only 46 percent of the Mexican-born male children without previous school experience in the United States. The result is overwhelming: dual citizenship and previous school experience in the United States raise school aspirations.

It is almost tautological to say that the children's academic aspirations are influenced by the opportunities to transform those ambitions into reality. That is why the children who studied in schools located in rural locations tend to express more modest aspirations such as finishing high school, attending high school, and pursuing a technical career. On the contrary, the students who study in urban locations, especially those who lived in large cities such as Guadalajara, Puebla, Cuernavaca, or Zacatecas, tend to have more ambitious aspirations. We observed the greatest contrast when comparing the Mexican-born children residing in rural areas of Puebla with the U.S.-children with previous school experience in the United States who resided in the metropolitan area of Guadalajara. Among the former only 48 percent aspired to pursue a higher education, compared to 74 percent of the latter.

Table 21 presents the percentage distribution of academic aspirations and clearly indicates that being U.S. born and having previous schooling in

Table 20   Percentage distribution of children's academic aspirations by country of birth, previous U.S. schooling, and gender (samples from Zacatecas, Puebla, Jalisco, and Morelos)

Country of birth and previous schooling	Gender	No aspirations to pursue college (%)	With aspirations to pursue college (%)	Number of students in the sample
Born in the U.S., without previous U.S. schooling	Girls	30	70	122
	Boys	33	67	115
Born in the U.S., with previous U.S schooling	Girls	20	80	108
	Boys	32	68	122
Born in Mexico, with previous U.S schooling	Girls	27	73	198
	Boys	37	63	191
Born in Mexico, without previous U.S. schooling	Girls	38	62	13,515
	Boys	46	54	13,224

SOURCE: Our elaboration is based on the databases of Universidad de Monterrey (2015).

U.S. schools significantly reduces the effect of rural-urban inequalities. In fact, the U.S. children with transnational schooling who live in rural towns are practically no different from those who live in urban areas (who are also U.S. born with previous school experience in that country). On the contrary, in the case of the mononational children, the effect of differences in rural versus urban school opportunities is very notable. Finally, the effect of the location size is greater on the Mexican-born international child migrants than on the U.S. born. Our data indicate that having the right to dual citizenship encourages children to pursue a college education, regardless of the size of the locality in which they attend elementary or junior high school.

The findings presented in this section indicate that the children's international migration experience encourages their desire to achieve higher

Table 21   Percentage distribution of children's academic aspirations by country of birth, previous U.S. schooling, and locality of the Mexican school (samples from Zacatecas, Puebla, Jalisco, and Morelos)

Country of birth and previous schooling	Type of locality	No aspirations to pursue college (%)	With aspirations to pursue college (%)	Number of students in the sample
Born in the U.S., without previous U.S. schooling	Rural	34	66	175
	Urban	28	72	115
Born in the U.S., with previous U.S. schooling	Rural	27	73	171
	Urban	25	75	60
Born in Mexico, with previous U.S. schooling	Rural	37	63	239
	Urban	29	71	164
Born in Mexico, without previous U.S. schooling	Rural	47	53	17,437
	Urban	32	68	9,372

SOURCE: Our elaboration is based on the databases of Universidad de Monterrey (2015).

levels of education. From our interviews with the U.S.-born children, we know as that many, but not all, aspire to achieve this goal by attending institutions of higher education in the United States. And they know that to achieve this goal, they will have the support of their parents, older siblings, aunts, uncles, grandparents, or godparents who reside in the United States. Whether or not they achieve these goals, having these school ambitions is a good starting point and an impetus that we must take advantage of in Mexico. We can safely infer that schools in the United States instill the aspiration to undertake university studies more effectively than those in Mexico.

MAKING THE "INVISIBLE" VISIBLE

At the beginning of this chapter, we referred to the invisibility of the children with previous school experience in the United States in most Mexican schools. The teachers and principals do not see them. The child migrants—

either U.S. or Mexican born—prefer to go unnoticed. Additionally, the statistics of the administrative records of the Mexican Secretary of Public Education either do not contain or do not present the students' information by place of birth, much less by their recent migratory experience. Consequently, it is difficult to design integration policies into a new school environment when this population of migrant minors is simply not seen.

The data from *2015 Intercensal Survey* and from the 1990, 2000, 2010, and 2020 censuses (INEGI 1990, 2000, 2010, 2020) allow us to approximate the size of the population of school-age child migrants enrolled in Mexican schools during the past three decades. In 1990 there were only 81,000 international child migrants between six and seventeen years old who attended school in Mexico. In 2000 the number of children rose to 150,000, and in 2010 it increased again to 348,000. According to data provided by the *2015 Intercensal Survey,* the size of this population peaked in 2015, reaching 420,969 migrants from the United States enrolled in Mexican schools, which included those born in the United States (n = 392,000) and those born in Mexico but who were living in the United States in 2010 (n = 28,000). In other words, in thirty-five years the school population (six to seventeen years old) with migratory experiences increased more than five times. More recently, the 2020 Mexican census reported a decrease of the school-age population enrolled in Mexico, either U.S. born or born in Mexico, who migrated back to the country. This decrease coincides with the drop in adult return migration during the past five years. By 2020 there were 321,885 children who moved from the United States to Mexico between the ages of six and seventeen enrolled in the Mexican educational system. Another trend in time is the increasing predominance of those born in the United States and moving to Mexico among the migrant school-age population (97.6 percent in 2020).

The data also suggest that, despite bureaucratic obstacles and possible delays depending on when they migrate, almost all migrant children enroll in the Mexican education system while they still are of elementary school entry age (in this case, between six and twelve years old). In fact, the level of school attendance is practically the same as that of minors who have not migrated to the United States (see figure 5). Around the age of thirteen is when the process of dropping out or not enrolling schools in Mexico

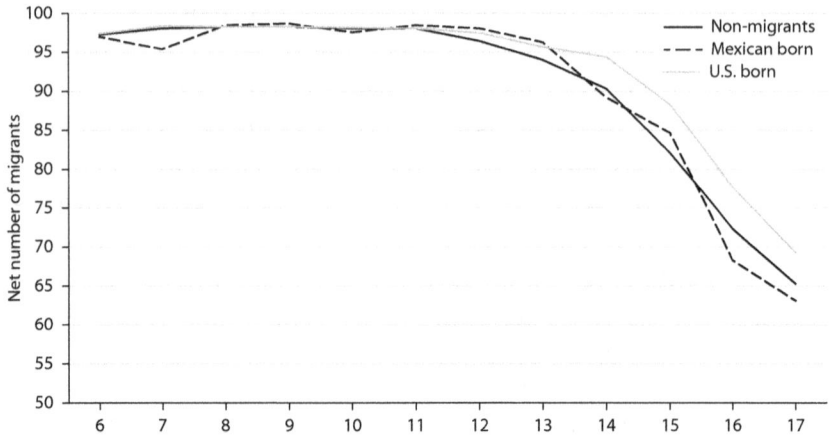

Figure 5. Percentage of population, ages six to seventeen, residing and attending school in Mexico, by Immigration status, 2015.

Note: International migrants are those born in the United States, regardless of when they arrived in Mexico (U.S. born) and those born in Mexico who were residing in the United States in 2010 (Mexican born).

Source: Our estimates are based on the *2015 Intercensal Survey* (INEGI 2015).

begins. The dropout rate by age is very similar between migrants and non-migrants. However, the data also show that there are different trends depending on the place of birth. There are some indications that those born in the United States are more likely to stay in school throughout adolescence; in contrast, those born in Mexico who lived in the United Stated will drop out of school sooner. It must be kept in mind that these children likely experienced more fractures in their schooling experience: they experienced at least two: leaving Mexico and leaving the United States. In contrast, those born in the United States may have stronger incentives and motivation to continue studying. These results are consistent with other studies (Aguilar Zepeda 2014; Giorguli and Gutiérrez 2011b) and suggest, as we saw throughout the chapter, that child migrants' experiences differ according to their place of birth.

This is a field of research still in development. The empirical evidence is diverse, and the findings across studies do not necessarily coincide. There is research that indicates that U.S.-born minors are more likely to stay in school than nonmigrant children and return migrant minors born in

Mexico (Aguilar Zepeda 2014; Giorguli and Gutiérrez 2011b). And there are studies that have been divergent in their conclusions.[23] For example, Elizabeth Camacho Rojas (2014) carried out an analysis of the data provided by Mexico's *Eleventh General Population and Housing Census, 2010* (INEGI 2011) regarding the state of Baja California with the objective of measuring the school dropout rate of international child migrants who had recently returned to Mexico. The author concludes that the percentage of returned child migrants ages eight to fifteen who did not attend school in Baja California was 11.7 percent versus only 4.0 percent of children who had never lived in the United States. Subsequently, Eunice Vargas Valle and Elizabeth Camacho Rojas replicated this analysis, using data from the 2010 census sample for the population of children between eleven and fifteen years of age in municipalities selected due to their high prevalence of return migration. They found that "recent immigrants have a higher probability of not attending school, compared to non-immigrants" (2015,168). In turn the authors observed a phenomenon that had been little explored until that time: the gaps in school attendance between migrants and nonmigrants are greater in urban settings compared to rural settings.[24]

A second potential effect of migratory itineraries among minors who circulate between Mexico and the United States could be the repetition and loss of years in school due either to the bureaucratic obstacles they face when enrolling in schools or to difficulties in integrating into and navigating through the system. To fully understand educational loss, longitudinal data is needed to see how the periods of nonattendance or the repetition of any grade are linked to the moment when the student changes residence from one country to the other. Unfortunately, we do not have this type of information at the national level. However, the *2015 Intercensal Survey* does allow for a cross-sectional approach to assess whether there are differences in school performance depending on the children's previous international migration experience. In table 22 we use information regarding the last completed school year of those children who continue to attend school and separate it to analyze who has less schooling than expected for their age. By this gross measurement, we try to understand the delay or grade repetition: if students have less schooling than expected for their age, this may be due to the periods spent out of school or to grade repetition. We present information about nonmigrants

Table 22   Percentage of the population, ages six to seventeen, residing in Mexico and enrolled in a lower grade than expected, by age and immigration status

Age (years)	Nonmigrants (%)	U.S. born (%)	Mexican born, living in the United States five years before the survey (%)
6	6.1	8.8	3.5
7	4.4	6.4	5.0
8	2.1	2.2	0.9
9	3.0	3.0	3.9
10	4.3	3.4	5.0
11	5.6	5.5	4.9
12	6.9	6.4	6.6
13	8.4	7.2	8.4
14	10.1	7.6	8.0
15	10.8	9.1	12.2
16	12.1	12.4	14.3
17	17.4	17.7	15.8

SOURCE: Our estimates are based on census samples (INEGI 1990, 2000, 2010) and the *2015 Intercensal Survey* (INEGI 2015).

and U.S.-born and Mexican-born minors who lived in the United States five years previous to the census date.

Our data suggest that there could be a late enrollment in elementary school among the U.S.-born children, which becomes visible when students are held back at ages six and seven. This difference could be a consequence of the fact that preschool is not compulsory in the United States, and, as the data show, this then influences at what age students enter Mexican schools and their age relative to their peers thereafter. For the three groups analyzed in table 22, as age increases, the probability of having less schooling than expected increases among those who continue to attend school. This process accentuates after the expected age for elementary school completion (around ages twelve and thirteen). With our fieldwork experience, we are well aware of the obstacles that international child migrants encounter when trying to enroll in Mexican schools, but national data suggest that this does not have a clear impact on how much schooling they accumulate. In fact, throughout the school year, child migrants—regardless of their place of birth—seem to behave similarly to the general population in terms of grade repetition and being held back a grade level.

As a hypothesis, the combination of data obtained during field work and nationally aggregated data could be indicating that, over time, child migrants develop effective strategies to compensate for any disadvantages they face when arriving in Mexico. The data also suggest that the problem of grade retention and repetition is common to the entire school population and requires specific policies. From our experience we could infer that the possible reasons for the child migrants being behind grade levels or repeating grades are different from those of the nonmigrant school population, and therefore measures tailored to the child migrants' own circumstances are required.

CONCLUSIONS

Throughout this chapter we have described and analyzed the context of how, in their role as mediating institutions between children and the nation-state, Mexican schools receive international migrant children. This context of reception is embedded in the teachers' visions and nonvisions, curricular norms, evaluation systems, and academic program sequences. The data point to the same conclusion: the uniqueness of the students who make the transition from the U.S. school system to the Mexican school system, including their skills, competencies, and abilities, is obscured or denied; consequently, Mexican schools do not respond to their needs, thus hindering their integration or reintegration into schools. There seems to be no single policy or protocol in Mexican schools to mediate the reception and integration of international migrant children. Instead, because the child migrants are defined by their deficits, deficiencies, or personality traits, it seems like their school success in Mexico is compromised from the start. Many teachers expressed their desire to academically support students who come to their classrooms after having completed part of their schooling in the United States; however, they admit that they have not been provided with the necessary training for supporting the migrant children's needs. The school does not embrace migrant children because the teachers have not been embraced by a school system that lacks a reception policy aimed at facilitating the transition from one country's school system to the other.

For many Mexican teachers, transnational students are both different and not different. Edmund Hamann, Víctor Zúñiga, and Juan Sánchez García explain this apparently contradictory statement as follows: "they are not like the others," but "they have to be like the others":

> Gaby [who started her schooling in Chicago] is not like the others; Gaby needs to be like the others. The dogma of a homogenous national identity in Mexico (Zúñiga 1998) has a clear manifestation in school practices and relations. Gaby's teachers do not know how many years Gaby attended school in Chicago. They do not know much about what she has studied, nor how well she did. Gaby's Mexican teachers appear to know practically nothing about her personal or educational history, but they do not find this absence problematic. From her teachers' perspective, Gaby is Mexican; she has no alternative. Part of who Gaby is is Mexican. She is welcome. But Gaby is not only Mexican and treating her as if that is all she is leaves out much that she knows and much that would engage her. She is also unwelcome. (2008, 78)

In response to these contradictions, we have emphasized more about the fractures and less about the transitions that migrant children experience, and this brings us to the dilemma about the integration or reintegration of children who migrated from the United States to schools in Mexico. As the teachers have observed, they are, at least partially, foreigners, while simultaneously being Mexican like their parents. Consequently, the mission of the Mexican schools is to make these children be like the others—that is, to transform them into Mexicans. This mission is justifiable from many points of view, and its fulfillment will ultimately benefit child migrants. Due to schooling in Mexico, they will gradually cease to feel, perceive themselves, relate, and act as foreigners. In this sense they experience transitions—not only ruptures—and will gradually become Mexican national citizens.[25] In this way the Mexican school contributes to the construction of biculturalism. Migrant children's abilities to speak, read, and write Mexican Spanish like their peers, know and identify with the history and geography of Mexico, and participate in Mexican patriotic liturgies are made possible through educational action in Mexican schools.

Therefore, future discussions should focus not on the mission of the Mexican school but on the way it fulfills its mission with this particular group of children. Currently, child migrants are experiencing schooling in Mexico more as a set of fractures than a series of transitions. Curriculum and pedagogy can change to facilitate the migrant children's linguistic, cognitive, and social transitions rather than hinder school success (Valdéz Gardea et al. 2018) and to support the construction of biculturalism, the strength of many of the children who have been educated in both school systems. This is the mission that Mexican schools share with U.S. schools for responding to the needs of the "students we share" (Gándara and Jensen 2021).

This chapter addresses the quintessential mediating institution for migrant children's integration and reintegration into Mexico: the school. In the following chapter, we address another central institution for the children's life—school trajectory—and integration into the new context: the family. We discuss a salient characteristic of the international migrant children's families: the fact that their members are often divided by the border, for short, long, or very long periods.

7 Families Divided by the Border

Migration is considered international when national borders are crossed. From the perspective of the sovereign, borders serve to mark the frontiers of the nation-state and its territory. They are understood as doors that can be opened or closed at the behest of the state, making them permeable or impermeable to people and goods, as the case may be (Foucher 1996). This brief overview of the invention of national borders establishes the legal, political, and ideological framework that explains why international child migrants live separated from their parents for periods of time. It also explains why the household composition of families that participate in international migration is constantly organized and reorganized by strategies designed to overcome obstacles inflicted by the border—hence our interest in studying the ways in which children respond and adapt to the changing contexts within their families as they follow the migratory paths forged by their immediate and extended families (Giorguli and Gutiérrez 2012; Zúñiga 2015).

At the peak of return migration to Mexico, Silvia Giorguli and Edith Gutiérrez (2012) analyzed the data provided by the *2010 General Population and Housing Census* with the aim of ascertaining whether the children and youth (ages zero to eighteen) residing in Mexico were living with one or both parents. They found that the majority (67 percent) of children whose families had no involvement in international migration were living with both parents in the same household, while only 30 percent of children from families who received remittances were living with both parents. Additionally, there is evidence that parents who migrate from Mexico to the United States will live separately from their children before the children turn thirteen. On average a family spends three years separated when the father migrates alone and only one year apart when both parents migrate (Giorguli, Jensen, and Angoa 2017). These approximations indicate that there is a strong association between exposure to international migration in its myriad forms (e.g., receiving remittances, return migration, etc.) and family dispersion that, in this case, is indicated by the children's coresidency with parents.

These data, along with the census statistics presented in chapter 2, represent quantitative evidence of how the border divides (Dreby 2010) and, as a result, separates families. Parents migrate to the United States without their families because the others lack documents to cross the border legally. The border also separates because, when the father or mother reside in the United States without authorization, they are afraid of being deported and so decide to bring their children to Mexico to not run the risk of them being left alone in the United States. The border also separates families when one member is deported to Mexico. Families often invoke a strategy to disperse the family, with some members staying behind in the United States while others returning to Mexico. They plan for reunification in the United States in stages while waiting to either fix their immigration status or find the necessary resources and contacts to cross the border clandestinely, resulting in periods of separation. In all cases the dispersion of international migrant families is the result of state restrictions that work to actively divide families (Fix and Zimmermann 2001; Taylor et al. 2011; Leal, Rodríguez, and Freeman 2016; Nobles 2011). Families, for their part, strategize to stay together, even amid subordinating conditions. International child migrants are aware that the state and its instruments derange families and that, in response, migrants do what they can to rearrange their families (Zúñiga 2018).

This chapter draws on data collected from surveys and interviews with international child migrants in Mexican schools to learn about how their experiences of separation characterized their migratory trajectory and to illuminate how they deal with familial dispersion. The surveys allow us to measure the separation experience at two moments: family dispersion at the time of the survey and past experiences of children living separated from their father or mother. (We asked the question: Have you ever lived separated from your father or mother?) The interviews carried out with the migrant children shed light on some of the strategies they employ while separated from their parents. We synthesize three of these interviews that are illustrative of the tactics that children develop throughout their geographically divided lives.

DIVIDED FAMILIES

The elementary and junior high students surveyed across the five Mexican states confirm and complement the findings from the *2010 General Population and Housing Census* data: that children with migratory experience often live in a home where their father or mother is absent, as we show in chapter 2 (INEGI 2010).[1] The data presented in tables 23 and 24 leave no room for doubt regarding this fact. In Zacatecas, at the time of the survey, 17.1 percent of girls and 20.3 percent of boys without migratory experience (i.e., they had never crossed the border) were living in households without their father. These percentages nearly doubled and tripled in the cases of children with international migratory experience. Noteworthy, almost half of the U.S.-born children in Zacatecas had been living in Mexico while their father continued to live in the United States. The percentage of households where the mother is absent is noticeably lower. According to the data collected in Zacatecas, around 2 percent of children without migratory experience had been living in Mexico while their mothers were in the United States. This proportion triples among those who crossed the border once (from the United States to Mexico) or twice (from Mexico to the United States and back to Mexico).

Our survey data also complement the information provided by the 2010 Mexican census (INEGI 2010). Tables 23 and 24 suggest that the phenomenon of child-parent separation in international migration has important regional variations. The percentage of children separated from

Table 23   Percentage of children, from fourth through ninth grade, residing in Mexico, whose fathers were living in the United States, by international migratory experience, country of birth, and gender

State (year)	Migratory experience	Girls (%)	Boys (%)	Both (%)	Number of students surveyed
Nuevo León (2004)	Without migratory experience	4.5	3.9	4.2	9,843
	Mexican-born child migrants	18.1	18.8	18.4	163
	U.S.-born child migrants	19.1	19.1	19.1	94
Zacatecas (2005)	Without migratory experience	17.1	20.3	18.8	5,850
	Mexican-born child migrants	30.0	26.1	28.1	96
	U.S.-born child migrants	48.9	47.2	48.0	102
Puebla (2009)	Without migratory experience	6.7	8.5	7.6	11,834
	Mexican-born child migrants	35.3	38.5	37.2	43
	U.S.-born child migrants	26.9	26.5	26.7	101
Jalisco (2010)	Without migratory experience	4.3	4.7	4.6	8,787
	Mexican-born child migrants	16.1	18.9	17.5	211
	U.S.-born child migrants	19.0	22.7	20.8	240
Morelos (2013)*	Without migratory experience	2.8	3.1	2.9	1,221
	Mexican-born child migrants	12.0	10.3	11.1	54
	U.S.-born child migrants	17.6	9.0	12.8	39

SOURCE: Our elaboration is based on the databases of Universidad de Monterrey (2015).

*The sample from Morelos is not representative of the students enrolled from fourth through ninth grade in the Morelos state school system.

Table 24   *Percentage of children, from fourth through ninth grade, residing in Mexico, whose mothers were living in the United States, by international migratory experience, country of birth, and gender*

State (year)	Migratory experience	Girls (%)	Boys (%)	Both (%)	Number of students surveyed
Nuevo León (2004)	Without migratory experience	0.4	0.6	0.5	9,843
	Mexican-born child migrants	4.8	6.2	5.5	163
	U.S.-born child migrants	8.5	6.4	7.4	94
Zacatecas (2005)	Without migratory experience	1.4	2.0	1.7	5,850
	Mexican-born child migrants	6.0	6.5	6.3	96
	U.S.-born child migrants	8.2	3.8	5.9	102
Puebla (2009)	Without migratory experience	1.2	2.2	1.9	11,834
	Mexican-born child migrants	23.5	11.5	16.3	43
	U.S.-born child migrants	5.8	8.2	6.9	101
Jalisco (2010)	Without migratory experience	0.6	0.7	0.6	8,787
	Mexican-born child migrants	3.8	4.7	4.2	211
	U.S.-born child migrants	2.5	5.0	3.8	240
Morelos (2013)*	Without migratory experience	1.5	0.9	1.2	1,221
	Mexican-born child migrants	16	6.7	11.1	54
	U.S.-born child migrants	5.9	4.5	5.1	39

SOURCE: Our elaboration is based on the databases of Universidad de Monterrey (2015).

*The Morelos sample is not representative of the students enrolled from fourth through ninth grade in the Morelos state school system.

their father is notably greater in Zacatecas and Puebla for children with *and* without migratory experience. Likewise, in Puebla the percentage of children living in Mexico while their mothers are in the United States is noteworthy: the population of children whose mother was absent in Puebla is proportionally greater than that observed across all three groups in the rest of the states. The data presented in the tables allow us to conclude that there are no differences by gender. There is no evidence that suggests there are more girls living in families divided by the border than there are boys. In nearly all cases the percentages by gender are similar.

In the group of children without migratory experiences, the surveys do not allow us to differentiate between those living in households that regularly receive remittances and those that do not. This limitation does not alter our conclusions because a regular reception of remittances is practically synonymous with the absence of at least the father or another family member shouldering the responsibility of providing for the children. To receive remittances, the immediate family members must migrate to the United States while the others stay in Mexico. Therefore, the regular reception of remittances is concomitant with the dispersal of the nuclear family: parents who migrate to the United States and leave their children in Mexico are among the families who have not been reunited (or at least they had not been reunited at the time the information was gathered). The children who are "left at home" are, by definition, children separated from their father or mother. These findings show the consistency and diversity of family's strategies and arrangements: some families seek to reunite in the United States, while others do so in Mexico. Still other families are scattered across both countries, and others in Mexico while one of the parents works in the United States. By definition, in these families the percentage of children separated from their parents is greater.

BIOGRAPHICAL EXPERIENCE OF SEPARATION

Instead of taking a synchronic approach to learn about family separation, as we had been doing up until this point, we used a diachronic approach to obtain a more comprehensive picture of the prevalence of family dispersal associated with international migration. We did so by asking the

Table 25   Percentage of children, fourth through ninth grade, separated from their father or mother, by migratory experience and gender, from survey in Jalisco, in 2010

	Girls		Boys		Number of students surveyed	
Migratory experience	Child-father separation (%)	Child-mother separation (%)	Child-father separation (%)	Child-mother separation (%)	Girls	Boys
Without migratory experience	25.3	3.2	26.7	3.4	4,466	4,286
Mexican-born child migrants	65.1	26.8	55.6	26.4	83	72
U.S.-born child migrants	53.9	20.7	66.3	29.5	178	169

SOURCE: Our elaboration is based on the databases of Universidad de Monterrey (2015).

children if, at some point in their lives, they had lived apart from their father or mother due to migration to the United States.

The comparison of the results obtained through the surveys in Jalisco (see table 25 and the previous tables) leads to strong conclusions.[2] The diachronic measurement (i.e., the experience of separation throughout life) is significantly higher than the synchronic one. Compared to the group of nonmigrant boys, the proportion of migrant boys separated from their father increases more than five times, from 4.7 percent to 26.7 percent. Similar results are obtained when comparing the data for girls. Likewise, in this subgroup, the comparison of the data regarding the experience of mother-child separation leads to the same conclusions. If we consider the entirety of children without migratory experience, we can conclude that, in Jalisco, a quarter of the children have experienced separation from their parents, and around three out of every hundred children have lived apart from their mothers due to migration to the United States at some point during their lives.

Both Mexican- and U.S.-born child migrants' biographical experience of separation is remarkably widespread. More than half of these children

Table 26   Duration of separation of children, fourth through ninth grade, from the
father or mother, by migratory experience, from survey in Jalisco, in 2010

Migratory experience	Separation	Never (%)	Less than 1 year (%)	From 1 to 3 years (%)	3 or more years (%)	Number of students surveyed
Without migratory experience	From the father	75.2	11.3	8.4	5.1	
	From the mother	96.9	1.9	0.5	0.7	8,451
Mexican-born child migrants	From the father	43.6	18.7	24.7	13.0	
	From the mother	75.7	6.8	11.4	6.1	143
U.S-born child migrants	From the father	48.0	23.1	14.9	14.0	
	From the mother	77.3	13.5	5.6	3.6	342

SOURCE: Our elaboration is based on the databases of Universidad de Monterrey (2015).

have lived in families separated by the border. Within these subgroups some differences are worth highlighting. Mexican-born girl migrants and U.S.-born boy migrants are the ones who spend more time throughout their lives separated from their parents. In both cases two-thirds have lived apart from their respective parents.

The data suggest that children with migratory experience frequently live apart from their mothers. The percentages indicate that being away from the mother for a period is an experience that is simply part of inter-national migrant families' lives. All the children surveyed were already in Mexico, and many of them were seeing their mothers again. However, throughout their short lives, migrant children already knew how family dispersion felt: they were keenly aware of the family arrangements and disruptions in which they had to participate and of the negotiations family members must assume according to gender, age, and immigration status.

Table 26 shows that child migrants have experienced longer periods of separation than the children without migratory experience. Almost a third of child migrants have experienced being away from their father for three, four, five, seven, nine, or even twelve years, while, in the group of children without migratory experience, the proportion who experienced prolonged periods of separation is visibly lower. Similarly, child-mother separation for long periods is significantly higher in the group of U.S.-born child migrants and even higher in the group of the Mexican-born child migrants. Most likely, having U.S. citizen status conferred by jus soli reduces the amount of time migrant children are separated from their mothers. These children can move freely across the border, making it possible for them to reunite with their mothers either when they decide to do so or when it is convenient for their family.

LEARNING HOW TO MAKE A FAMILY WHILE SEPARATED

The literature on the dispersion of international migrant families high-lights the effects of family separation on children: it can cause suffering, sacrifice, deprivation, resentment, dilution of paternal authority, school abandonment, stress, defiance, untimely changes in roles within the fam-ily, and the breakdown of family ties (Suárez-Orozco and Suárez-Orozco 2001; Jensen and McKee 2003; Schneider and Waite 2005; López Castro 2006; Coe 2008; Parreñas Salazar 2008; Lahaie et al. 2009; Glick 2010; Suárez-Orozco, Jin Bang, and Yean Kim 2011; Ensor and Gozdziak 2010; Dreby 2010, 2012; Jensen, Giorguli, and Hernández 2016). The litera-ture indicates that these are unavoidable consequences that leave lasting marks on the lives of children who participate in international migration.

In this section we extend what has been comprehensively studied by scholars by exploring two elements related to the migrant children's knowledge and experiences that complement these findings. The first is linked to the fact that, for nearly all the children interviewed, the disper-sion of their family is an inherent part of their daily knowledge and is considered concomitant with migration. The children know that the bor-der divides their families, and, when discussing their lives, they report this separation as something natural and not as a tragic or fatal event.[3]

The data from the Jalisco sample show that more than half of the migrant children know what it is like to be separated from their father due to international migration, while a quarter of them have experienced separation from their mother. If we were to include siblings and grandparents in our calculations, the increase in the percentages of migrants who have experienced separation would lead us to conclude that international migration inevitably leads to geographic dispersion of the family either because the border prevents family members from migrating at the same time or because the family's return to Mexico must be strategized and organized in stages. In any case what we want to emphasize here is that international migration creates a dispersed geography of families and that, as a result, migrant children develop sui generis competencies that enable them to better deal with the separation of their family. Children of the 0.5 generation know a world in which significant components of their lives are divided; subsequently, children become increasingly better at managing the divisions embedded in their lives.

To illustrate the unique skills and competences that the members of the 0.5 generation have developed and how naturally they manage the geographic fractures in their short lives, we present the case of Itzcalli, a student in Atlixco, Puebla, and our youngest interviewee to date. Here are interview segments from February 2010, when Itzcalli was six years old.[4]

INTERVIEWER: Where were you born?

ITZCALLI: In the United States.

INTERVIEWER: Where exactly?

ITZCALLI: I don't remember, but in the United States.[5]

·   ·   ·   ·   ·

INTERVIEWER: Have you recently been in the United States?

ITZCALLI: It was just until I was like three, and after that we came [here].

INTERVIEWER: So you were born there, and it was when you turned . . .

ITZCALLI: Three, that's when we came here.

·   ·   ·   ·   ·

INTERVIEWER: And who was with you there?

ITZCALLI: My dad, my mom, my grandmother.

INTERVIEWER: Your grandmother too, and do you have brothers who were also there?

ITZCALLI: Just one, but he's not there; he's here. . . . He's younger. . . . He's going to be three years old.

INTERVIEWER: And was your whole family happy there?

ITZCALLI: Yes, but some are here now.

INTERVIEWER: And why did they come [to Mexico]?

ITZCALLI: Because my dad had problems, that's why he told us to come here.

INTERVIEWER: He didn't want to work there anymore?

ITZCALLI: No, he did, but there was no money for my milk. . . . We were going to Atlixco, Mexico, he said, because here they give him money to buy my milk, and also work, so both food and work.

INTERVIEWER: And right now is your mom working too?

ITZCALLI: Yes, but she came [here] when I finished kindergarten. She came by car when I was going to start elementary school, but then she left. She struggled to cross the border because she was not born there.

INTERVIEWER: And your dad, was he born there?

ITZCALLI: I don't remember. Oh, he's from Cholula. I think so.

INTERVIEWER: Do you ever want to go back to the United States?

ITZCALLI: Yes, because it's more beautiful there.

.   .   .   .   .

INTERVIEWER: Who looks after your little brother? Your mother?

ITZCALLI: No, because my mom has left. Only my grandmother and I look after him.

INTERVIEWER: Is your mom going to come at a later time?

ITZCALLI: Yes. [For now] she calls me on the phone.

INTERVIEWER: And what does she tell you?

ITZCALLI: That when she has more money she will send me my toy box, for me and my little brother.

.   .   .   .   .

ITZCALLI: My grandmother tells me that they are going to leave me here, but I also want to go.

INTERVIEWER: Is your grandmother going to take you?

ITZCALLI: We can just leave the house secured or sell it.

INTERVIEWER: And when everybody gets back together, where would you like to live? There [in the United States]?

ITZCALLI: Yes.

INTERVIEWER: Would you like to study there?

ITZCALLI: Yes.

INTERVIEWER: What would you like to study?

ITZCALLI: Computers.

INTERVIEWER: Your mom, is she going to come back, or are you going to go there?

ITZCALLI: I'm going there and also my little brother and my grandmother.

Itzcalli was three years old when she arrived in Atlixco, accompanied by her mother, grandmother, and her younger brother. After some time her mother returned to the United States, where she lived with Itzcalli's father. We do not know if the parents' decision to send their children to Mexico was motivated by the risk of deportation, by the father's unemployment, or by other circumstances. What we do know is that both the father and the mother were undocumented, so the mother "struggled to cross the border." Under these circumstances it is surprising how naturally a six-year-old girl narrates the separation from her family and how aware she is of the fact that the border divides her family—as she explains, it is because her parents and grandmother were not born there, like she and her brother were. Itzcalli also makes plans to fix this anomalous situation by stating, "I'm going there and also my little brother and my grandmother." To achieve this Itzcalli even proposed selling the house in Atlixco. Itzcalli is currently nineteen years old. We do not know whether her parents continue to live in the United States, or whether Itzcalli and her brother returned to the United States. What we do know is that a binational girl in the first year of elementary school had already developed the initial ability to maneuver the significant challenges brought about by the geographic fractures in her life. For obvious reasons children without migratory experience do not develop these capacities, nor do they need to.

Next let's examine Gabriel's story. We met him at a junior high school in Tepanco, Puebla, where we interviewed three students who had lived through the experience of being separated from their families by the border. Gabriel's account of his experiences was quite eloquent and included a good sense of humor. He told us about his family negotiations, how he was participating in them, and the way in which he imagined that things could work out. He was born in Cacaloapan and migrated to Valley View, California, when he was seven years old. His family's migration to the United States was organized in stages. First his father migrated, then Gabriel's older brother, then Gabriel, and finally his mother and younger sister. During the interview we did not discuss how they crossed the border, only how the family was eventually reunited in California. Gabriel also shared that an U.S. owner of a "100-hectare" ranch wanted to adopt him. He explained, "He liked me very much, and [by now] I would have had my documents."

The thirteen years of Gabriel's life are divided as follows: he spent seven years in Cacaloapan, four in Valley View (between 2004 and 2008), and the remaining two in Tepanco. Gabriel began his school career in California, where he explained that "no teacher spoke Spanish" and that "there was a very racist child who did not like Mexicans." When he resumed schooling in Tepanco, he repeated the fourth grade. Things were difficult for him after his arrival at the Mexican school because, in his words, "I arrived, and I was very afraid of failing. I didn't know how to read very well, and I don't like to fail. I took a long time to read."

Why did Gabriel, his mother, and his younger sister return to Puebla? The year they returned is important: they came to Puebla in the middle of 2008, when the Great Recession (2007–9) was already wreaking havoc on many regions of the United States. As economic conditions deteriorated, life in California became difficult, and Gabriel's family made the decision to separate. Gabriel told us that it was during that time when his father's boss explained that "the hard times were coming," concluding, "that's why we came here." His father had been working for a company that built houses and buildings. Life in California became undesirable and unsafe. The neighborhood where the family was living became more dangerous because, as Gabriel explained, "There were a lot of men drinking beer in Valley View," and "we had to move to Santa Clarita." Furthermore, living expenses were increasing, while the family's income was decreasing. Sending some of the family to live in Puebla was the only option they had. Between 2008 and

2010, Gabriel's father and his older brother stayed in California. However, this configuration of family separation had changed a week before our interview. Gabriel's seventeen-year-old brother had recently returned to Tepanco and was planning to work as a truck driver in Puebla.

Within this context we began to see how Gabriel had begun to weave together strategies regarding his and his family's future. When we asked him if he wanted to return to California, he replied, "Sometimes I do; sometimes I don't." As he weighed the pros and cons of this question, he considered many circumstances. Sometimes he wanted to go back because his father had informed them that the employment situation was improving and that he would soon receive two large checks of four thousand dollars each. Gabriel not only included his father's economic improvement in his evaluation but also recalled that, in California, he had spent more time with his father. In Puebla his father had worked as a truck driver, and Gabriel often spent weeks without seeing him. He explained that "we only saw him when we went on vacation." Sometimes Gabriel also wanted to go back to California because there was a possibility of changing his father's immigration status, as his "father is getting his papers fixed; his employer is going to fix his papers."

On the other hand, Gabriel explained that sometimes he did not want to return to the United States. According to his memory, his mother was largely absent when they were living in California. "There [in the United States], my mother was hardly ever with us. She would leave us with a babysitter. My mother took care of other children and cleaned houses." Sometimes Gabriel did not want to go back because he felt like he was forgetting English and that it would be difficult for him to return to school in the United States. He also worried that his younger sister had forgotten the little English she had learned. He explained, "My little sister, she doesn't even know how to say hi." Likewise, sometimes he did not want to go back because many of his maternal cousins, aunts, and uncles were living in Tepanco, and he would miss them if he returned to the United States. He also considered that many of his friends from Valley View had moved to other parts of the United States or had returned to Mexico and would not be there if he returned. Memories of his parents sharing an apartment with another couple, unrelated to his family, who slept in the living room also made Gabriel hesitate about returning to California.

By carefully weighing the pros and cons, Gabriel found a solution. He knew that his father had learned auto mechanics and realized that his father had been sending "a lot of tools" to Tepanco. All this suggested that, as long as nothing changed, his father would return and set up an auto shop in Tepanco. This is why Gabriel had decided to finish high school and then enroll in a technical school, where he would learn auto mechanics. While all these events were taking place, Gabriel was witnessing the way in which they were doing family (Suárez-Orozco, Todorova, and Louie 2002; Cherlin 2006; Hertz 2006; Thao and Agergaard 2012; Nobles 2013): "My dad talks to my mom three times a day, and they talk, talk, talk, and talk."[6]

Gabriel's story depicts the mastery of family management while separated. Family members disperse, reunite, and disperse again, all the while being responsible for each other and looking for opportunities to reunite within the context of the borders and economic realities affecting their lives. Within these contexts the children of the 0.5 generation, like Gabriel or Itzcalli, become strategists of their geography by imagining how they could bring their separated family together and by working to maintain family ties.

Gabriel and Itzcalli negotiate two distinct national territories. Their geography is linear: one point here, Tepanco or Atlixco, and the other one there, in California and (likely) New Jersey. This linearity is not common for many children of the 0.5 generation, whose geographies resemble spider webs (Ma Mung 2000; Zúñiga and Hernández-León 2005b). The latter is the case of Andrés, who was born in Chicago in 1993. We interviewed him in Villanueva, Zacatecas, in 2005, when he was twelve years old.[7] He spent the first years of his life in Idaho and Illinois. His family consisted of two members born in Zacatecas (his father and mother), one born in Idaho (his older sister), and three born in Chicago (Andrés and his two younger brothers). When we asked Andrés how he imagined his adult life, we were surprised by how geography permeated his thinking. He had aunts in Massachusetts, uncles and cousins in Idaho and California, his father's cousins in Illinois, and four other uncles (his father's brothers) in Zacatecas. To Andrés, all these relatives represented study or work opportunities. At his young age, he had not made a decision about where he would end up, but he could afford to play with various options because he knew he had U.S citizenship. What reassured him the most about his future was the fact that he was maintaining, not forgetting, English.

CONCLUSIONS

The typical migratory pattern of Mexicans heading to the United States between 1965 and 1985, as described by Douglas Massey, Jorge Durand, and Nolan Malone (2002), included the following stages: traveling, crossing (the border), arriving to the destination, working, sending remittances, returning to Mexico, and then going back to the United States. This pattern is what is identified in literature as circular migration, something in which mostly young adult men participated and that entailed some form of family separation: the men migrated while their families stayed behind in Mexico. However, the periods of separation were not long because the last phase, going back to the United States, was not a major obstacle due to the possibility of reentry.

Toward the end of the 1980s, the circularity was affected by the increasing militarization of the border and by the strengthening of migration policies (Durand and Massey 2003; Bustamante and Alemán 2007; Terán, Giorguli, and Sánchez 2015; Sandoval and Zúñiga 2016). As a result, migrants who managed to cross the border without authorization would extend their stay due to the stratospheric costs and high risks associated with crossing the border without documents. The prolongation of their stay in the United States made many Mexican migrants decide to bring their wives and children (and other extended family members), thus initiating a process of family reunification outside of Mexico.[8] This explains the increase in the number of children born in the United States to Mexican parents (Batalova and Fix 2010). However, during the early twenty-first century, the story reversed: a process of return to Mexico began and families became dispersed throughout Mexico and the United States (Hernández-León and Zúñiga 2016).

These migration processes are not linear or homogeneous; instead, they include myriad familial strategies that materialize into more heterogeneous migratory patterns than those previously observed (Giorguli and Gutiérrez 2011b; Terán, Giorguli, and Sánchez 2015). The children of the

0.5 generation are heirs of this heterogeneity that involves arrangements, disruptions, and new family configurations between parents, children, siblings, grandparents, and sometimes members of the extended family. Thus, many migrant children are learning how to do family in new contexts. By the mid-1990s, the dispersion of migrant families became a constant factor of migration, along with its share of suffering, frustration, and resentment. Despite all of this, the children of the 0.5 generation are developing competencies and skills to negotiate the multiple and changing geographic contexts in which they are being educated. Family dispersion is a burden imposed by legislation and mechanisms of deportation; at the same time, it becomes an unexpected resource available to migrant families. Most definitely, the children of the 0.5 generation are learning how to live through political, legislative, and economic conditions that separate them from their parents and siblings.

This analysis of some of the most distinguishing characteristics of the typical dynamics of migrant children's immediate families leaves us wanting to delve more deeply into the children's subjective experiences during their transition from the United States to Mexico. In the next chapter, we draw on survey and interview data to present the intrinsic life stories of migrant children that we have collected since 2004.

8 Subjective Affiliations and Identifications

While they were living and attending schools in the United States, international child migrants gradually formed images of themselves by using the categories and labels assigned to and instilled in them within the social contexts of their development: their nuclear families, extended families, schools, neighborhoods, shopping centers, places of recreation, churches, community celebrations, and sports activities.[1] Likewise, given the conditions of segregation and resegregation that prevail in large metropolises and medium-sized cities in the United States (Orfield 2001, 2005), many children arrive in Mexico after having formed images of themselves as members of ethnic minorities in accordance with the U.S. racial stratifications and specific to the region and locality in which they lived. They have internalized labels such as "Hispanics," "Mexican Americans," "Mexicans," "Latinos," "migrants," and "English learners" and have experienced the notion of "illegality" or "legality" either directly or through their parents and siblings (Dreby 2015).

With this in mind, we return to Lulú. She was born in Arkansas and spent much of her childhood in San Diego, California, in a neighborhood called Clairemont. In 2013 Clairemont was predominantly white, with a growing population of migrants making up approximately one-fifth of all residents (Urban Mapping 2013). This neighborhood and its schools constituted Lulú's urban and institutional framework of socialization. Lulú's older sister was also born in Arkansas, while her two younger sisters were born in San Diego, making all four siblings U.S. citizens by jus soli and Mexican by jus sanguinis. Lulú's parents lived as undocumented citizens in the United States for more than sixteen years.

Lulú's family decided to move from San Diego to Tlaltizapán, Morelos, in 2013 because her uncle, her mother's brother, was deported earlier that year. This event shocked the family and motivated all six members to reassess their situation and decide whether they should continue living in the United States (running the risk that one of the two family members living without authorization be deported) or if they should move to Mexico together, as a family. The option of separating the family had never been put up for discussion, although it would have been feasible because Lulú's maternal grandmother and great aunts were living—and are still living—in California and would have been able to house their granddaughters so that they could continue their schooling in the United States. The unanimous decision, as Lulú's parents describe it, was to move together as a family to Tlaltizapán: "We didn't take long to pack our things; that same week we were leaving California and moving to Mexico" (interview with Lulú, Zacatepec, Morelos, March 2014).

Until she was thirteen years old, Lulú perceived herself as a young girl from Southern California and the daughter of Mexican migrants. She had developed strong linguistic skills in English (this was the language in which she was able to best express herself) and at the same time spoke Spanish with her parents at home. Drawing on their linguistic capital, she and her older sister became interpreters for their parents and close relatives (Valdés 2003). Through these experiences Lulú began adopting the labels that were inculcated in her in school, in public places, and in recreational, commercial, and sports activities. As a result, as she grew into adolescence, Lulú began perceiving herself as a Mexican American, a Californian, and a member of the second generation of immigrants. Additionally, she defined herself as a bilingual, urban youth and a member of California's working class.

The decision to migrate to Morelos, the municipality where her father was born, meant a bifurcation in Lulú's biographical trajectory (Román

González 2017). In Morelos she was still Mexican American, but this label did not carry the same meaning as it did in San Diego. She was still Californian, but this nickname carried little to no value as she attempted to form social relationships with her extended family members and classmates in Mexico. She was still an urban youth, but this label—and its derivatives—was rather uncomfortable in the context of a small, rural town. On the other hand, Lulú was still bilingual—one does not simply stop being bilingual—and she continued to speak English with her sisters; however, this skill turned out to be a problem when she enrolled in school in Mexico. She ceased to be a member of California's working class and instead became part of the working class in Morelos. Upon her arrival in Mexico, she was no longer a member of second-generation migrants in the United States but a member of the 0.5 generation. At the age of thirteen, Lulú's trajectory had bifurcated, and she began a new chapter in her life surrounded by relatives who were unknown to her, by neighbors who did not know what her past life had been like, by schoolmates with whom she had little in common, and by teachers who, in some cases, disparaged the knowledge that Lulú had gained in the United States.

Lulú and her sisters' reception in Morelos by their relatives was not remotely what they had imagined. Their cousins did not want to play with them because they considered them to be *fresas* (Román González, Carrillo, and Hernández-León 2016).[2] They were met with suspicion and resentment because their relatives assumed they had a lot of money. A few months after arriving in Morelos, Lulú's parents organized a party for the eldest daughter's fifteenth birthday, and this further fueled the rumor that they were wealthy. When the family arrived in Morelos, they did not have a home of their own, so Lulú's parents decided to rent one from her aunt. They paid a year's rent in advance. To their surprise the house was in horrible condition and was inhabitable: it had a leaking roof, water damage, and deteriorating walls. According to Lulú, strange noises were heard at night, frightening her younger sister and making her burst into tears. After about a month, they decided to move to another house, and, as part of their "welcome" from the family in Morelos, the aunt refused to return the money they had paid her for rent.

Lulú's accounts included a mix of the pros and cons of living in both the United States and Mexico. She missed their comfortable life in San Diego, and at the same time she cherished the time she spent with her father, despite the hardships, in her new home in Mexico. While they were living in California, her father was usually absent because he would work overtime and, often, the nightshift. During our interviews Lulú would bring up her father's grueling shifts in California and how they caused him continuous discomfort and even illness. In contrast, according to Lulú, in Morelos her father seemed much healthier, more youthful, and more attentive to his daughters' needs.

Lulú enrolled in seventh grade in Zacatepec. Her first schooling experience in Mexico set her life on a course with an ending still unknown. Because reading in Spanish was difficult for Lulú, she was soon labeled as dyslexic. This news dampened her spirits and worried her parents. To make things worse, a middle high school teacher publicly called her a *burra* (donkey).[3] This event prompted an angry protest by Lulú's parents and older sister, who showed up at the principal's office, demanding an explanation. The principal extended his apologies and demanded that the teacher apologize publicly during the flag-honoring ceremony. However, the principal's prompt response and the teacher's public apology were not enough to remedy the situation and its lasting effects on Lulú. Eventually, Lulú told her parents she wished to pause her education and instead help them with the small businesses they were setting up. All this happened between 2013 and 2014.

Before she dropped out of middle high school, Lulú had shown an interest in a career in the U.S. military. Her parents and her older sister rejected the idea, saying that they would not accept her going to the United States to join the army because the country was permanently at war, and they feared for her life. In exchange they suggested that she study at the Cuernavaca Women's Military School, where she would also have the option of attending high school.

In 2015, and more notably in 2016, Lulú gave up on her outward appearance of a young urban woman educated in California and started to dress, wear makeup, and fix her hair like a girl from Tlaltizapán. In fact, in 2016 she pointed this out to us by saying, "I know I have that [U.S.] nationality but to tell you the truth I feel more Mexican than anyone here" (Román González, Carrillo, and Hernández-León 2016, 266). Likewise, and as expected, her accuracy and efficiency in communicating in Spanish had notably improved and included the use of colloquial expressions; although, as of September 2016 she still found it difficult to communicate some of her feelings and ideas in Spanish. Furthermore, at her mother's insistence, Lulú returned to school at a local technical junior high school. Here her integration process seemed more positive, and she was more optimistic about her academic performance. In short, Lulú went from being a foreign girl to gradually becoming a member of the local and national Mexican society. Still, she did not rule out the possibility of returning to California as an adult to earn money and financially support her family.

Over three and a half years, Lulú underwent a subjective journey that consisted of the following stages: (1) her family's decision to move to Mexico, a country she did not know; (2) the difficult transition from an urban to a rural community; (3) familial, social, and schooling adjustments and readjustments that interfered with the continuity of her biography; (4) subjective negotiations undertaken to accommodate disjointed biographical fragments, and (5) the construction of new forms of belonging and identification with new labels, among which feeling "more Mexican than anyone here" was most notable.

While studying the return to Mexico of young adults who had been members of the 1.5 generation in the United States, Shinji Hirai and Rebeca Sandoval (2016) showed how the notion of subjective itineraries is a tool used by migrants to accommodate the complex process of integration into Mexican society. The noun "itinerary" represents a procedural component, while the adjective "subjective" refers to the frictions and negotiations experienced emotionally as a resignification of the past, present, and future (Clifford 1999; Hirai, 2014). Hirai and Sandoval (2016) articulate the need to document the paradoxical aspects that young people experience as they go through the adjustments and negotiations that lead them to new forms of belonging to their society of origin (i.e., Mexico), which, in many ways, they first perceive as a strange society. The notion of subjective itineraries highlights the processual dimensions through which life projects are continuously adapted and how a migrant child's past life (i.e., in the United States) is periodically reinterpreted. Lulú's story is precisely that of a subjective itinerary still unfinished.

Our current research focuses on documenting international migrant children's subjective itineraries. This study is ongoing and includes ten children, born either in the United States or in Mexico, who arrived in Morelos in 2012. Lulú, who turned fifteen in September 2016, is one of these children. Some of our participants continue to live in Morelos, while others have moved to different regions of Mexico or have returned to the United States. Their complete life stories are the focus of other publications. However, in this chapter we present the data we have gathered thus far on two of the stages in the children's subjective itineraries, with emphasis on the first stage. We acknowledge that what is captured here is no more than photographs representing mere moments of these migrant youths' integration process. These snapshots are complemented with the children's narration of their subjective journeys.

The first moment is a statement made by the children at our request. One of the questions in the survey asked students to make a choice about one of the most influential identifications in contemporary life: national and ethnic affiliation.[4] To analyze this moment, we draw on the data from the five surveys administered in Mexican schools. The written responses in the questionnaire provide data that must be read and analyzed carefully because they depict a crucial moment in the migrant children's trajectory and of their arrival in Mexico. These results do not lead to any firm conclusions; however, they do serve to develop and elaborate initial hypotheses.

The second moment refers to the negotiations that migrant children carry out to reconcile the various legacies they inherit (in both the United States and Mexico) from their families, schools, and other contexts in which they had been socialized. The interviews are particularly useful to observe the subjective ways in which children attempt, many times successfully, to put together pieces of their bifurcated biographies.

NATIONAL AND ETHNIC AFFILIATIONS

We asked the migrant children with prior school experience in the United States to choose an affiliation from a list to answer the following multiple-choice question: "What do you consider yourself to be?" With the exceptions of the surveys administered in Nuevo León and Zacatecas, the options were "Mexican, Mexican American, American, Nahuatl, Zapotec, Mixtec, Otomí, Huichol, Purépecha, other (fill in the blank), and some of the above

Table 27   National and ethnic affiliations of students, fourth through ninth grade, by country of birth, in schools in Nuevo León, Zacatecas, Puebla, Jalisco, and Morelos, with previous school experience in the United States

Country of birth	Mexican (%)	Mexican American (%)	American (%)	Ethnic affiliation (%)	Number of students surveyed
Mexico	74.7	20.3	2.3	2.7	444
United States	19.5	58.9	11.7	9.9	282
Both	53.5	35.3	5.2	6.0	726

SOURCE: Our elaboration is based on the databases of Universidad de Monterrey (2015).

(identify which ones)."[5] This was, undoubtedly, a partially arbitrary procedure because it was the researchers who selected which national and subnational ethnic labels to include and make available to the students. Nevertheless, the exercise revealed novel findings. All international child migrants with previous schooling experience in the United States usually identified with one of these labels, and their selection was closely associated with their international travel trajectory. These findings must be read and interpreted carefully because the questionnaire required respondents to choose a label from a preselected list of options as opposed to generating their own. Thus, we offer our observations to serve only as material for formulating initial hypotheses that can be used and refined in future studies.

Of the total survey responses across the five Mexican states (n = 726), we found that a little more than half of the migrant children identified with the label "Mexican" and over a third with that of "Mexican American."[6] Less than 10 percent chose either "American" or one of the ethnic affiliations (see table 27). Noteworthy is the fact that many of the international child migrants born in the United States do not identify as "Mexican"—that is, over 80 percent of these children chose options other than Mexican.[7]

Mexicans?

Identifying as "Mexican" is clearly linked to the child migrants' country of birth and less exposure to schooling in the United States. Table 27 shows

Table 28   National and ethnic affiliations of students, fourth through ninth grade, by selected characteristics, in schools in Nuevo León, Zacatecas, Puebla, Jalisco, and Morelos, with previous school experience in the United States

	Mexican (%)	Mexican American (%)	American (%)	Ethnic affiliation (%)	Number of students surveyed
Length of schooling in the United States					
Short-term (from 1 to 2 years)	62.3	29.9	4.5	3.3	425
Long-term (3 or more years)	40.5	42.9	8.0	8.6	301
Gender					
Girls	54.4	36.2	4.0	5.4	373
Boys	52.1	34.3	8.0	5.6	353

SOURCE: Our elaboration is based on the databases of Universidad de Monterrey (2015).

that three-quarters of the children born in Mexico identified themselves as Mexican as opposed to only one-fifth of those born in the United States. The difference is so great that there is no doubt that the country of birth determines the way in which children identify themselves, at least in terms of national belonging. Similarly, as table 28 shows, a higher proportion of the children with short-term schooling in the United States chose the affiliation of Mexican as opposed to those who spent three, four, five, or more years in U.S. schools. As illustrated in table 29, 83 percent of the Mexican-born girls with short-term schooling in the United States selected Mexican, representing a notably higher proportion than what was observed in other subgroups.

The subjective itineraries of the children who identify as Mexicans are likely less meandering while they are in Mexico because, to an extent, they are indicating that their time in the United States and their passage through U.S. schools do not make them different from the rest of their peers, neighbors, friends, and family in Mexico. However, whether or not children selected the label "Mexican" is clearly mediated through other circumstances of their childhood migration experiences: a quarter of the

Table 29   National and ethnic affiliations of students, fourth through ninth grade, by country of birth, length of schooling in the United States, and gender, from schools in Nuevo León, Zacatecas, Puebla, Jalisco, and Morelos, with previous schooling in the United States

Country of birth	Schooling in the United States	Gender	Mexican (%)	Mexican American (%)	American (%)	Ethnic affiliation (%)	Number of students surveyed
Mexico	Short	Girls	83.2	14.7	1.4	0.7	155
		Boys	74.2	22.6	3.2	0.0	66
	Long	Girls	63.6	31.8	3.0	1.6	53
		Boys	65.5	31.0	3.5	0.0	64
United States	Short	Girls	15.1	79.2	5.7	0.0	124
		Boys	26.7	56.7	16.6	0.0	58
	Long	Girls	10.9	76.5	12.6	0.0	60
		Boys	17.2	64.0	18.8	0.0	64

SOURCE: Our elaboration is based on the databases of Universidad de Monterrey (2015).

children who were born in Mexico did not consider this label to fully represented them (see table 27). In other words, some migrant children who have only Mexican citizenship did not select the label "Mexican" on the survey. Regarding these cases, we infer that some of the fragments that they experienced in their migratory trajectories are not reflected in the word "Mexican" and that these children are still in the process of figuring out what shape will result from their migratory puzzle.

Mexican Americans?

The dual affiliation of Mexican and American is equally associated with the migrant children's country of birth and their exposure to school in the United States. Almost 60 percent of the U.S-born children (see table 27) and 43 percent of those with long-term schooling in the United States (see table 28) selected the label "Mexican American" on the survey. Approximately a third of the Mexican-born boys and girls with long-term schooling in the United States identified themselves as "Mexican Americans," exceeding the number of Mexican-born girls and boys with short-term schooling in the United States by about 15 and 10 percent (see table 29). Undoubtedly, attending school instills feelings, emotions, allegiances, and relatively lasting attachments that child migrants carry with them to Mexico. The label "Mexican American" indicates, in some cases, that the children feel both "Mexican" and "American." This does not necessarily mean that the children affirm a binationality (as many have citizenship in only one country) but rather that their biculturalism is intricately associated with their bilingualism, which resulted from their previous schooling in the United States.

Now let's turn our attention exclusively to the U.S.-born children. These children are binational, and they feel binational. Taking on dual affiliation is by far the most frequent response among the U.S.-born children regardless of the amount of time they spent in U.S. schools or their gender, indicated by the data presented in table 29. The highest subgroup of the Mexican Americans were U.S.-born girls with short-term schooling in the United States: almost 80 percent of these migrant children selected Mexican American.

Americans

The selection of the label "American" is the most differentiated finding from our dataset. By selecting this label, children state that they are foreigners in Mexico. The data show that a small proportion of the Mexican-born children and only 12 percent of the U.S.-born children identify themselves as American (see table 27). The differentiation among the subcategories of children is not as clear-cut, as there are many complicating factors influencing this data, including that most of the migrant children's parents are Mexican citizens who were born in Mexico; the children are living in Mexico; the children have Mexican citizenship, regardless of the country of birth; and, at the time of the survey, they were being educated in Mexican schools. These characteristics subjectively indicate that the children who chose this label do not consider that the demonym "Mexican" fully describes them. They undergo a sort of process of alienation from the national society in which they live.

In this regard, it is worth looking more closely at how the characteristics presented in table 28 are distributed. Most noticeable is the fact that the percentages for most of the identification labels are similar for boys and girls except for when we analyze the section of "American." The proportion of boys who identified themselves as American while in Mexico is twice that of girls. This finding is further confirmed in table 29. The girls who chose the American affiliation are an exception: among those who were born in the United States and spent three or more years in U.S. schools, only 12.6 percent selected the option "American." This could indicate that migrant girls are raised by their families to be guarantors of the preservation of cultural, linguistic, and social heritages, which include gastronomy, a manner of speaking, and a set of values and practices inherited from their parents and grandparents. It is perhaps because of this gender differentiation that girls are more reluctant to adopt the American national label than are boys (Curran et al. 2006).

Ethnic Affiliations

The data regarding the choice of an indigenous affiliation, mainly Mixtec, turned out to be an unexpected finding for a few reasons. First, children who chose subnational ethnic affiliations were almost exclusively children from Puebla, with the exception of one from Jalisco and another from Morelos. Even more interesting was that none of the child migrants in Puebla chose the options "Mexican American" or "American" (see table 30). These two affiliations were discarded, thus indicating that they are not representative of the children's itineraries as starting points, intermediate stops, or destinations. With regard to the labels, the migrant children from Puebla were divided into two groups: about half of them selected "Mexican" and the other half "ethnic affiliation."

Second, the data from the Puebla survey showed that identification with ethnic affiliations (generally Mixtec) is relatively higher among the U.S.-born children and lower among Mexican-born child migrants. Although the subgroups in the Puebla sample are numerically small, the trend that U.S.-born children are more prone to adopt ethnic affiliations appears to be clear. It is not the children born in Mexico who identify as Mixtec but mainly the U.S.-born children.

Table 30   National and ethnic affiliations of students, fourth through ninth grade, by country of birth, length of schooling in the United States, and gender, from schools in Puebla, with previous schooling in the United States

Country of birth	Schooling in the United States	Gender	Mexican (%)	Ethnic affiliation (%)	Number of students surveyed
Mexico	Short	Girls	83.3	16.7	6
		Boys	81.8	18.2	11
	Long	Girls	63.6	36.4	11
		Boys	76.9	23.1	13
United States	Short	Girls	40.0	60.0	5
		Boys	36.4	63.6	11
	Long	Girls	23.1	76.9	13
		Boys	33.0	67.0	12

SOURCE: Our elaboration is based on the databases of Universidad de Monterrey (2015).

In a similar vein, we also found that the more time migrant children spent in U.S. schools, the greater the percentage identified as Mixtec. This seems to be a salient paradox because it indicates that the U.S. schools, not Mexican schools, promote, encourage, or facilitate adherence to and pride of belonging to their parents and grandparents' indigenous ethnic affiliation(s). Many of the children who identified as Mixtec responded in the survey that English was the language in which they communicated most effectively. These findings indicate that the diverse context of California or New York, where most of the child migrants in Puebla come from, supports indigenous ethnic identification because half of the children in Puebla chose it instead of Mexican. Judging from their migratory experiences, they feel more Mixtec than Mexican.[8] Finally, in this respect, gender is also important, especially due to the high percentage (nearly 77 percent) of U.S.-born girls with long-term schooling experience in the United States who identified themselves as Mixtec. These data reinforce what was previously stated about gender differentiation in preserving family cultural heritage.

Summary

The data presented in the tables in this chapter were collected in 2005, 2009, 2010, and 2013. If the number of the U.S.-born children who arrive in Mexico grows in the future, then the Mexican society and its institutions will have an increasing presence of minors who see themselves, while living in Mexico, as Mexican American, American, Mixtec, Zapotec, and so on, and not as Mexican. Migrant children born in Mexico tend to identify themselves as Mexican, while U.S.-born children's identifications are dispersed across many labels. These ways of defining themselves are not definitive and can morph according to the children's subjective process. However, our findings indicate that, if the prognoses are correct, there will be ever more children in the Mexican society who will not identify simply as Mexicans, and schools, along with other institutions, will have to learn to receive and support children who have adopted other affiliations.

NEGOTIATING MULTIPLE FRAGMENTS

The pioneering studies of Fredrik Barth (1969) have established that national and ethnic identifications are not hermetically sealed boxes containing symbolic, homogeneous, and perennial substances. However, for many of those who adopt these labels, and especially for those who promote them, national affiliations are often defined as a set of revered and resolved symbols that are antagonistic to foreign affiliations. According to this belief, it is assumed that one is "Mexican" and therefore cannot be "American" and vice versa.

In U.S. society dual labels have acquired a certain legitimacy and have a relatively understandable meaning (i.e., Native American, Italian American, Asian American). In this context the label "Mexican American" indicates that one is a U.S. citizen descendant of Mexican-born parents, grandparents, or great-grandparents who were born in Mexico. As defined, the label does not imply a double affiliation but rather makes visible the migratory, generational sequence and belonging to a specific segment in U.S. society. In his essay "The Mexican Americans: Who We Are and Who We Will Be," Néstor Rodríguez establishes this term as "a social group of Mexican descent that was formed in the United States in a historical context of minority, of social exclusion, with a subculture based on that experience and, in many cases, with an immense separation from the Mexican society" (2008, 63).

Two components of Rodríguez's definition are not fulfilled in the case of the child migrants who come to Mexico from the United States. First, these children are not separated from Mexican society. On the contrary, they live in Mexico and are developing significant ties with Mexican society. Second, in Mexico they do not constitute a minority segregated or subjugated by Anglo-Americans—they are not even considered a formal social group. Despite this, many international child migrants residing in Mexico felt comfortable identifying as "Mexican Americans." What does this mean to them and how are they building this affiliation? To answer this question, we look at the conversations we had with six children, four born in the United States and two in Mexico. Their stories outline a dual affiliation that seems to bring with it the ingredients of subjective innovation that, at this point in their itinerary, appear to have different (actual or potential) objective uses.

Mexican Americans: Born in the United States

Let's begin with an interview in which a child migrant eloquently addressed the subjective intricacies between her national affiliations. Nanys was born in Los Angeles, California, and we interviewed her in Jolalpan, Puebla, in February 2010, when she was fifteen years old. Nanys had spent most of her childhood in Los Angeles in the company of her father, mother, and younger brother, who was also born in Los Angeles. Her parents were originally from Jolalpan, Puebla, and they migrated to the United States, first to California and then later to Aurora, Colorado, where Nanys finished middle high school and completed one year of high school. When we met her, she had been in Puebla for no more than a month and was enrolled in ninth grade. In chapter 5 we presented the circumstances that led Nanys's entire family to move to Jolalpan. During the interview, which was conducted entirely in English, she told us that the life they led in the United States prevented her and her siblings from spending time with their parents due to the intensity and long hours of their jobs. As things were in the United States, "we weren't really a family anymore."

Within a month of their arrival in Jolalpan, Nanys's parents and aunts began analyzing the different educational options available to her in Mexico and in the United States. Once in Puebla the revalidation of Nanys's studies in the United States had been complicated due to the state's requirements and procedures. As a result, the adults in Nanys's family were comparing the two most attractive options for her once she obtained the Mexican junior high school certificate (a level of education that she had already completed in Colorado): either enroll in a high school in Mexico City, where she had some relatives to support her, or return to Denver, where some of her relatives lived, and go back to high school. As Nanys recounted these possibilities, one of the interviewers asked her, "Do you feel Mexican or American?" The question made sense within this part of the interview because Nanys had practically never lived in Mexico. Nanys replied, "I feel a little bit of both, but here I've become more Mexican because *he convivido* [I've lived] more with their culture, and it's really helped me to bring out what I call my Mexicanism." Since she used the term "Mexicanism," we thought we could introduce the corresponding term for the United States and asked her what she understood by "Americanism." Nanys answered without any hesitation, "[Americanism is] how I speak English, what I know about the culture, and what they celebrate and what I studied over there."

At that point during the interview, we pointed out that she used the third-person plural pronoun or possessive adjective when referring to both Mexicans (*they, their* culture) and Americans ("what *they* celebrate"). Given this observation, Nanys offered an explanation that synthesized not only her own itinerary but also that of many other migrant children in Mexico born and educated in the United States. "I'm like in between both of them because I can't really, there is one poem my teacher showed us over there by, I forgot his name, but it says like 'when you're in America, people look at you and say you may be from here, but you don't look like me, and when you're in Mexico, they say you look like me, but you're not like me.'"

The conviction of being "in the middle," or at an intermediate point between two national societies, is the nodal point in Nanys's explanation.[9] There is no contradiction: she places herself in the middle to establish a dialogue between both symbolic worlds that she feels as her own; however neither of the two comprises her whole biography (Hamann, Zúñiga, and Sánchez 2006). What Nanys points out is that she finds herself amid the process of building a synthesis of identification. That explains why this subjective experience is a process for her ("I've become more Mexican"). Essentially, this is the difference between the experience of the international child migrants in Mexico and the historical experience of the Mexican Americans in the United States. In Mexico they are extracting their Mexicanism, as Nanys called it. Historically, Mexican Americans belong to the second, third, or fourth generation of migrants; however, the children living in Mexico are now members of the 0.5 generation. As members of this generation, they are undergoing the subjective itinerary to elaborate their identification and construct a synthesis among the emerging characteristics.

The subjective dialogue established by Nanys in Jolalpan denotes a subculture that does not yet exist or that is partially coming into existence as an embryonic state in Mexico. It is a subculture that is binational and bicultural, indicating that international migrant children who have been, still are, or will be arriving in Mexico will continue constructing and negotiating elements of their biography and identification.[10] It is relevant to add that, in the case of Nanys, a dual affiliation not only is subjective but also includes objective, very real possibilities, such as circulating (e.g., returning to the United States to study in Denver) or continuing to live in Mexico (e.g., studying high school in Mexico City). For any of these to happen, Nanys will make use of a certain symbolic capital that consists of her binationality and developing biculturalism, which includes her bilingualism.

This sort of subjective dialogue that works to construct biculturalism is what Jazmín related during her interview. Jazmín was born in Sun Valley, California, and was interviewed in Jerez, Zacatecas, in November 2005, when she was thirteen. She explained,

> [When I was in Sun Valley,] I felt both [Mexican and American], [but] right now I have my Mexican documents. I'm not from here or there anymore. I'm from both places. . . . I was born there. I lived there until I was six years old, then I came here. They called me a *gringa* from the start, but I knew that if my parents were Mexican, then I was not a *gringa*. Then later I began to make it clear to them too, and they no longer called me [*gringa*].

Jazmín's perspective is similar to Nanys's in the sense that she had been constructing a synthesis of identification (i.e., "I felt both"), but she added a new element: Jazmín's dialogue is not only internal but also external, as she indicated by letting her classmates and neighbors that she was not a *gringa*. While declaring her biculturalism and binationality, she refused to be defined by others in terms of only one of the two facets of her biographical experience. Jazmín's synthesis has not yet been shaped into a well-defined form, but a part of it is becoming more clearly defined, as she knows who and what she is *not*.

Jazmín was enrolled in sixth grade and expressed her intention to continue her schooling in Jerez and later study chemistry at a university. During the interview she repeatedly told us that she and her family were very happy to live in Jerez ("I am very comfortable here, in Mexico"). Jazmín's father had worked for several years as a chef in "a very big factory," and he was going to return to Mexico soon to open his own restaurant, so Jazmín felt sure that Jerez was her new home. Under these circumstances Jazmín reiterated that she would go to California and Nevada only to visit her relatives, but she did not intend to live and work in the United States. However, these plans did not prevent her from defining herself as possessing a certain form of biculturalism, even though she was losing her bilingual skills. Apparently, Jazmín was not planning to make use of the bicultural, binational, and bilingual capital that she has developed, as she did not foresee the possibility of moving between the two countries or returning to the United States. For this reason, throughout her life (if her current circumstances do not change), Jazmín will likely use her rights and acquired knowledge differently than Nanys.

The refusal to be classified as a *gringa* appeared explicitly in another interview we conducted in Lagos de Moreno, Jalisco, in March 2011. At a junior high school, we chatted with thirteen-year-old Estefania. She was born in Chicago, and, when she was eight years old, she moved with her parents and siblings to Georgia, where she repeated a school year. In Georgia her parents got divorced, which resulted in Estefania and her younger sister moving to Lagos de Moreno to live with their paternal grandmother. Unlike Jazmín, Estefania belonged to a dispersed family: her father was living in Georgia with her older brother, and her mother had returned to Mexico and was living in Jalisco, where she had remarried.

Her family's dispersion made it difficult for Estefania to determine her life trajectory in the near future. She and her sister were fond of the idea of staying in Lagos instead of returning to Georgia, but their paternal grandmother persuaded them to return to be with their father because the girls were an economic burden, and the little remittance that she was receiving from her son (Estefania's father) was not enough to cover their needs.

Ambivalence was present throughout Estefania's interview. She described life in the United States as an undesirable routine. She explained, "Yes, I want to stay. I like it here [Lagos de Moreno]. It's very nice here, and yes, I do want to [stay here], because there [the United States] we are staying indoors all the time.... There [people] don't go out." However, her grandmother did not seem to agree with these plans. Estefania continued,

> My grandmother wants us to go back there, because my dad doesn't have a job, or he's not doing well at work, [so] he can't keep sending us money as he used to, and my grandmother tells me it makes it harder for her, [and] that, maybe, we're going to return, but we are not sure.

At that point during the interview, we asked Estefania if she *felt* she like was from the United States or if she *felt* like she was from Mexico. She answered,

> Sometimes they just make fun of me. They call me *gringa*, but, no, it's just the way they mock people here. *Na*, but it's just from time to time they say that, but ... no, when they tell me, "You are *gringa*," [I answer] "No, I'm not. I'm Chicana. My parents are from Mexico, and I come from there [the United States], but I'm Mexican."

Estefania's answer does not describe a subjective quest, but rather it seems like she has come to understand two appropriate syntheses in her identification. First, just like Jazmín, she knows what she is not and does not allow others to mistake what she is not. She states the second synthesis explicitly in the way she defines herself: she comes from there (that is why she calls herself Chicana), but she is not entirely from *there*. She conceives herself as fully Mexican, but as a sui generis Mexican: she was born in the United States, she was raised in that country, then she migrated to Mexico, and she would like to continue living in Mexico. The interview was carried out entirely in Spanish, showing that Estefania spoke the language fluently as a native speaker. At the same time, she also recounted her difficulties in writing and reading in Spanish and still spoke English with her younger sister.

How Estefania will objectively use her biculturalism, binationality, and bilingualism seems uncertain. She does not want (at least as of March 2011) to return to the United States. In this regard her itinerary is similar to that of Jazmín's. However, Estefania's family circumstances are diametrically different, and for this reason, regardless of her wishes, she may have to make use of her rights and knowledge to resume a life in the United States.

Omar's itinerary depicts the story of a child who will likely make conscious and effective use of his rights and knowledge. This is the story of someone preparing to circulate between the two countries and who would take advantage of his binationality, biculturalism, and bilingualism in the most effective way. We met him in February 2010 at a school in Izúcar de Matamoros, when he was twelve years old. At the beginning of the interview, he introduced himself in Spanish, as follows:

> My name is Omar. I am from the United States, from the state of New York. I'm in seventh grade. There [in the United States], I finished all primary school, from kindergarten to sixth grade. I came here, to Mexico. I also like it here. I had been here [before]. I returned on June 27; I came here . . . because my mother wanted to come and because we wanted to see our house in Mexico. . . . It's finished. We just wanted to see it because we had not been here for eight years.

Omar had lived in Houston for two years before arriving in Izúcar. According to him, his mother had grown weary of living in New York because of the weather and because "there, we were barely free." Additionally, his mother told him that Houston reminded her of Mexico. When describing his life in the United States, Omar almost automatically switched to English, clarifying that he liked Spanish more than English: "To be honest, I like Spanish better than English. I don't know why." He summarized his subjective itinerary in English, as follows:

> Well, I always say that I'm Mexican American because I was born over there. I'm not going to make a big deal about who I am, but I obviously am Mexican because of my parents' heritage. I've learned Spanish since I was born.

> When I went to school I learned English, but when I started I only spoke Spanish. . . . I really want to live in the United States because I want to help my parents. They work hard for my future, and also I want to live here. I want to have a house. I want to do stuff here. I want to help my parents over there.

At this point during the interview, we asked him, "So do you want to live there and here?" Omar replied firmly, "Yeah, I want to do stuff here." Omar's itinerary incorporates another element of synthesis that is partially outlined in Nanys's narrative: that of migratory circulation. Omar does not make a big deal of his identification: he identified himself as a Mexican American and as a Mexican and found no contradiction in this. This synthesis of identification includes his filial love, which prepares him for his integration into adult life in the United States; a firm will to maintain ties with his parents' region of origin; circulation between the two countries; and an imagined life in both countries. To be able to circulate successfully and enact these forms of identification, Omar must take advantage of his biculturalism and bilingualism. When compared to Omar's pragmatic synthesis, Jazmín's synthesis looks rather rhetorical. While she was cognizant that she was from both places, Omar will likely make use of his dual affiliation. This is probably why he clearly told us that he did not want to make a big deal about national affiliation: he defined himself as Mexican American because he was born in the United States and "obviously" as a Mexican because his parents are Mexican.

Born in Mexico: Polarized Experiences

The children born in Mexico generally identify themselves as "Mexicans," as we previously established. However, a quarter of these children chose the category "Mexican American" in our survey. To present the rationales and experiences of the Mexican-born children, we draw on two interviews that represent the two extremes of the continuum on which the rest of the Mexican-born child migrants fall.

Andrea stands at one end of the extremes. She was born in Jerez, Zacatecas. We met her in November 2005, in a Jerez junior high school, where she was enrolled in eighth grade. Andrea migrated to Wichita, Kansas, when she was four years old and returned to Jerez a few months before our interview, when she was fourteen. She had received all of her previous schooling in Wichita, from kindergarten through seventh grade. In fact, during the interview she stated that she spoke English better than Spanish. During the conversation she alternated between English and Spanish, selecting each language according to her preference.

A significant part of Andrea's story focused on describing how U.S. schools instill patriotism through the Pledge of Allegiance. During many of the interviews, the migrant children remembered this experience, but none recalled it in as much detail as Andrea. She showed us how the hand is placed on the heart, recounted the words they had to repeat every morning, and explained how the students stood and showed respect, although, she added, many students would fall asleep. For her the flag-salute ceremony in Mexican schools was intriguing not only because she did not know what to do or say but because of the seriousness with which the weekly ceremony was conducted. In addition to these patriotic experiences, Andrea described her eight years of schooling in Wichita as an incredibly positive experience. Particularly, she emphasized that her teachers were "fabulous."

Andrea arrived in Jerez in the company of her mother and her two sisters. Her father had previously returned by himself because he had separated from her mother a year before. Andrea had arrived in Mexico only two months before our interview with her was conducted, which explains why she felt she had not fully integrated into the school community and why she was missing her friends in Wichita.

The three girls, their mother, and their father had returned to Mexico for the same reason: "Because they wanted to fix their *papeles*." In fact, Andrea told us that her father had already started the paperwork and that soon the other family members would do the same. She had no doubts that everyone would get a resident visa, no matter how long they had to wait. "Maybe we will stay here for two, three, or even four years, but we will definitely return." During another point of the interview, she reaffirmed this statement but, this time, using the first person: "I'm going to return to live there. I don't know where, but maybe I'm going to live somewhere else, right, and so we're going to go."

Andrea imagined her life in the United States even if she clearly identified herself, and all of her family members, as Mexican: "In my family everybody is Mexican, and we all speak Spanish." She had been educated in the United States since the age of four, and she came to Mexico because neither she nor her parents and siblings were authorized to reside in the United States, and they were looking for a legal solution to return to the United States. As soon as she obtained a visa, she saw herself circulating between the two countries, working in one country and taking vacations in the other. We do not know if she managed to fulfill her plans, but we do know that she was a young woman who identified as Mexican and was planning her future in the United States. At the time of the interview, these plans had not been questioned at all. She stated boldly, "That is what we are planning. These are our plans."

Norma, a teenage girl from Monterrey, is at the other extreme of the continuum. Norma lived in Garland, Texas, for one year. She arrived there when she was eleven years old and returned to Mexico when she was thirteen. She moved to Texas with her mother and two sisters because her mother had decided to separate from her father. The girls settled in their aunt's home while the mother was living in Dallas with a new partner. When the maternal aunt enrolled her nieces in school, she declared that she was their mother. So in Texas Norma lived separated from both her father and mother. Throughout her short stay, she developed animosity toward the United States, its schools, and its society for the following reasons:

1. She thought that migrants were discriminated against and that the discrimination (a term she used three times) was particularly marked against Mexicans.

2. She realized that educational opportunities were available to Anglo-Americans but not to other social groups.

3. She disliked the daily patriotic ceremony at school every morning at eight o'clock, in which she had to salute the U.S. flag and sing the national anthem.

4. She considered some school practices as comical, such as "sock day" (when students and teachers wore socks of different colors), "hat day" (when everyone wore a hat), and "Teddy day" (when everyone brought their favorite stuffed animal to school). Norma concluded, "It was a culture like that. Not very, well, it doesn't convince me at all. It's a lot of fun, but since it doesn't go much with the culture of a country, it seemed like a game to me, but that's what it is." For Norma school practices were not serious at all.

5. She was intrigued by the food served at the school cafeteria and explained, "Over there they eat plain flour more than anything else, a lot of pizza."

6. She was not directly affected by racism, but on several occasions she could identify the weight of skin color in social relations in the United States.

7. She contrasted the coldness of social relations in the United States with the warmth of Mexican society. She explained, "Here [in Mexico] they celebrate you, *posada* (very popular religious plays to prepare for the Christmas holiday). I don't know, they congratulate you on your grades, and there [in the United States] they rarely do so. Here [in Mexico] the atmosphere is cheerful, and there in the United States] it's very cold."

8. She concluded that the U.S. people believed they live in a country of freedom; however, in her opinion, they were deluded. Ironically, she affirmed that they were free, but free to leave their homes to get in their cars and go shopping, but nothing else.

With these characteristics Norma emphatically defined herself as Mexican by stating, "I have always been a Mexican," and characterized the United States as "a different world; the United States is something else." Apparently, Norma's subjective itinerary had come to an end, and she had no intention of returning to the United States, much less did she identify as Mexican American. However, she acknowledged her achievements in learning English and told us that she wanted to study applied linguistics.

CONCLUSIONS

This chapter provides an account, at least in part, of the migrant children's subjective itineraries as they continue their journey of living and adapting to life in Mexico. For all migrant children, the journey includes an encounter—or reunion—with the Mexican society and its institutions, among which the school is the most important. In this way the children no longer feel like strangers in the society with which they had a distant bond while they were living in the United States. From beginning as partial foreigners, they gradually become full members of an abstract community (i.e., the nation) presented to them in its more concrete local and regional manifestations: ways of speaking, dressing, celebrating, interacting, denominating, appreciating, and disapproving—that is, all the subtleties of everyday life that ensure the fluency of practical social relationships.

The learning path seems winding, especially for the children who have never lived in Mexico, who have received most of their schooling in the United States, and who speak English as native speakers. These children are forced to conduct more elaborate negotiations, including preserving the skills they acquired while living in the United States. By preserving and developing these skills, the children are building a future that will allow them to move between Mexico and the United States more effectively. Their most visible and valuable skill is their bilingualism. Without it life in one of the two countries will be limited, even for the binational children, as they need to speak English *and* Spanish like native speakers in order not to be treated as foreigners in either country.

Some of the migrant children plan their future in the United States, but, once in close contact with Mexican society, they become instilled with the desire to maintain concrete ties with regions and localities in Mexico. This especially applies to those who are binational, but it is not exclusive to this group, as the same desire can be observed in some children who have only Mexican citizenship. The same can be said about those children who want to build their lives in Mexico. They want to maintain ties with their relatives and friends in the United States. Their choice for wanting to stay in Mexico does not imply rejecting the United States, except in the extreme case of Norma.

For the children who have lived in the United States, living in Mexico represents an opportunity to build their biculturalism according to their personal circumstances. Biculturalism is not one-size-fits-all: national labels serve migrant children only as trail markers, not as enduring attributions, throughout this complex process. Having migrated at an early age, these children have all been socialized in two societies, and it is in their interest to construct a synthesis of what they can call their own, unique "Mexicanism/Americanism." Regardless of which label they select, they all (some more, others less) have internalized components of both U.S. and Mexican societies and are in the process of developing the synthesis of the two.

The migrant children's synthesis of identification is still unfinished and will be an ongoing process as they develop into adults. Along the way many children feel as if they are "from both places" or "in the middle." They do not feel like aliens in the societies in which they are being educated, but as architects of an internal and external dialogue in which disconnected biographical pieces are being put into place, similar to completing a puzzle. Because migrant children's itineraries vary depending on their country of birth, the number of years they lived in the United States, the influence of schools, and their gender, their final syntheses will not be homogeneous. In the end there will be many forms of "Mexicanism/ Americanism," as different children forge distinct paths throughout their journey.

What about the children who were born in the United States and arrived in Mexico before reaching school age? If they never return to the United States, it is very likely that they will not be immersed in subjective itineraries like those analyzed in this chapter. All their socialization will have taken place in Mexico. If they decide to migrate to the United States as adults, they will be part of a rare category of migrants that has U.S. citizenship by jus soli but that act like migrants in their birth country. However, this outcome seems highly unlikely. Many working-class Mexican parents know that a child who has both nationalities represents a type of capital for the family. They will do everything in their power to help their children, who came to Mexico while still very young, develop their own biculturalism and learn English. To do this they will turn to relatives and friends living in the United States to offer these children the opportunity to be educated, at least for a few years, in U.S. schools. If this plays out, the children who arrived in Mexico at a young age will experience similar migration itineraries to those analyzed in this chapter.

At the end of this story, when the hundreds of thousands of children become adults, they will take up Rodríguez's description of a segment of the U.S. society as Mexican Americans intricately linked to Mexican society or of a segment of the Mexican society as Mexican Americans intricately linked to U.S. society. They are children of the Great Expulsion and will be participants in the New Circulation.

Conclusion

HISTORICAL AND POLITICAL IMPLICATIONS

We wrote this book during a historical conjuncture of international migration not exclusive to Mexico. Traditional migratory patterns have been interrupted as individuals and families who were residing in countries that have typically received migrants are now migrating to those that have historically been considered as migrant-sending countries.[1] The immigration patterns between the United States and Mexico have shifted. Instead of primarily migrating to the United States from Mexico, many Mexican families, after years of living in the United States, migrate in the opposite direction and settle in Mexico. Thus, from 2005 to 2020, Mexico has increasingly become more of a receiving country for migrants and less of a sending country (at least not to the same scale that it has sent migrants to the United States in past decades). Migration scholars, media, and some leaders are just beginning to focus their attention on return migration to Mexico.

Although this type of return migration from the United States to Mexico is a relatively recent phenomenon, we have begun to identify some of the most important realities that these international migrants navigate. We conclude this book by highlighting these realities. First, we know that international migrants are vulnerable and find themselves in conditions that exacerbate their vulnerability. Many arrive in Mexico with little foresight and planning; they have limited options and experience difficulties in making decisions and responding to the demands of their new context. This could be because they were imprisoned, humiliated, and then deported (Golash-Boza 2015) or because the living conditions in the United States had become adverse and hostile for them and their families (Dreby 2015; Jones-Correa 2012). Vulnerability also manifests in the forced separation of family members, as some settle in Mexico while others continue their lives in the United States. For many migrants their return to Mexico represents a complex, sudden transition that often is as risky as their initial migration to United States (Durand 2004).

Second, we realize that, for many Mexican migrants, their extended stay in the United States almost inevitably entailed the weakening and, in some cases, the loss of networks of relationships and meaningful connections with Mexico (Hagan, Hernández-León, and Demonsant 2015). In the past most Mexicans participated in circular migration, and their stay in the United States was short while their families remained in Mexico. Since 1986 historical and structural circumstances caused a shift in migration patterns.[2] Circular migration turned into permanent migration, in the case not only of young adults, as had been the typical practice in preceding migratory patterns, but of entire nuclear and extended families. This explains why the total number of Mexicans born in Mexico and living in the United States increased from 0.8 million in 1970 to about 12.5 million in 2007 (González-Barrera and López 2013; Zong and Batalova 2016).

Between 1986 and 2004, many Mexicans moved to the United States with the intention to settle permanently. Their children were born there, and families established roots in various regions of the country. Abruptly (and due to circumstances that we need not repeat here), these families were caught up in a new sociopolitical context that brought them back to Mexico after five, ten, fifteen, or more years of residing in the United States. Inevitably, upon their arrival in Mexico, they discovered that their relationships, their support systems, and the reciprocity they expected from others in their community had weakened or disappeared and further complicated their integration into the country. This is a *new* pattern of return migration. It is considered new because it frequently involves the family; familial migration is a pattern that now coexists with that of young, single men. The configurations of migrant families are often characterized as a mix of members with distinct attributes, which include varied lengths of stay in the United States, different documentation statuses, and uncertainties regarding their eventual return to the United States.

The findings from our research suggest that Mexican migrant families maintain continuities relevant to their realities, such as support networks on both sides of the border, to be drawn on when necessary. For the children we interviewed, the family was fundamental in shaping their experiences and expectations. In some cases familial networks have broken down as a result of the disruptive effect of migration and long periods of separation. These circumstances generate tension, conflict, abandonment, reorganization, and redistribution of responsibilities within households. This does not mean that the role of the family is diminished; on the contrary, the transnational family's ties are recomposed and renewed in the emerging context of international migration. It is quite possible that they are even reinforced, which would go against a trend described in various studies that suggest that family networks in Mexico and Latin America, which serve as support networks to supplement the lack of or ineffective state social security, are being exhausted and nearing depletion.

Third, we now know that migrants who return to Mexico do not necessarily go back to the places from where they migrated. Data from different sources show that some regions in Mexico are attracting return migrants and that these are not necessarily the regions where the migrants were born. For example, migrants from Morelos who lived in California for several years decided to settle in Chihuahua, Baja California, or Sonora, depending on the opportunities that they encountered in those states (Giorguli and Gutiérrez 2012; Masferrer and Roberts 2012; Jacobo Suárez 2017b; Masferrer 2021). Currently, our data has revealed only the broad trends of this new geography of return, and we are just beginning to understand the challenges and opportunities that the arrival of Mexicans from the United States entails for cities, municipalities, and particular regions of Mexico. Nevertheless, the children in this study taught us that arrival in Mexico is composed of heterogenous itineraries and experiences that include different family situations, support networks, and educational opportunities.

A fourth reality is the types of mobility deployed by return migrants. For epistemological reasons it is much easier to interpret and study migration from a single place (an origin or a destination) and as a permanent phenomenon—until the opposite occurs. Our research indicates that this is with a mobile population that frequently migrates internally within the country in which they are living (i.e., they change their state of residence while living in the United States or in Mexico) and that has a high probability of migrating either to other cities in Mexico in search of better education and work opportunities or, when legal conditions permit, to destinations in the United States, where, in many cases, family members still reside. Just as social networks have operated to sustain Mexican migration to the United States (Durand and Massey 2003), many child migrants will rely on their wide support network in the United States and their knowledge of U.S. institutions, language, and culture to remigrate in the near future, either as children or as young adults.

Finally, the social institutions that international migrants encounter such as healthcare, education, housing, certification of job skills, and civil registration (to mention only the most important) were not designed to facilitate the integration of Mexican families who arrive in Mexico after having resided in the United States. For this reason institutional responses are limited and are being constructed only as international migrants become more visible, and social organizations request changes to facilitate their integration into the institutional dynamics of Mexico (Jacobo Suárez 2017a). Thus, the geographic concentration of return migrants calls for public policy that focuses on the integration and reintegration of international migrants—policies that do not yet exist at the national level, let alone at local levels.

Over the past decade, the demographic characteristics of over one million Mexicans who moved from the United States to Mexico raise questions about the scope of any national and state public policies that have been implemented thus far. In matters of social institutions in the United States, the meek measures that have been adopted fall short of the immense challenge. Of particular interest to our research is the role of the school, the institution that plays an instrumental role in the integration and reintegration of child migrants. The educational challenge is even greater when we consider the persistent inequalities across the educational system in Mexico. Defining effective policies that will reverse general inequities seems impossible, let alone imagining policies that privilege the skills and knowledge that migrant children bring with them and that support the culturally diverse spaces created by their presence.

Mexico, as a society and as a government, has not been able to adopt a political vision that aligns with the new conjuncture of migration. We must reimagine Mexico as a migrant-receiving country and, consequently, call for clear public policies to integrate or reintegrate those who return or arrive for the first time in Mexico, like the children of Mexicans born in the United States. We are referring, then, to a reconversion of the national political imagination that would shift the idea of Mexico being a migrant-sending country to that of Mexico being a migrant-receiving country. This shift in vision involves a change of the parameters we use to define migratory events. In fact, the return of the Mexicans is often considered a *problem* and is rarely viewed as an *opportunity*. If we renew our political perspective and the semantics derived from it, we will be able to appreciate the value of demographic growth, human capital, multicultural wealth, expansion of political horizons, and forms of social organization. As such, the return of international migrants to Mexico would cease to be seen as a problem and, instead, would be conceived as an opportunity. This can happen only if we create the social and institutional conditions that permit us to take advantage of this situation.

Mexico and its institutions have the opportunity to overcome the policy (and ideology) established during the forced repatriation of Mexicans in the 1920s and 1930s, synthesized by the words of Fernando Alanís Enciso (2007): "They should stay there." The current, historical conjuncture of migration calls on us to gradually imagine, create, and work toward a collective creed that asserts, "They should stay here" and feel like a part of the national community.

Finally, we must be attentive to the multiple forms of return migration. Return migration varies according to factors like the number of years spent in the United States, the dispersion and reunification of families, the economic context of the receiving regions of Mexico, the conditions of reception in either country, and other individual and contextual dimensions. Return migration includes the return of single men who left their families in the United States, mothers who came to Mexico with their young children while their older ones stay in the United States, the sudden and unexpected return as a result of deportation, the planned or unplanned return, and the desired or undesired return. Some migrants return from large cities in the United States to small rural towns in Mexico, while others return to big cities such as León, Guadalajara, Tijuana, Mexico City, or Monterrey. While we know that there are multiple forms of return migration, we do not yet have enough information, at least at this time, to fully describe each of these variants.

The 0.5 Generation: Children Moving from the United States to Mexico is a book that addresses the "return" migration of minors who arrive in Mexico from the United States. The fact that they arrive as children or adolescents is important both scientifically and politically. The new generation of Mexicans, those we are currently educating to build the future of Mexican society, includes a significant number of children and adolescents who were born, lived, and studied in the United States. We are dealing with the first generation of Mexican children who are, to a varying extent, legally, institutionally, symbolically, and subjectively binational, bicultural, and bilingual. These international child migrants living in Mexico are already forming an important chapter in the history of Mexico during the twenty-first century.

Of course, before we draw our reflections to an end, we must note that a significant percentage of these migrant children are also U.S. citizens by jus soli. Regardless of what they decide to do as adults (e.g., live in Mexico or in the United States or circulate between both countries), they will continue to be either a conceptual or authentic part of the U.S. political society simply because of their citizenship. Their fate cannot be ignored by U.S. government officials, decision-makers, producers of opinion, or the society in general (Gándara and Jensen 2021). The fact that many of these children are living in Mexican communities, being educated in Mexican schools, and internalizing Mexican cultures does not make them less American. In the near future, these children will represent a type of U.S. citizen that has never existed in history, at least not to the demographic degree we analyze in this book.

Forward-looking leaders in the United States may agree that this generation of children could become a bridge that brings Mexico and the United States closer together in a much more effective and enduring way than the well-intended rhetoric of the past, which has sought only to establish good neighborly relations between both countries and societies. We assert that the subject matter of this book not only is a domestic concern for Mexico but also addresses an important item on the binational agenda writ large. The experiences and realities of international migrant children are not, and cannot become, solely a Mexican issue. This is a responsibility that both countries share and must act on as equal partners, without a power imbalance. We close this book by reiterating the demographic data presented in the second chapter: as of 2015 one million U.S.-born individuals of all ages were residing in Mexico, most of them children, adolescents, and youth.[3]

Children's Responses to the Question: "Why Have You Returned to Mexico?"

PART 1: FAMILY REUNIFICATION IN MEXICO

My father was deported.

I came to visit our family and to see everyone and because everyone in my family wanted to come.

To see my mother.

The police were looking for my dad.

My parents wanted me to come here, and I could not stand not seeing them.

My mother decided to return for my brothers.

She was afraid they would send us to Mexico, and I would be alone there.

My mother would not leave me alone in Los Angeles.

My father was transported, and my mother wanted to come here so the family could be together.

My mother brought us here to see my father.

My dad got deported.

To meet my dad and stay.

For my parents, who didn't want me to stay in the United States.

My dad got caught.

My dad lives here.

My dad is in jail, and he came back one Wednesday, and my mother, my sister, and I went to the day care, and the lady told my mother that we could be together.

My father was happy, and he went to have beer, and the policemen caught him.

They couldn't stay there because they deported my mother.

I wanted to come visit my family and get to know them.

My mother told us or suggested that, according to the police, they were going to look for those who didn't have papers, and they were going to put them in jail or something like that, I don't remember, and that's why we went back because we didn't have papers.

My father was a drinker, and they put him in jail, and then they sent him to Alabama, and then we went to visit him, and they told him they were going to send him to Mexico, and then we came here.

PART 2: FILIAL DUTIES

I came back because my grandfather was sick.

To take care of my grandmother because my mother's father died.

My great-grandmother died, and we came here and didn't leave anymore, because we had already lived there for a long time, and my parents wanted to return here to see their parents.

My mother's grandfather was dying, and he was asking to see her.

My parents came here because my grandfather was dying.

My grandmother doesn't want to be alone.

My mother has not seen her mother in nine years.

My grandfather was very ill, and my mother was desperate and wanted us to come here.

PART 3: LIVING CONDITIONS

There I stayed with some uncles, and we hardly ever went out.

My mother thinks that life is better in Mexico.

[Life] is very boring, and you can't ride a bike.

Freedom.

To be able to live.

There were many problems in the United States.

My mom and dad got tired of working there.

My mom's job there was too difficult for her.

I liked Mexico more

The economic crisis in the United States.

I wasn't happy in the United States.

The September 11th attack.

Lack of work, and we wanted to come here.

The crisis, it is severe.

The rent was very expensive, and we were bored there.

I really like my country, where I am now.

I missed everything.

My parents were tired of living there; they had already built our house, some apartments, and they had bought a ranch [in Mexico].

We had no money, and my dad got fired, and they took our house away from us.

There my dad got beaten up.

My brother was about to be born, and my mother was afraid because there they send some of the children to war.

It is very nice here.

PART 4: CONFLICTING FAMILY SITUATIONS

The problems with my grandparents.

My mother's health.

My mother passed away, and I had to return.

My mother and my father, they had problems.

My father is sick, and we came to see what was wrong with his stomach.

We couldn't stay with my uncle.

My mommy and my daddy fought a lot, so we came here.

My mom threatened to turn us in to the immigration authorities.

My brother died, and my sister was ill.

My mother was very ill and could not be cured; she had hemorrhages.

My parents got divorced and because my father was sent to jail.

My father went to live with another lady, and my mother decided to come to Mexico.

My brother was using [drugs], and they sent him to Mexico, and he was doing the same thing here, and that's why we came.

My stepfather is here.

I didn't get along with my stepmother.

My mother got angry with my father because he was working all day.

For a family and intimate cause.

My mom was being abused, and I was going to be placed in foster care.

My dad found a mom for me.

PART 5: WORKING CONDITIONS

My dad had a better job [in Mexico].

My mother went to study [in the United States], and now she is a teacher here, in Mexico.

My father finished his work.

To help cultivate the land and get the job done.

My dad was sold a small shop.

My dad couldn't get a good job.

My dad is a teacher and has to work here.

Because of my dad's job we came back.

They had work here, in Mexico.

My dad was laid off in the United States.

They offered him another job.

My mom asked for a leave in hospital no. 46 [and the leave ended].

My father's job, he worked legally there, and the company offered him a better job in Mexico.

In the United States my dad stopped working because the company went bankrupt.

Work was over in the United States.

My father couldn't find a job.

My father didn't work there.

Notes

1. In general, we use the terms *girls* and *boys* as equivalent to *children*. In some chapters this category covers the age group of zero to seventeen years old, while in others it refers only to those who are school age (six to seventeen years old). The terms are clarified to the reader in each of the cases.

2. A different group of child migrants arriving in Mexico is composed of those born in Central America. According to a 2015 population survey, that same year 11,274 children born in Central America were living in Mexico (Aguilar and Giorguli 2016). Our research does not include this group, which remains largely unexplored at the time of our writing.

3. According to the data from the population and housing censuses from 2000 and 2010, the number of Mexicans who immigrated to the United States was gradually decreasing while the number of Mexicans who returned to Mexico was increasing every year (Passel, Cohn, and González-Barrera 2012; BBVA Research 2011, 2012; Ramírez and Meza González 2011; Giorguli and Angoa 2019).

4. The number of Mexicans (born in Mexico) residing in the United States went from 0.8 million in 1970 to more than 10 million in 2000 (Giorguli and Angoa 2019), which is why we speak of the Great Migration.

5. Children who arrive in a new country where the spoken language is the same as their country of origin also face significant linguistic changes. This is

the case of Bolivian children who migrate to Argentina or Chile (Cavagnoud, Suremain, and Riva González 2013).

6. One of the contemporary academic and political debates about children who are members of the 1.5 generation is that of those who entered the destination country without authorization—that is to say, they arrived in the United States as undocumented children. By country of birth, they are not citizens of the country where their parents take them (unless one of their parents is a citizen of that country). While not all of them are unauthorized migrants, many arrive in the new country and live their childhood without possessing documents to prove their residency (Gonzales 2007, 2011; Gonzales and Chavez 2012). While still underage, these children and adolescents are protected because they are not subject to deportation. The outcomes of these debates will greatly affect this group of child migrants' futures.

7. One example of how international child migrants lack visibility is the fact the secretary of public education of Mexico has virtually no information on the number of foreign-born students or the number of students born in Mexico who have migratory experience at the basic education level (i.e., kindergarten through ninth grade). There is no data or reference whatsoever to this kind of information in the 911 form that is filled out by Mexican school authorities. The 911 form for the 2015–16 school year includes the student's nationality but not the birthplace. However, those children born in another country to a Mexican father or mother (part of our focal population) may and probably will be registered as Mexicans, making it difficult to determine who has migrant status. The *Mexican Education Census* that INEGI (National Institute of Statistics and Geography) conducted during the 2014–15 school year and the context questionnaires included in the standardized tests carried out each year in large samples of schools nationwide also do not record this type of data.

8. Children who moved to Canada represent a very small group in our samples.

9. One exception is represented by the work of Enrique T. Trueba, who poses the following questions: "How do children adjust back in Mexico, and how do they perform in Mexican schools? For those who return to Mexico for extended periods of time, what is the impact of the socioeconomic, political, and cultural changes they have experienced as they engage in daily life in Mexico?" (1998, 267).

10. Instead of applying the questionnaire and interviewing the children, we decided to conduct a collective interview for all first, second, and third graders. In the classroom the interviewer posed several questions to the whole group, including if any of them had lived in the United States and when they had arrived in Mexico.

11. All the children in our studies have been referred to in publications with pseudonyms.

12. In the total numbers, we included in the sample students from four schools in the state of Morelos, where we applied the questionnaire in September 2013.

That small sample was not representative of the primary and secondary schools in that state, but those students' experiences also shed light on the whole phenomenon of migration and reacting to migration.

CHAPTER 1

1. Commuters here are individuals who cross national boundaries on a daily basis to work or study in another country.

2. Migrant parents are well aware of this function of the school. In an interview conducted in Ameca, Jalisco, by Enrique Martínez Curiel in January 1995, one of the workers at the sugar mill explained why he decided not to migrate to the United States: "At some point, I thought I would leave my job at the mill to go work in the United States, but I did not do it because I had to take the whole family with me and it was very difficult to do it. . . . I did not want to take my family with me, because there, children, from primary school, are inured to things that are very different from ours" (2016, 118–19).

3. When referring to the maximization of opportunities and minimization of risks, we take inspiration from the military and political metaphor that follows the grammar of war described by Pierre Tripier (2010). We do not refer to the notion of "goal-oriented action" nor to the economic logic of cost-benefit. International migrant workers often move in hostile contexts, so they are not investors seeking profits. Roger Waldinger synthesizes this perspective eloquently: "The history of the strategies of migrants [shows] that, in order to solve their problems, they use the most important resource they possess—that is, themselves—to consolidate the networks which allow them to link the 'here' and 'there'" (2006, 29; our translation).

4. Nicholas De Genova (2005) shows, in a quality ethnographic study carried out in Chicago, how immigration policies in the United States have resulted in Mexicans' becoming the "illegals" par excellence and therefore the most desirable candidates for deportation. Genova's work gives continuity to the historical findings of Rodolfo Acuña (1972).

5. The subjective dimension is not ethereal but concrete. The children know the geography of the United States and its history and patriotic signs and have recited the Pledge of Allegiance numerous times, but their subjectivity lacks transnational characteristics.

CHAPTER 2

1. For an account of the changes in Mexican migration to the United States, see Durand (2016).

2. U.S.-born children include children born to both U.S. and Mexican parents. However, in the vast majority of the cases, these are children of Mexican parents or children in households headed by a Mexican parent. In 2015, 97 percent of the U.S.-born children were living in households headed by a Mexican parent. This chapter presents the information on two population groups between zero and seventeen years of age. The U.S.-born population is the "stock"—that is, the total population regardless of when they entered Mexico. The information we have on the Mexican-born children's migratory experience is limited to the cases that occurred five years prior to the census or to the *2015 Intercensal Survey* because these instruments include a question that asks about place of residence five years prior. By capturing only the experience of the past five years, the number is lower than if we had information on all the Mexican-born individuals who have ever migrated to the United States and not only on those who had migrated to the United States five years prior to the census survey date. The question about the place of residence five years prior to the census is the most used for the study of migration in Latin America, and there is no other source in Mexico with similar representation to that of the census samples and of the *2015 Intercensal Survey* that would allow us to obtain more details about whether Mexican-born children ever migrated to the United States, much less information about the duration of their stay in the United States or if they attended school during their stay.

3. The data in figure 1 show that in 2015 there was a sharp decrease in the number of U.S.- born children and adolescents fifteen years of age and older—the age that coincides with the completion of lower secondary education and entrance into high school. The possible circularity related to the educational trajectories of the U.S.-born children and adolescents remains a hypothesis to be explored in the future, when we have more information on this generation of child migrants or other longitudinal data sources.

4. The difference in the percentages, as referred to here, is significant (p <0.01).

5. According to the *2015 Intercensal Survey*, 23 percent of the Mexican population lived in communities of fewer than 2,500 people (INEGI 2015).

6. The difference in the percentages is significant (p <0.01).

7. For a review of the age distribution of the U.S.-born population residing in Mexico in 2000 and 2010, see Castillo (2012).

CHAPTER 3

1. The analysis and theoretical discussion would be different if the children returned to the United States as adults. Certainly, they were born in the United States and may enter the country as citizens, but what kind of citizens would they

be if, for example, they received their entire schooling in Mexico? In many respects, they would be citizens very similar to first-generation immigrants. Mexican-born minors who moved to the United States and, at some point, obtained legal residency documents or are eligible for the U.S. citizenship face a similar dilemma. That is to say, among those who were born in and later returned to Mexico, there are many (and we believe they represent the majority) who live within irregular migratory circumstances. However, there are others who, at some point in their lives, may be able to attend to their situation, obtain legal documentation, and live in the United States.

2. Translator's note: "Junior high school" corresponds to *secundaria* in Mexico, which comprises three years (grades seven through nine). The first year of *secundaria* is equivalent to seventh grade.

3. The "immobility effect" is described by the author as follows: "What struck me about this segment of the Monterrey origin population in Houston was not their transnational orientation but their social and physical immobility.... [These conditions] appeared to trap undocumented immigrants inside the United States, significantly limiting their ability to move and travel—if not impeding their cross-border mobility altogether" (Hernández-León 2008, 141–42). Abel's case is illustrative of the same situation, but this time in Mexico, not in the United States.

4. The main objective of this law and its decree was so that Mexicans living in the United States would not lose Mexican nationality in case they decided to become a naturalized U.S. citizen. An unforeseen consequence of this law is related precisely to the dual nationality of the children born in the United States to Mexican parents.

5. This number does not include nine children who were born in other countries: Germany, Cuba, Canada, Uruguay, Chile, and Colombia.

6. The fact that, until recently, there was no information in the administrative records of the schools to identify those born outside of Mexico is a reflection of the invisibility of international child migrants in the Mexican education system.

7. In Zacatecas the foreign-born children were all born in the United States. However, some of them were born to parents from Costa Rica, El Salvador, Canada, the Dominican Republic, Guatemala, and Nicaragua.

8. Only two foreign-born children were born in a country outside of the United States: Spain and Peru.

9. The survey identified twenty-three children born in other countries: Argentina, Canada, China, Colombia, Korea, Costa Rica, Cuba, Ecuador, El Salvador, Spain, Japan, Panama, Peru, and Poland.

10. These explanations are reinforced by the findings of María Eugenia D'Aubeterre Buznego (2015) in the northern sierra of Puebla, where single women's migration to the United States (with or without children) has been a constant since the beginning of the 1990s. Although Itzcalli's mother was not single,

generally speaking, single mothers are more likely to use the preventive strategy deployed by Itzcalli's parents, and this is reflected in the high percentage of U.S.-born children who arrive in Puebla at an early age.

11. It is precisely because they have dual nationality that these children can become transnational students, if they have relatives in the United States willing to receive them. The ethnographic study in Morelos illustrates the following: four out of the ten children whose life stories we have been following since 2013 have already returned to the United States and are continuing their schooling in that country. All of them were born in the United States.

12. Theoretically speaking, there can be a type 6, but no such case was found in the surveys. This would be the case of a child born in Mexico, who moves to the United States before reaching school age and later returns to Mexico without ever having been enrolled in schools in the United States.

13. Percentages in table 9 are calculated taking into account the data of the subsample of children enrolled in schools from the fourth grade of elementary school through the third year of junior high school. (Translator's note: the third year of junior high school in Mexico corresponds to ninth grade in the United States.) Children enrolled in the first three years of elementary school are not included because, due to their age, they could not possibly have been enrolled in schools in the United States for a long period. For these children the maximum accumulated number of school years is three: one of preschool and the first two years of elementary school. All, without exception, would fall into the category of "shorter experience in U.S. schools." The percentage does include, of course, children from the fourth grade of elementary school through the third year of junior high (ninth grade in the United States) who were born in the United States and have never been enrolled in U.S. schools. The data of these children are presented in the column labeled "without previous experience in U.S. schools."

14. The return experiences of these youth are not addressed in this book because they are no longer children when they arrive in Mexico and therefore not included in our data. We refer to them as a way to highlight the uniqueness of child migration. In this case we emphasize the fact that migrant children can experience fragmented socialization as young adults upon their arrival in Mexico and begin a process of resocialization, according to Peter Berger and Thomas Luckmann's (1991) definition of this notion.

CHAPTER 4

1. Unfortunately, there are no data sources available in the United States or Mexico that allow us to draw a relation between the states of origin and destination among migrants. The microlevel approaches, such as those included in the

following sections, facilitate a rapprochement with the child migrants' itineraries but are not representative at the state or national level.

2. These labels are not used by the children, nor by their parents or teachers. We use them as a resource that allows us to abbreviate expressions such as "native Texas children," "children from California," "children who lived in New York," and so on.

CHAPTER 5

1. A version of the academic adult-centrism has certainly paid attention to migrant children, but they are represented as victims, subjects of protection, needy, and devoid of knowledge and agency. According to this perspective, children are "sources of anxiety" (Dobson 2009, 357). Examples of this perspective are found in Byrne (2008), Ceriani (2012), Mancillas Bazán (2009), Gallo (2005), Villaseñor and Moreno (2006), Capps et al. (2007), and Ensor and Gozdziak (2010).

2. This change in semantics and syntax is an example of the methodological dialogue that we announced in the introduction. It is a dialogue between the "sciences of calculus" *(sciences du calcul)* and the "sciences of narration" *(sciences du recit),* according to the classification put forward by Louis-André Gérard-Varet and Jean-Claude Passeron (1995), who include demography, economics, and quantitative sociology among the former, and anthropology, history, and interpretive sociology among the latter.

3. The children chose their preferred language in which to conduct the interview. It was not a surprise to us how the children switched from one language to the other. Here our focus is on content as opposed to a deeper linguistic analysis of translanguaging.

4. Erasmo did not know what type of factory his father worked in.

5. Similar conclusions appear in the work of Seth Gitter, Robert Gitter, and Douglas Southgate (2008), who observed that the migrants who have the highest probability of employment are those who return to the northern part of Mexico (not to the border cities) and those who return to the central region of the country.

CHAPTER 6

1. See chapter 3, in which we discuss the diversity of school experiences and the variation in the importance of previous schooling in the United States for international child migrants.

2. In fact, at that time we still were not sure if we would find any international child migrants enrolled in those schools.

3. That explains why the spoken Spanish acquired by many of these children in the United States is limited to basic interpersonal communication.

4. Similar observations carried out in schools in Sonora in 2004 reached very similar conclusions (Valdéz et al. 2018).

5. The fact that the international child migrants are invisible in Mexican schools is the result not of teachers' or principals' ignorance or blindness but rather of the lack of an educational policy aimed at increasing their visibility. International child migrants are completely overlooked in *The National Development Plan, 2013–2018* (Secretaría de Gobernación 2013), the *Sectoral Program of Education, 2013–2018* (Secretaría de Educación Pública 2013), and the *2016 Educational Model: The Pedagogical Approach in the Educational Reform* (Secretaría de Educación Pública 2016), which are all documents that support Mexico's 2016 Educational Reform. In other words, international child migrants do not exist for those who design the educational policies in Mexico. Contrarily, in the Mexican states where committed groups of professionals deploy effective actions to respond to the educational needs of children from the United States, the visibility of international child migrants increases significantly in schools.

6. The authors classify the various forms of social disdain observed in Quebec elementary schools, which include humiliation, violation of dignity, symbolic elimination of the other, disdain for ignorance, social invisibility, and false recognition (Lenoir and Froelich 2016).

7. The exception is a social worker who worked in a school in Lagos de Moreno, Jalisco. She was not a teacher but provided support to migrant families.

8. Norma González reached this conclusion as follows: "It took a while for me to realize that what needed to change radically was the implicit ideology that had insidiously crept into my thinking: that to fix teachers was to fix schools. Although I continue to have the deepest respect for the teachers who have struggled through this process, I now wince as I recall my naïveté regarding the burdens under which teachers work. . . . An emancipatory social research agenda calls for empowering approaches that encourage and enable participants to change through self-reflection and a deeper understanding of their situations. Yet these empowering approaches must contend with a context that isolates practitioners, mutes autonomy, and pushes for standardization and homogenization" (2005, 3).

9. Translator's note: *Telesecundarias* are middle schools equivalent to the seventh, eighth, and ninth grades in junior high schools in the United States. This kind of school operates in small rural towns, where students receive televised lessons instead of regular classes. After the televised class is over, students are required to complete assignments with the support of a teacher or paraeducator.

10. The 2011 documentary directed by Eugenio Polgovsky, with a script by Mara Polgovsky, *Learning from Here and There*, produced with the sponsorship

of the Federal Ministry of Public Education through the Basic Education without Borders Program, masterfully expresses what we describe in this section.

11. The teachers were unaware of these programs because they were not offered during those years, at the state or federal level.

12. We remind the reader that the sample of the students in Morelos is not representative.

13. It is probable that what we observed in Morelos (the percentage of repeaters is lower than in the other states, and the students repeated grades mainly in the United States, not in Mexico) is the result of the attention provided in that state through the successful support program for international migrant children, underway since 2010.

14. The differences may seem small; however, in all cases the analysis of variance (ANOVA) reveals that the differences are significant with a very small degree of error.

15. Sometimes the loss of years in school is a consequence of the admission requirements in Mexico. Documented evidence indicates that child migrants and their families frequently face bureaucratic difficulties to enroll in Mexican schools, despite the 2015 regulatory modifications approved by Secretarial Agreement 286 in the Federal Ministry of Public Education (Secretaría de Educación Pública 2015). For more information on these types of obstacles, see Jacobo Suárez (2017a).

16. In 2019 we conducted two surveys that provided information about this issue: at least from our eight hundred households of Jalisco's random representative sample (n = 2798 individuals), we got clear evidence about the relation between international migration and school dropout rates (Zúñiga and Carrillo 2020; Carrillo and Zúñiga 2022).

17. Translator's note: *Sótano* means "basement," with the emphasis on the first syllable. This student emphasized the second syllable.

18. Let us not dwell on this topic, although it is of great importance. The children usually receive the support they need during the linguistic transition from written English to written Spanish from their families, not from their teachers.

19. For child migrants the letters and letter combinations that represent important challenges are *h, v, z, k,* double *r,* and double *l* and the digraph *ch.*

20. Feed-forward activation refers to the activation of two phonological codes that relate to one grapheme (Hino, Lupker, and Pexman 2002). Feed-backward activation is a process that refers to a phonological code that relates to multiple graphical codes: "When we asked Julio [transnational student in Nuevo León] to write Monterrey, his answer was 'Monteray.' This is a clear case of feed-backward activation.... Bilingual students ... may activate phonological and graphical representations from both languages. So, when we asked him to write Monterrey, Julio probably associated the phonemes /ei/ with its possible written forms

in English, like ay, as in hay; or ey, as in they. Therefore, the written form of the word, according to Julio, was 'Monteray'" (Panait and Zúñiga 2016, 242).

21. We did not find significant differences by gender. Both boys and girls indicated that the most difficult subjects in Mexican schools were mathematics and history.

22. This question was not included in the Nuevo León survey.

23. The differences between the various studies are explained partly by the varied methodological designs, the selection of different populations, or the definition of different variables of educational attainment.

24. Eunice Vargas Valle and Elizabeth Camacho Rojas's 2015 study also addresses educational delays and suggests a higher frequency of grade repetition and loss of school years. According to the data presented by the authors, children of recent immigration have more profound losses compared to the nonmigrants.

25. We use the notion of foreigner in the sense given by Alfred Schutz (1944, 501): "The stranger, therefore, approaches the other group as a newcomer in the true meaning of the term. At best he may be willing and able to share the present and the future with the approached group. . . . However, he remains excluded from such experiences of its past." The author clarifies that this applies only to adult individuals.

CHAPTER 7

1. Table 5 in chapter 2 shows that, in 2015, almost 30 percent of the U.S.-born children under six years old were living separated from one or both parents. Among the children ages twelve to fifteen, the proportion was around 37 percent for both U.S.- and Mexican-born international child migrants.

2. We have drawn on the Jalisco study only, because the survey administered in the schools of this state makes it possible to compare the parent-child separation among the families of children with migratory experience to those of children without migratory experience. The previous surveys do not provide data on the family dispersion among the second group of children.

3. This is true except for the cases where migration included imprisonment, deportation, illness, or the death of one parent. Inevitably, the interviews of the children who have lived through such circumstances express suffering and grief.

4. For a more detailed analysis of Itzcalli's trajectory, see Sánchez-Garcia, Hamann, and Zúñiga (2012).

5. Due to some of the details provided by Itzcalli during the interview, we think that she was born in New Jersey.

6. In Gabriel's case phone calls were a means, among others, of doing family from a distance. What the literature emphasizes is that families are permanently built and rebuilt; they do not exist, nor do they subsist, in a static way.

7. For a more detailed analysis of Andrés's trajectory, see Zúñiga and Hamann (2011).

8. Throughout this period the migration of single women who sometimes left their children in Mexico or were accompanied by them to the United States, began (Hondagneu-Sotelo 1994; Itzigsohn and Giorguli-Saucedo 2005; D'Aubeterre Buznego 2015).

CHAPTER 8

1. We use the terms "categories," "tags," "labels," and "nicknames" interchangeably to designate national or ethnic identifications. By doing this we adopt the theoretical positions elaborated by Rogers Brubaker (2004) and Andreas Wimmer (2013), who warn against the temptation to reify social groups and "identities," a temptation to which many contemporary sociological studies frequently succumb. Of the total number of children surveyed in Zacatecas in 2005, 84 percent lived in the United States with their father and/or mother. This is the case of 95 percent of the children in Puebla in 2009, 89 percent of the children in Jalisco, and 85 percent of the children in Morelos.

2. Translator's note: *Fresa* literally means "strawberry." However, *fresa* in Mexican slang means "smug" or "preppy."

3. Translator's note: Mexican slang. *Burro/burra* (donkey) is a derogatory term that means "fool."

4. We avoid the use of the noun "identity" and its derivatives. Our entire analysis follows the critical approaches elaborated by Brubaker (2004) under the proposal "beyond identity."

5. In the surveys used in Nuevo León and Zacatecas, only the national affiliations were included and not the subnational ethnic ones. We noticed this error just when we were designing the questionnaire to be administered in Puebla.

6. Certainly, the category "Mexican American" stems from the ethnoracial hierarchies of U.S. society. However, a significant proportion of the children who moved from the United States to Mexico have assimilated this label and, at least at the time of the survey, chose it because it somehow described their own experiences.

7. Among the options in the survey were also two categories of "other." The first asked respondents to fill in the blank with a category not on the list of options, and the second asked respondents to indicate "some of the above." Except in a few cases, these two options were not chosen by the children surveyed.

8. Unfortunately, we have not gathered enough data on the itineraries of the child migrants who adopt ethnic affiliations; this is a pending chapter in our research.

9. The literature is abundant on what is denominated "in-betweenness" in English, and we do not address it here because it would involve a long discussion. This notion is inspired by the works devoted to the analysis of the intersection of cultures. See McFee (1968) and Karttunen (1994).

10. The experience of the international child migrants in Mexico differs entirely from that described by David Pollock and Ruth Van Reken in their book about third-culture kids, the children of expatriates, missionaries, military officers, executives, or diplomats. During their childhood, they move to various countries around the world. The authors explicitly state, "the Third World does not have a specific relationship with the concept of the third culture," although some of the third-culture children have lived in a "third-world" country. In other words, according to the authors, the third-culture children are "first world" (whatever that is) and are part of an elite that the authors call "global nomads" (2001, 14).

CONCLUSION

1. See McCormick and Wahba (2003) and Chan and Tran (2011) for the return to Egypt and Vietnam; Christou (2006) for the return to Greece; Phillips and Potter (2009) for the return to Barbados; Vadean and Piracha (2009) for the return to Albania; López de Lera (2011) for the return to Chile and Argentina; Teerling (2011) for the return to Cyprus; Castro and Mejía (2013) for the return to the Andean countries; Jáuregui Díaz and Ávila Sánchez (2013) for the return to South America; Silveira, Siqueira, and Dominguez (2013) for the return to Brazil; Biao, Yeoh, and Toyota (2013) for the return to China; Robila (2012) for the return to Moldova; and Ní Laoire (2011) for the return of children to the Republic of Ireland.

2. See Hernández-León and Zúñiga (2016) for a deeper analysis of this historical context.

3. This figure does not include the retired U.S. population who live in Mexico only during certain periods of the year. They are not permanent residents, and therefore it is very likely that they are not included in large national surveys or censuses.

References

Acuña, Rodolfo. 1972. *Occupied America: The Chicano's Struggle toward Liberation*. New York: Harper and Row.

Aguilar, Rodrigo, and Silvia Giorguli. 2016. *Escolaridad en niños y jóvenes centroamericanos en México: Generaciones 1.5 y 2.0*. Central America–North America Migration Dialogue. Policy Brief Series. PB#10. Guadalajara: Centro de Investigaciones y Estudios Superiores en Antropología Social.

Aguilar Zepeda, Rodrigo. 2014. "Nos regresamos pa´tras: Diferencias en el desempeño escolar de niños y jóvenes en un contexto de migración de retorno." PhD diss., El Colegio de México.

Alanís Enciso, Fernando. 2007. *Que se queden allá: El gobierno de México y la repatriación de mexicanos en Estados Unidos (1934–1940)*. Tijuana: Colegio de la Frontera Norte/Colegio de San Luis.

Alvírez, David. 1973. "Consecuencias de la migración a los Estados Unidos: Los migrantes que regresan a México." In *Migración, estructura ocupacional y movilidad social*, edited by Jorge Balán, 114–31. Mexico City: Instituto de Investigaciones Sociales, UNAM.

Anderson, Benedict. 1991. *Imagined Communities: Reflections on the Origin and Spread of Nationalism*. New York: Verso.

Anderson, Jill, and Nin Solis. 2014. *Los Otros Dreamers*. Mexico City: Iniciativa Ciudadana/U.S.-Mexico Foundation.

Barth, Fredrik, ed. 1969. *Ethnic Groups and Boundaries: The Social Organization of Cultural Differences*. London: Allen and Unwin.

Batalova, Jeanne, and Michael Fix. 2010. *Children of Immigrants in US Schools: A Portrait*. Washington, DC: Migration Policy Institute, National Center on Immigrant Integration Policy.

BBVA Research. 2011. *Situación migración: México*. Mexico City: Fundación BBVA Bancomer/Servicio de Estudios Económicos del Grupo BBVA.

———. 2012. *Situación migración: México*. Mexico City: Fundación BBVA Bancomer/Servicio de Estudios Económicos del Grupo BBVA.

Berger, Peter L., and Thomas Luckmann. 1991. *The Social Construction of Reality*. Harlow, UK: Penguin Books.

Biao, Xiang, Brenda S. A. Yeoh, and Mika Toyota, eds. 2013. *Return: Nationalizing Transnational Mobility in Asia*. Durham, NC: Duke University Press.

Boehm, Deborah A. 2008. "'For My Children': Constructing Family and Navigating the State in the U.S.-Mexico Transnation." *Anthropological Quarterly* 81:777–802.

———. 2016. *Returned: Going and Coming in an Age of Deportation*. Berkeley: University of California Press.

Bressoux, Pascal, and Pascal Pansu. 2003. *Quand les enseignants jugent leurs élèves*. Paris: Presses Universitaires de France.

Brubaker, Rogers. 2004. *Ethnicity without Groups*. Cambridge, MA: Harvard University Press.

Bustamante, Juan José, and Carlos Alemán. 2007. "Perpetuating Split-Household Families: The Case of Mexican Sojourners in Mid-Michigan and Their Transnational Fatherhood Practices." *Migraciones Internacionales* 4:65–86.

Byrne, Olga. 2008. *Unaccompanied Children in the United States: A Literature Review*. New York: Vera Institute of Justice.

Camacho Rojas, Elizabeth. 2014. "Inserción escolar de niños de inmigración reciente de Estados Unidos a Baja California, México." Master's thesis, El Colegio de la Frontera Norte.

Capps, Randolph, Rosa María Castañeda, Ajay Cjaudry, and Robert Santos. 2007. *Paying the Price: The Impact of Immigration Raids on America's Children*. Washington, DC: National Council of La Raza/Urban Institute.

Carrillo, Eduardo, and Víctor Zúñiga. 2022. "Parcours scolaires fracturés des enfants migrant depuis les États-Unis vers le Mexique." In *Enfances et jeunesses en migration*, edited by Virginie Baby-Collin and Farida Souiah, 275–91. Paris: Cavalier Bleu.

Castillo, Manuel Ángel. 2012. "Extranjeros en México, 2000–2010." *Coyuntura Demográfica* 2:57–61.

Castro, Yeim, and William Mejía. 2013. "Retorno de migrantes a la comunidad andina (CAN): Diagnóstico de los procesos de retorno de colombianos, ecuatorianos, peruanos y bolivianos hacia sus países de origen." Paper presented at el Seminario Internacional sobre Migración de Retorno, El Colegio de México, CISAN, UNAM, Mexico City, May 6–7.

Cavagnoud Robin, Charles-Édouard de Suremain, and Palmira La Riva González. 2013. "Infancia y niños en las sociedades andinas contemporáneas." *Bulletin de l'Institut Français d'Études Andines* 42 (3): 323–585.

Ceriani, Pablo, ed. 2012. *Niñez detenida: Los derechos de los niños, niñas y adolescentes migrantes en la frontera México-Guatemala; Diagnóstico y propuestas para pasar del control migratorio a la protección integral de la niñez.* Mexico City: Fontamara/UNLA/Centro de Derechos Humanos Fray Matías de Córdova/Ford Foundation.

Chan, Yuk Wah, and Thi Le Thu Tran. 2011. "Recycling Migration and Changing Nationalisms: The Vietnamese Return Diaspora and Reconstruction of Vietnamese Nationhood." *Journal of Ethnic and Migration Studies* 37 (7): 1101–17.

Chavez, Leo R. 1988. "Sojourners and Settlers: The Case of Mexicans in the United States." *Human Organization* 47:95–108.

Cherlin, Andrew J. 2006. "On Single Mothers 'Doing' Family." *Journal of Marriage and Family* 68 (4): 800–803.

Christou, Anastasia. 2006. "American Dreams and European Nightmares: Experiences and Polemics of Second-Generation Greek-American Returning Migrants." *Journal of Ethnic and Migration Studies* 32 (5): 831–45.

Clifford, James. 1999. *Itinerarios transculturales.* Barcelona: Gedisa.

Coe, Cati. 2008. "The Structuring of Feeling in Ghanaian Transnational Families." *City and Society* 20:222–50.

Cortina, Regina, and Mónica Gendreau, eds. 2004. *Poblanos en Nueva York: Migración rural, educación y bienestar.* Mexico City: Universidad Iberoamericana Puebla.

Crawford, James. 2004. *Educating English Learners: Language Diversity in the Classroom.* Los Angeles: Bilingual Education Services.

Curran, Sara R., Steven Shafer, Katharine M. Donato, and Filiz Garip. 2006. "Mapping Gender and Migration in Sociological Scholarship: Is It Segregation or Integration?" *International Migration Review* 40 (1): 199–223.

D'Aubeterre Buznego, María Eugenia. 2015. "¡Aquí estamos las pahuatecas para hacerles el trabajo! Migración acelerada a Estados Unidos en la sierra norte de Puebla y transiciones en el patrón de movilidad de las mujeres." In *Lo que dejamos atrás . . . lo que vinimos a encontrar: Trabajo precario, nuevos patrones de asentamiento en Estados Unidos y retorno a México,* edited by María Eugenia D'Aubeterre Buznego and María Leticia Rivermar Pérez, 31–76. Puebla: Benemérita Universidad Autónoma de Puebla.

Despagne, Collete, and Mónica Jacobo. 2016. "Desafíos actuales de la escuela monolítica mexicana: El caso de los alumnos migrantes transnacionales." *Sinéctica* 47. https://sinectica.iteso.mx/index.php/SINECTICA/article /view/645.

Dobson, Madeleine E. 2009. "Unpacking Children in Migration Research." *Children's Geographies* 7 (3): 355–60.

Dreby, Joanna. 2010. *Divided by Borders: Mexican Migrants and Their Children*. Berkeley: University of California Press.

———. 2012. "The Burden of Deportation on Children in Mexican Immigrant Families." *Journal of Marriage and Family* 74:829–45.

———. 2015. *Everyday Illegal: When Policies Undermine Immigrant Families*. Oakland: University of California Press.

Dubar, Claude. 2000. *La socialisation*. Paris: Colin.

Dubet, François. 2007. "Injustices et reconnaissance." In *La quête de reconnaissance : Nouveau phénomène social total*, edited by Alain Caillé, 17–43. Paris: Découverte.

Durand, Jorge. 2002. "Sistema geográfico de distribución de la población migrante mexicana en Estados Unidos." *Espiral* 8 (23): 141–56.

———. 2004. "Ensayo teórico sobre la migración de retorno: El principio del rendimiento decreciente." *Cuadernos Geográficos* 35 (2): 103–16.

———. 2016. *Historia mínima de la migración México–Estados Unidos*. Mexico City: El Colegio de México.

Durand, Jorge, and Douglas S. Massey. 2003. *Clandestinos: Migración México–Estados Unidos en los albores del siglo XXI*. Mexico City: Universidad Autónoma de Zacatecas/Porrúa.

Durand, Jorge, Douglas S. Massey, and Chiara Capoferro. 2005. "The New Geography of Mexican Immigration." In Zúñiga and Hernández-León 2005, 1–20.

Durkheim, Émile. 1922. *Éducation et sociologie*. Paris : Librairie Félix Alcan.

Ensor, Marisa O., and Elzbieta M. Gozdziak, eds. 2010. *Children and Migration: At the Crossroads of Resiliency and Vulnerability*. New York: Palgrave Macmillan.

Fass, Paula S. 2007. *Children of a New World: Society, Culture, and Globalization*. New York: New York University Press.

Fitzgerald, David. 2008. *A Nation of Emigrants: How Mexico Manages Its Migration*. Berkeley: University of California Press.

Fix, Michael, and Wendy Zimmermann. 2001. "All under One Roof: Mixed-Status Families in an Era of Reform." *International Migration Review* 35 (2): 397–419.

Foucher, Michel. 1996. *L'invention de frontières*. Paris: Fondation pour les Études de Défense Nationale.

———. 2007. *L'obsession de frontières*. Saint-Amand-Montrond, France: Perrin.

Fuller, Richard C. 1939. "Social Problems." In *An Outline of the Principles of Sociology*, edited by Robert E. Park, 18–52. New York: Barnes and Noble.

Gallo, Karla. 2005. "Niñez migrante: Blanco fácil para la discriminación." In *Derechos humanos de los migrantes,* edited by Juan Carlos Gutiérrez, 133–44. Mexico City: Programa de Cooperación sobre Derechos Humanos, Comisión Europea y Secretaría de Relaciones Exteriores.

Gándara, Patricia. 2002. "Learning English in California: Guideposts for the Nation." In *Latinos Remaking America,* edited by Marcelo Suárez-Orozco and Mariela Páez, 339–58. Los Angeles: University of California Press.

Gándara, Patricia, and Frances Contreras. 2009. *The Latino Education Crisis: The Consequences of Failed Social Policies.* Cambridge, MA: Harvard University Press.

Gándara, Patricia, and Bryan Jensen, eds. 2021. *The Students We Share: Preparing US and Mexican Educators for Our Transnational Future.* Albany: State University of New York Press.

Gellner, Ernst. 1988. *Naciones y nacionalismo.* Mexico City: CONACULTA /Alianza.

Genova, Nicholas De. 2005. *Working the Boundaries: Race, Space, and "Illegality" in Mexican Chicago.* Durham, NC: Duke University Press.

Gérard-Varet, Louis-André, and Jean-Claude Passeron, eds. 1995. *Le modèle et l'enquête : Les usages du principe de rationalité dans les sciences sociales.* Paris : L'École des Hautes Études en Sciences Sociales.

Giorguli, Silvia. 2011. "Caminos divergentes hacia la adultez en México." In *Nupcialidad y familia en la América Latina actual,* edited by Georgina Binstock and Joice Melo Vieira, 123–63. Campinas: Universidade Estatual de Campinas/Asociación Latinoamericana de Población.

Giorguli, Silvia, and Adela Angoa. 2019. "¿Una nueva era de la migración internacional entre México y Estados Unidos?" In *La dinámica demográfica de México en el siglo XXI,* edited by Silvia Giorguli and Jaime Sobrino, 83–128. Mexico City: El Colegio de México.

Giorguli, Silvia, Víctor M. García, and Claudia Masferrer. 2016. *A Migration System in the Making: Demographic Dynamics and Migration Policies in North America and the Northern Triangle of Central America.* Mexico City: El Colegio de México.

Giorguli, Silvia, and Edith Y. Gutiérrez. 2011a. "Is There Any Evidence of Changes in the Patterns of Mexican Migration to US? A Very Preliminary Analysis Using the 2010 Mexican Census." Paper presented at Reunión del Estudio Binacional, Mexico City, May 23.

———. 2011b. "Niños y jóvenes en el contexto de la migración internacional entre México y Estados Unidos." *Coyuntura Demográfica* 1:21–25.

———. 2012. "Children and Youth in the Context of International Mobility in Mexico." Paper presented at the Annual Meeting of Population Association of America, San Francisco, CA, May 3–5.

Giorguli, Silvia, Bryant Jensen, and Adela Angoa. 2017. "Las interacciones entre las experiencias migratorias de los padres y el logro educativo de los hijos." Paper presented at Seminario 30 Años del Mexican Migration Project, El Colegio de México, Mexico City, October 26.

Giorguli, Silvia, Bryant Jensen, Frank Bean, Susan Brown, Adam Sawyer, and Víctor Zúñiga. 2021. "Bienestar educativo para los hijos de inmigrantes mexicanos en Estados Unidos y en México." In *La década en que cambió la migración: Enfoque binacional del bienestar de los migrantes mexicanos en Estados Unidos y México*, edited by Agustín Escobar Latapí and Claudia Masferrer, 183–276. Mexico City: El Colegio de México/CIESAS.

Giorguli, Silvia, and Itzam Serratos López. 2009. "El impacto de la migración internacional sobre la asistencia escolar, ¿paradojas de la migración?" In Leite and Giorguli 2009, 313–44.

Gitter, Seth R., Robert J. Gitter, and Douglas Southgate. 2008. "The Impact of Return Migration to Mexico." *Estudios Económicos* 23 (1): 3–23.

Glick, Jennifer E. 2010. "Connecting Complex Processes: A Decade of Research on Immigrant Families." *Journal of Marriage and Family* 72 (3): 498–515.

Golash-Boza, Tanya. 2015. *Deported: Immigrant Policing, Disposable Labor and Global Capitalism*. New York: New York University Press.

Gonzales, Roberto G. 2007. *Wasted Talent and Broken Dreams: The Lost Potential of Undocumented Students*. Washington, DC: Immigration Policy Center, American Immigration Law Foundation.

———. 2011. "Learning to Be Illegal: Undocumented Youth and Shifting Legal Contexts in the Transition to Adulthood." *American Sociological Review* 76 (4): 602–19.

Gonzales, Roberto G., and Leo R. Chavez. 2012. "'Awakening to a Nightmare': Abjectivity and Illegality in the Lives of Undocumented 1.5-Generation Latino Immigrants in the United States." *Current Anthropology* 53 (3): 255–81.

González, Norma. 2005. "The Anthropologist's View, Introduction: Theorizing Practices." In *Funds of Knowledge: Theorizing Practices in Households, Communities and Classrooms*, edited by Norma González, Luis C. Moll and Cathy Amanti, 2–3. Mahwah, NJ: Erlbaum.

González-Barrera, Ana, and Mark Hugo López. 2013. "A Demographic Portrait of Mexican-Origin Hispanics in the United States." Pew Research Center. May 21, 2006. www.pewhispanic.org/2013/05/01/a-demographic-portrait-of-mexican-originhispanics-in-the-united-states/.

González Quiroga, Miguel. 1993. "La puerta de México: Los comerciantes texanos y el noreste mexicano, 1850–1880." *Estudios Sociológicos* 11 (31): 209–36.

Goode, Judith G., Jo Anne Schneider, and Suzanne Blanc. 1992. "Transcending Boundaries and Closing Ranks: How Schools Shape Interrelations." In Lamphere 1992b, 173–213.

Hackenberg, Robert A. 1995. "Joe Hill Died For Your Sins." In *Any Way You Cut It: Meat-Processing and Small-Town America*, edited by Donald D. Stull, Michael J. Broadway, and David Griffith, 232–64. Lawrence: University Press of Kansas.

Hagan, Jacqueline, Brianna Castro, and Nestor Rodriguez. 2010. "The Effects of U.S. Deportation Policies on Immigrant Families and Communities: Cross-Border Perspectives." *North Carolina Law Review* 88:1799–824.

Hagan, Jaqueline, Rubén Hernández-León, and Jean-Luc Demonsant. 2015. *Skills of the Unskilled: Work and Mobility among Mexican Migrants.* Oakland: University of California Press.

Hamann, Edmund T. 2001. "Theorizing the Sojourner Student (with a Sketch of Appropriate School Responsiveness)." In *Negotiating Transnationalism: Selected Papers on Refugees and Immigrants*, edited by Mary Carol Hopkins and Nancy Wellmeier, 32–71. Arlington, VA: American Anthropological Association.

———. 2003. *The Educational Welcome of Latinos in the New South.* Westport, CT: Praeger.

Hamann, Edmund T., and Víctor Zúñiga. 2011. "Schooling, National Affinity(ies), and Transnational Students in Mexico." In *Hyphenated Selves: Construction, Negotiation and Mediation of Immigrant Identity within schools; Transnational Dialogues*, edited by Saloshna Vandeyar, 57–72. Amsterdam: Pretoria, Rozenberg/University of South Africa Press.

Hamann, Edmund T., Víctor Zúñiga, and Juan Sánchez García. 2006. "Pensando en Cynthia y su hermana: Educational Implications of U.S./Mexico Transnationalism for Children." *Journal of Latinos and Education* 5 (4): 253–74.

———. 2008. "From Nuevo León to the USA and Back Again: Transnational Students in Mexico." *Journal of Immigrant and Refugee Studies* 6 (1): 60–84.

———. 2017. "Identifying the Anthropological in the Mixed Methods Study of Transnational Student in Mexican Schools." *Current Anthropology* 58 (1): 124–32.

———. 2022. *Lo que los maestros mexicanos conviene que conozcan sobre la educación en Estados Unidos.* Monterrey: Universidad Autónoma de Nuevo León; Lincoln: University of Nebraska Press.

Hamilton, Erin R., Claudia Masferrer, and Paola Langer. 2023. "U.S. Citizen Children De Facto Deported to Mexico." *Population and Development Review* 49 (1): 175–203.

Harklau, Linda, Kay Mi Losey, and Meryl Siegal, eds. 2009. *Generation 1.5 Meets College Composition: Issues in the Teaching of Writing to U.S.-Educated Learned of ESL.* Mahwah, NJ: Erlbaum.

Heller, Agnes. 1977. *Sociología de la vida cotidiana.* Barcelona: Península.

Hernández-León, Rubén. 2008. *Metropolitan Migrants: The Migration of Urban Mexicans to the United States*. Oakland: University of California Press.

Hernández-León, Rubén, and Víctor Zúñiga. 2016. "Contemporary Return Migration from the United States to Mexico: Focus on Children, Youth, Schools and Families." *Mexican Studies/Estudios Mexicanos* 32 (2): 171–98.

Hertz, Rosanna. 2006. "Talking about 'Doing' Family." *Journal of Marriage and Family* 68 (4): 796–99.

Hino, Yashushi, Stephen J. Lupker, and Penny M. Pexman. 2002. "Ambiguity and Synonymy Effects in Lexical Decision, Naming, and Semantic Categorization Tasks: Interactions between Orthography, Phonology, and Semantics." *Journal of Experimental Psychology: Learning, Memory and Cognition* 28 (4): 686–713.

Hirai, Shinji. 2014. "La nostalgia: Emociones y significados en la migración transnacional." *Nueva Antropología* 27 (81): 77–94.

Hirai, Shinji, and Rebeca Sandoval. 2016. "El itinerario subjetivo como herramienta de análisis: Las experiencias de los jóvenes de la generación 1.5 que retornan a México." *Mexican Studies/Estudios Mexicanos* 32 (2): 276–301.

Hobsbawm, Eric J. 1990. *Nations and Nationalism since 1780*. Cambridge: Cambridge University Press.

Hondagneu-Sotelo, Pierrette. 1994. *Gendered Transitions: Mexican Experiences of Immigration*. Berkeley: University of California Press.

INEGI (Instituto Nacional de Estadística, Geografía e Informática). 1990. *XI Censo General de Población y Vivienda, 1990*. Mexico City: INEGI.

———. 2000. *XII Censo General de Población y Vivienda, 2000*. Mexico City: INEGI.

———. 2010. *XIII Censo General de Población y Vivienda, 2010*. Mexico City: INEGI.

———. 2011. *XI Censo General de Población y Vivienda, 2011*. Mexico City: INEGI.

———. 2014. *Encuesta Nacional de Dinámica Demográfica 2014*. Mexico City: INEGI.

———. 2015. *Encuesta Intercensal 2015*. Mexico City: INEGI.

———. 2020. *XIV Censo General de Población y Vivienda, 2020*. Mexico City: INEGI.

Itzigsohn, José, and Silvia Giorguli-Saucedo. 2005. "Incorporation, Transnationalism, and Gender: Immigrant Incorporation and Transnational Participation as Gendered Processes." *International Migration Review* 39 (4): 895–920.

Jacobo Suárez, Mónica. 2017a. "De regreso a 'casa' y sin apostilla: Estudiantes mexicoamericanos en México." *Sinéctica* 48. https://sinectica.iteso.mx/index.php/SINECTICA/article/view/712.

————. 2017b. "Desafíos para estudiantes binacionales y transnacionales."
Paper presented at Education Summit: Bilateral Relations between Mexico
and California, Mexico City, June 14–16.

Jáuregui Díaz, José Alfredo, and María de Jesús Ávila Sánchez. 2013. "Tenden-
cias en la migración de retorno de los latinoamericanos desde España
2002–11." Unpublished paper. Universidad Autónoma de Nuevo León,
Instituto de Investigaciones Sociales.

Jensen, An-Margritt, and Lorna McKee. 2003. *Children and the Changing
Family: Between Transformation and Negotiation.* New York: Routledge
Falmer.

Jensen, Bryant, Silvia Giorguli, and Eduardo Hernández. 2013. "International
Family Migration and the Academic Achievement of the 9th Grade Students
in Mexico." Paper presented at the Annual Meeting of Population Association of America, New Orleans, April 11–13.

————. 2016. "International Migration and the Academic Performance of
Mexican Adolescents." *International Migration Review* 50 (3): doi:10.1111/
imre.12307.

Jensen, Bryant, Rebeca Mejía Arauz, and Rodrigo Aguilar Zepeda. 2017. "La
enseñanza equitativa para los niños retornados a México." *Sinéctica* 48.
https://sinectica.iteso.mx/index.php/SINECTICA/article/view/756.

Jones-Correa, Michael. 2012. *Contested Ground: Immigration in the United
States.* Washington, DC: Migration Policy Institute.

Jones-Correa, Michael, and Els de Graauw. 2013. "The Illegality Trap: The
Politics of Immigration and the Lens of Illegality." *Daedalus: The Journal of
the American Academy of Arts and Sciences* 142 (3): 185–98.

Kandel, William, and Douglas S. Massey. 2002. "The Culture of Mexican
Migration: A Theoretical and Empirical Analysis." *Social Forces* 80 (3):
981–1004.

Karttunen, Frances. 1994. *Between Worlds: Interpreters, Guides, and Survi-
vors.* New Brunswick, NJ: Rutgers University Press.

Kleyn, Tatyana. 2022. *Leaving, Learning, and Languaging across Borders:
Students between the US and Mexico.* New York: Taylor and Francis.

Lahaie, Claudia, Jeffrey A. Hayes, Tinka Markham Piper, and Jody Heymann.
2009. "Work and Family Divided across Borders: The Impact of Parental
Migration on Mexican Children in Transnational Families." *Community,
Work and Family* 12 (3): 299–312.

Lamphere, Louise. 1992a. "Introduction: The Shaping of Diversity." In Lamphere 1992b, 1–34.

Lamphere, Louise, ed. 1992b. *Structuring Diversity: Ethnographic Perspectives on the New Immigration.* Chicago: University of Chicago Press.

Leal, David L., Nestor P. Rodríguez, and Gary P. Freeman. 2016. "Introduction:
The New Era of Restriction." In *Migration in an Era of Restriction and*

Recession: Sending and Receiving Nations in a Changing Global Environment, edited by David L. Leal and Nestor P. Rodriguez, 1–23. New York: Springer.

Le Blanc, Guillaume. 2009. *L'invisibilité sociale.* Paris: Presses Universitaires de France.

Leite, Paula, and Silvia E. Giorguli, eds. 2009. *El estado de la migración: Las políticas públicas ante los retos de la migración mexicana a Estados Unidos.* Mexico City: CONAPO.

Lenoir, Yves, and Alessandra Froelich. 2016. "La socialisation scolaire à l'aune des processus de reconnaissance dans les classes du primaire au Québec." In Lenoir, Froelich, and Zúñiga, *Reconnaissance à l'école*, 79–108.

Lenoir, Yves, Alessandra Froelich, and Víctor Zúñiga. 2016. *La reconnaissance à l'école: Perspectives internationales.* Québec: Presses de l'Université Laval.

Light, Ivan. 2006. *Deflecting Immigration: Networks, Markets and Regulation in Los Angeles.* New York: Sage.

Llopis Goig, Ramón. 2007. "El 'nacionalismo metodológico' como obstáculo en la investigación sociológica sobre migraciones internacionales." *EMPIRIA: Revista de Metodología de Ciencias Sociales* 13:101–17.

López Castro, Gustavo. 2006. "Migración, educación y socialización: Adolescentes mexicanos en la migración exterior." *Ethos Educativo* 36–37:61–78.

López de Lera, Diego. 2011. "Migración de retorno: El caso de España." Paper presented at Seminario Permanente sobre Migración Internacional, El Colegio de la Frontera Norte, Tijuana, May 29.

Loredo, Maggie. 2016. "Otros dreamers en acción (ODA): The Experiences of Student Returnees." Paper presented at Simposio Binacional: The Students We Share/Los Estudiantes que Compartimos, University of California, Mexico Iniciative, Mexico City, September 12–13.

Ma Mung, Emmanuel. 2000. *La diaspora chinoise: Géographie d'une migration.* Paris: Ophrys.

Mancillas Bazán, Celia. 2009. "Migración de menores mexicanos a Estados Unidos." In Leite and Giorguli 2009, 211–46.

Martínez Curiel, Enrique. 2016. *Los que se van y los que se quedan: Familia, migración, educación y jóvenes en transición a la adultez en contextos binacionales.* Guadalajara: JAL, Universidad de Guadalajara.

Masferrer, Claudia. 2012. "Cuando el origen no es destino: Ciclo de vida y el retorno como posibles vínculos entre la migración interna e internacional." *Coyuntura Demográfica* 2:45–50.

———. 2021. *Atlas of Return Migration: From the United States to Mexico.* Mexico City: El Colegio de México.

Masferrer, Claudia, and Bryan Roberts. 2012. "Going Back Home? Changing Demography and Geography of Mexican Return Migration." *Population Research and Policy Review* 31 (4): 465–96.

Massey, Douglas S., Jorge Durand, and Nolan J. Malone. 2002. *Beyond Smoke and Mirrors: Mexican Immigration in an Era of Economic Integration*. New York: Sage Foundation.

Massey, Douglas S., Jorge Durand, and Karen Pren. 2016. "Why Border Enforcement Backfired?" *American Journal of Sociology* 121 (5): 1557–600.

McCormick, Barry, and Jackline Wahba. 2003. "Return International Migration and Geographical Inequality: The Case of Egypt." *Journal of African Economies* 12 (4): 500–532.

McFee, Malcom. 1968. "The 150% Man: A Product of Blackfeet Acculturation." *American Anthropologist* 70 (6): 1096–107.

Mead, Margaret. 1972. *Educación y cultura en Nueva Guinea*. Mexico City: Paidós.

Mier y Terán, María, and Cecilia Rabell. 2003. "Inequalities in Mexican Children Schooling." *Journal of Comparative Family Studies* 34:435–54.

Mummert, Gail. 2012. "Pensando las familias transnacionales desde los relatos de vida: Análisis longitudinal de la convivencia intergeneracional." In *Métodos cualitativos y su aplicación empírica: Por los caminos de la investigación sobre migración internacional*, edited by Marina Ariza and Laura Velasco, 151–86. Mexico City: UNAM/Colegio de la Frontera Norte.

Ní Laoire, Caitriona. 2011. "Narratives of 'Innocent Irish Childhoods': Return Migration and Intergenerational Family Dynamics." *Journal of Ethnic and Migration Studies* 37 (8): 1253–71.

Ní Laoire, Caitriona, Naomi Tyrrel, and Fina Carpena Méndez. 2012. "Children and Young People on the Move: Geographies of Child and Youth Migration." *Geography* 97 (3): 129–34.

Nobles, Jenna. 2011. "Parenting from Abroad: Migration, Nonresident Father Involvement, and Children's Education in Mexico." *Journal of Marriage and Family* 73 (4): 729–46.

———. 2013. "Migration and Father Absence: Shifting Family Structure in Mexico." *Demography* 50 (4): 1303–14.

Olvera, José Juan, and Carolina Muela. 2016. "Sin familia en México: Redes sociales alternativas para la migración de retorno de jóvenes mexicanos deportados con experiencia carcelaria en Texas." *Mexican Studies/Estudios Mexicanos* 32 (2): 302–27.

Ordaz, José Luis, and Juan José Li Ng. 2013. *Perfil socioeconómico y de inserción laboral de los migrantes mexicanos de retorno, análisis comparativo entre 2005-2007 y 2008-2012*. Mexico City: BBVA Research/Fundación Bancomer.

Orellana, Marjorie Faulstich. 2001. "The Work Kids Do: Mexican and Central American Immigrant Children's Contributions to Households, Schools, and Community in California." *Harvard Educational Review* 7 (3): 366–89.

———. 2016. *Immigrant Children in Transcultural Spaces: Language, Learning and Love.* New York: Routledge.

Orellana, Marjorie Faulstich, Barrie Thorne, Anna Chee, and Wan Shun Eva Lam. 2001. "Transnational Childhoods, the Participation of Children in Processes of Family Migration." *Social Problems* 48 (4): 572–91.

Orfield, Gary. 1998. "Commentary." In M. Suárez-Orozco 1998, 276–80.

———. 2001. *Schools More Separate: Consequences of a Decade of Resegregation.* Cambridge, MA: Civil Rights Project, Harvard University.

———. 2005. "Introduction: The Southern Dilemma." In *School Resegregation: Must the South Turn Back?,* edited by John Charles Boger and Gary Orfield, 1–25. Chapel Hill: University of North Carolina Press.

Panait, Catalina. 2011. "Cuentos de mis escuelitas: La princesa y el hombre de hojalata; Transiciones, rupturas e identidades lingüísticas en alumnos con escolaridad circular." Master's thesis, Universidad de Monterrey.

Panait, Catalina, and Víctor Zúñiga. 2016. "Children Circulating between the U.S. and Mexico: Fractured Schooling and Linguistic Ruptures." *Mexican Studies/Estudios Mexicanos* 32 (2): 226–51.

Park, Robert E. 1950. *Race and Culture.* Glencoe, IL: Free Press.

Park, Robert E., and Eduard Burgess. 1921. *Introduction to the Science of Sociology.* Chicago: University of Chicago Press.

Parreñas Salazar, Rhacel. 2005. *Children of Global Migration: Transnational Families and Gendered Woes.* Stanford, CA: Stanford University Press.

———. 2008. "Transnational Fathering: Gendered Conflicts, Distant Disciplining, and Emotional Gaps." *Ethnic and Migration Studies* 34:1057–72.

Passel, Jeffrey S. 2011. "Flujos migratorios México-Estados Unidos de 1990 a 2010: Un análisis preliminar basado en las fuentes de información estadounidenses." *Coyuntura Demográfica* 1:15–20.

Passel, Jeffrey, D'vera Cohn, and Ana González-Barrera. 2012. "Net Migration from Mexico Falls to Zero and Perhaps Less." Pew Research Center. April 23, 2012. www.pewhispanic.org/2012/04/23/net-migration-from-mexico-falls-tozero-and-perhaps-less/.

Payet, Jean-Paul. 2016. "Les cadres de référence de l'agir scolaire: Égalité, équité, reconnaissance." In Lenoir, Froelich, and Zúñiga 2016, 109–28.

Payet, Jean-Paul, Frédérique Giuliani, and Denis Laforgue, eds. 2008. *La voix des acteurs faibles: De l'indignité à la reconnaissance.* Rennes, France: Presses Universitaires de Rennes.

Péquignot, Bruno, and Pierre Tripier. 2000. *Les fondements de la sociologie.* Paris: Nathan.

Péquignot, Bruno, Pierre Tripier, Víctor Zúñiga, and Roland Pfefferkorn. 2022. *Les sources de la sociologie.* Brussels: Éditions de l'Université de Bruxelle.

Pérez Amador, Julieta, and Silvia Giorguli. 2018. "Child Marriage and Early Transitions to Adulthood in Mexico." In *Developmental Science and Sustain-*

able Development Goals for Children and Youth, edited by Suman Verma and Ann Petersen, 239–56. Cham, Switzerland: Springer.

Perlmann, Joel, and Roger Waldinger. 1999. "Immigrants, Past and Present." In *The Handbook of International Migration: The American Experience,* edited by Charles Hirschman, Philip Kasinitz, and Josh DeWind, 223–38. New York: Sage Foundation.

Phillips, Joan, and Robert B. Potter. 2009. "Questions of Friendship and Degrees of Transnationality among Second-Generation Return Migrants to Barbados." *Journal of Ethnic and Migration Studies* 35 (4): 669–88.

Polgovsky, Eugenio, and Mara Polgovsky. 2011. *Aprendiendo de aquí y de allá.* Mexico City: Secretaría de Educación Pública, Programa de Educación Básica sin Fronteras.

Pollock, David, and Ruth Van Reken. 2001. *Third Culture Kids: Growing Up among Worlds.* Boston: Brealey.

Portes, Alejandro, ed. 1996. *The New Second Generation.* New York: Sage Foundation.

Quiroz, Pamela A. 2001. "The Silencing of Latino Student 'Voice': Puerto Rican and Mexican Narratives in Eight Grade and High School." *Anthropology and Education Quarterly* 32 (3): 326–49.

Ramírez, Jorge Ariel. 2013. "La construcción de expectativas del curso de vida en los jóvenes de familias con actividad migratoria en Axochiapan, Morelos." PhD diss., El Colegio de México.

Ramírez García, Telésforo, and Liliana Meza González. 2011. "Emigración México–Estados Unidos antes y después de la recesión económica estadounidense." In *La situación demográfica en México,* edited by Consejo Nacional de Población, 241–60. Mexico City: CONAPO.

Rendall, Michael S., and Berna M. Torr. 2008. "Emigration and Schooling among Second-Generation Mexican-American Children." *International Migration Review* 42 (3): 729–38.

Richek, Margaret Ann, Joanne Schudt Caldwell, Joyce Holt Jennings, and Janet W. Lerner. 2001. *Reading Problems: Assessment and Teaching Strategies.* Boston: Allyn and Bacon.

Robila, Mihaela. 2012. "The Impact of Migration on Children's Psychological and Academic Functioning in the Republic of Moldova." *International Migration* 52 (3): 221–35.

Rodríguez, Néstor. 1996. "The Battle for the Border: Notes on Autonomous Migration, Transnational Communities, and the State." *Social Justice* 23 (3): 21–37.

———. 2008. "Los mexicoamericanos: Quiénes somos y quiénes seremos." In Zúñiga 2008, 63–70.

Rojas-García, Georgina. 2013. "Transitioning from School Work as a Mexican 1.5er: Upward Mobility and Glass-Ceiling Assimilation among College

Students in California." *Annals of the American Academy of Political and Social Science* 648 (1): 87–101.

Román González, Betsabé. 2017. "'Pa' cuando me regrese': Can We Speak in English? Trayectorias de menores migrantes que llegan a México." PhD diss., Tecnológico de Monterrey.

Román González, Betsabé, Eduardo Carrillo, and Rubén Hernández-León. 2016. "Moving to the 'Homeland': Children's Narratives of Migration from the United States to Mexico." *Mexican Studies/Estudios Mexicanos* 32 (2): 252–75.

Ruiz, Richard. 1984. "Orientations in Language Planning." *NABE Journal* 8 (2): 15–34.

Rumbaut, Ruben G. 1994. "The Crucible Within: Ethnic, Identity, Self-Esteem, and Segmented Assimilation among Children of Immigrants." *International Migration Review* 28 (4): 748–94.

———. 2004. "Ages, Life Stages, and Generational Cohorts: Decomposing the Immigrant First and Second Generations in the United States." *International Migration Review* 38 (3): 1160–205.

Rumbaut, Ruben G., and Kenji Ima. 1988. *The Adaptation of Southeast Asian Refugee Youth: A Comparative Study*. Washington, DC: Office of Refugee Resettlement.

Sánchez-Garcia, Juan, Edmund T. Hamann, and Víctor Zúñiga. 2012. "What the Youngest Transnational Students Have to Say about Their Transition from U.S. Schools to Mexican Ones." *Diaspora, Indigenous, and Minority Education* 6 (3): 157–71.

Sandoval, Rebeca, and Víctor Zúñiga. 2016. "¿Quiénes están retornando de Estados Unidos a México? Una revisión crítica de la literatura reciente (2008–2015)." *Mexican Studies/Estudios Mexicanos* 32 (2): 328–56.

Sawyer, Adam. 2014. "Is Money Enough? The Effect of Migrant Remittances on Parental Aspirations and Youth Educational Attainment in Rural Mexico." *International Migration Review* 50 (1): 231–66.

Schneider, Barbara, and Linda J. Waite. 2005. *Being Together, Working Apart: Dual-Career Families and the Work-Life Balance*. Cambridge: Cambridge University Press.

Schutz, Alfred. 1944. "The Stranger: An Essay in Social Psychology." *American Journal of Sociology* 49 (6): 499–507.

Schwartz, Ana, Judith Kroll, and Michele Diaz. 2007. "Reading Words in Spanish and English: Mapping Orthography to Phonology in Two Languages." *Language and Cognitive Processes* 22 (1): 106–29.

Secretaría de Educación Pública. 2013. *Plan sectorial de educación, 2013–2018*. Mexico City: SEP.

———. 2015. *Acuerdo número 07/06/15 por el que se modifica el diverso 286 por el que se establecen los lineamientos que determinan las normas y criterios generales a que se ajustarán la revalidación de estudios realizados en el extranjero.* Mexico City: Diario Oficial de la Federación.

———. 2016. *El modelo educativo 2016: El planteamiento pedagógico de la reforma educativa.* Mexico City: Secretaría de Educación Pública.

Secretaría de Gobernación. 2013. *Plan nacional de desarrollo, 2013–2018.* Mexico City: Diario Oficial de la Federación.

Silveira Moreira, Júlio Da, Sueli Siqueira, and Devani Tomaz Dominguez. 2013. "El retorno de Estados Unidos a Brasil: Panorama de la reintegración de los migrantes en la región de Governador Valadares." Paper presented at Seminario Internacional sobre Migración de Retorno, CISAN, UNAM, Mexico City, May 6–7.

Smith, Michael Peter. 1994. "Can You Imagine? Transnational Migration and the Globalization of Grassroots Politics." *Social Text* 39:15–33.

Smith, Michael Peter, and Luis Eduardo Guarnizo. 1998. "The Locations of Transnationalism." In *Transnationalism from Below,* edited by Michael Peter Smith and Luis Eduardo Guarnizo, 3–34. New Brunswick, NJ: Transaction.

Smith, Robert C. 2006. *Mexican New York: Transnational Lives of New Immigrants.* Berkeley: University of California Press.

Suárez-Orozco, Carola, Hee Jin Bang, and Ha Yean Kim. 2011. "I Felt Like My Heart Was Staying Behind: Psychological Implications of Family Separations and Reunifications for Immigrant Youth." *Journal of Adolescent Research* 26 (2): 222–57.

Suárez-Orozco, Carola, and Marcelo M. Suárez-Orozco. 2001. *Children of Immigration.* Cambridge, MA: Harvard University Press.

Suárez-Orozco, Carola, Irina L. G. Todorova, and Josephine Louie. 2002. "Making Up for Lost Time: The Experience of Separation and Reunification among Immigrant Families." *Family Process* 41 (4): 625–43.

Suárez-Orozco, Marcelo, ed. 1998. *Crossings: Mexican Immigration in Interdisciplinary Perspectives.* Cambridge, MA: Harvard University Press.

Taylor, Paul, Mark Hugo Lopez, Jeffrey S. Passel, and Seth Motel. 2011. *Unauthorized Immigrants: Length of Residency, Patterns of Parenthood.* Washington, DC: Pew Hispanic Center.

Tedesco, Juan Carlos. 2011. "La escuela justa." In *La escuela incluyente y justa: Antología comentada al servicio de los maestros de México,* edited by Víctor Zúñiga, 22–27. Monterrey: Fondo Editorial Nuevo León.

Teerling, Janine. 2011. "The Development of New 'Third-Cultural Spaces of Belonging': British-Born Cypriot 'Return' Migrants in Cyprus." *Journal of Ethnic and Migration Studies* 37 (7): 1079–99.

Terán, J. Diego, Silvia E. Giorguli, and Landy Sánchez. 2015. "Reconfiguraciones de la geografía del retorno de Estados Unidos a México, 2000–2010: Un reto para las políticas públicas." In *La situación demográfica en México,* edited by Consejo Nacional de Población, 285–305. Mexico City: CONAPO, 2015.

Terrail, Jean-Pierre. 2009. *De l'oralité: Essai sur l'égalité des intelligences.* Paris: La Dispute.

Thao, Vu Thi, and Jytte Agergaard. 2012. "'Doing' Family: Female Migrants and Family Transition in Rural Vietnam." *Asian Population Studies* 8 (1): 103–19.

Thomas, William Isaac, and Florian Znaniecki. 1958. *The Polish Peasant in Europe and in America.* New York: Dover.

Tripier, Pierre. 2010. "Gramáticas de acción, retorno de experiencia y arte para resolver los problemas." *Confines* 6 (11): 13–36.

Trueba, Enrique T. 1998. "The Education of Mexican Immigrant Children." In M. Suárez-Orozco 1998, 253–75.

Universidad de Monterrey. 2015. *Databases of the International Migration: Interinstitutional Seminar; School, Family, and Return (2005–2015).* Monterrey: CIESAS, IIEPE, ITESM, UCLA, UNL, and UDEM.

Urban Mapping. 2013. "San Diego, California Neighborhood Map." Accessed September 9, 2018. www.city-data.com/neighborhood/Clairemont-San-Diego-CA.html.

U.S. Census Bureau. 2016. *Current Population Survey, 2015 and 2016.* Washington, DC: U.S. Census Bureau.

Vadean, Florin P., and Matloob Piracha. 2009. *Circular Migration or Permanent Return: What Determines Different Forms of Migration?* Discussion Paper 4287. Bonn, Germany: Forschungsinstitut zur Zukunft der Arbeit.

Valdés, Guadalupe. 2001. *Learning and Not Learning English.* New York: Teachers College Press.

———. 2003. *Expanding Definitions of Giftedness: The Case of Young Interpreters from Immigrant Communities.* Mahwah, NJ: Erlbaum.

Valdés, Guadalupe, Sarah Capitelli, and Laura Alvarez. 2011. *Latino Children Learning English: Steps in the Journey.* New York: Teachers College Press/Columbia University.

Valdéz Gardea, Gloria Ciria. 2011. "Antropología, migración y niñez." In *La antropología de la migración: Niños y jóvenes migrantes de la globalización,* edited by Gloria Ciria Valdéz Gardea, 11–19. Hermosillo: El Colegio de Sonora/Universidad Autónoma de Sinaloa.

Valdéz Gardea, Gloria Ciria, and Ismael García Castro, eds. 2017. *Tránsito y retorno de la niñez migrante: Epílogo en la administración Trump.* Hermosillo: El Colegio de Sonora/Universidad Autónoma de Sinaloa.

Valdéz Gardea, Gloria Ciria, Liza Fabiola Ruiz Peralta, Óscar Bernardo Rivera García, and Ramiro Antonio López. 2018. "Menores migrantes de retorno: problemática académica y proceso administrativo en el sistema escolar sonorense." *Región y Sociedad* 30 (72). https://doi.org/10.22198/rys.2018.72. a904.

Vargas Valle, Eunice, and Elizabeth Camacho Rojas. 2015. "¿Cambiarse de escuela? Inasistencia y rezago escolar de los niños de migración reciente de Estados Unidos a México." *Norteamérica* 10 (2): 157–86.

Vázquez, Josefina Zoraida. 1975. *Nacionalismo y educación en México.* Mexico City: El Colegio de México.

Villaseñor, Blanca, and José Moreno, eds. 2006. *La esperanza truncada: Menores deportados por la garita Mexicali-Caléxico.* Mexico City: Albergue del Desierto/SEDESOL.

Waldinger, Roger. 2006. "Transnationalisme des immigrants et présence du pasée." *Revue Européenne des Migrations Internationales* 22 (2): 23–41.

———. 2008a. "El aquí y el allá: Los migrantes entre su país de origen y el país de destino." In Zúñiga 2008, 49–61.

———. 2008b. "Between 'Here' and 'There': Immigrant Cross-Border Activities and Loyalties." *International Migration Review* 42 (1): 3–29.

———. 2015. *The Cross-Border Connection: Immigrants, Emigrants, and Their Homelands.* Cambridge, MA: Harvard University Press.

———. 2021. "Niñas y niños en la migración de Estados Unidos a México: La generación 0.5." *Ethnic and Racial Studies* 44 (3): 524–27.

Waldinger, Roger, and David Fitzgerald. 2004. "Transnationalism in Question." *American Journal of Sociology* 109 (5): 1177–95.

Warner, William L., and Leo Srole. 1945. *The Social Systems of American Ethnic Groups.* New Haven, CT: Yale University Press.

Wimmer, Andreas. 2013. *Ethnic Boundary Making: Institutions, Power, Networks.* Oxford: Oxford University Press.

Wimmer, Andreas, and Nina Glick Schiller. 2002. "Methodological Nationalism and Beyond: Nation-State Building, Migration, and Social Sciences." *Global Networks* 2 (4): 301–34.

Zhou, Min. 1997. "Segmented Assimilation: Issues, Controversies, and Recent Research on the New Second Generation." *International Migration Review* 31 (4): 975–1008.

Zong, Jie, and Jeanne Batalova. 2016. "Mexican Immigrants in the United States." Migration Information Source. May 22, 2016. www.migrationpolicy.org/article/mexican-immigrants-united-states.

Zúñiga, Víctor. 1992. "Tradiciones migratorias internacionales y socialización familiar." *Frontera Norte* 7:45–74.

———. 1993. "Evolución de la migración internacional en un municipio de la zona metropolitana de Monterrey." In *TLC: Impactos en la frontera norte,* edited by Ajejandro Dávila, 205–27. Mexico City: UNAM.

———. 1998. "Nations and Borders: Romantic Nationalism and the Project of Modernity." In *The U.S.-Mexico Border: Transcending Divisions, Contesting*

Identities, edited by David Spener and Kathleen Staudt, 35–55. Boulder: Rienner.

———, ed. 2008. *Dilemas de la diversidad cultural*. Monterrey: Fondo Editorial Nuevo Léon.

———. 2015. "Niños y adolescentes separados de sus familias por la migración internacional: El caso de cuatro estados de México." *Estudios Sociológicos* 33 (97): 145–68.

———. 2018. "The 0.5 Generation: What Children Know about International Migration." *Migraciones Internacionales* 10 (1): 93–120.

Zúñiga, Víctor, and Eduardo Carrillo. 2020. "Migración y exclusión escolar: Truncamiento de la educación básica en menores migrantes de Estados Unidos a México." *Estudios Sociológicos* 38 (114): 655–88.

Zúñiga, Víctor, and Edmund T. Hamann. 2008. "Escuelas nacionales, alumnos transnacionales: La migración México/Estados Unidos como fenómeno escolar." *Estudios Sociológicos* 26 (76): 65–85.

———. 2011. "Volviendo a visitar la noción de transnacionalidad: Comunicación transfronteriza y redes diaspóricas en alumnos migrantes internacionales en las escuelas de México." In *Procesos comunicativos en la migración: De la escuela a la feria popular*, edited by José Juan Olvera and Blanca Vázquez Delgado, 29–59. Mexico City: El Colegio de la Frontera Norte.

Zúñiga, Víctor, Edmund T. Hamann, and Juan Sánchez García. 2008. *Alumnos transnacionales: Escuelas mexicanas frente a la globalización*. Mexico City: Secretaría de Educación Pública.

———. 2016. "Students We Share Are Also in Puebla, Mexico: Preliminary Findings from a 2009–2010 Survey." In *Mexican Migration to the United States: Perspectives from Both Sides of the Border*, edited by Harriet D. Romo and Olivia Mogollón-López, 248–64. Austin: University of Texas Press.

Zúñiga, Víctor, and Rubén Hernández-León, eds. 2005a. *New Destinations: Mexican Immigration in the United States*. New York: Sage Foundation.

———. 2005b. "Peut-on parler d'une diaspora mexicaine aux États-Unis?" *Géographie et Cultures* 53:89–104.

———. 2017. "Due decenni di ricerca sulla migrazione messicana in una nuova destinazione non-metropolitana: Riflessioni di campo dagli Stati Uniti." *Mondi Migranti* 1:7–28.

Zúñiga, Víctor, and Miguel Reyes. 2006. "La cultura de los pasaporteados: Cultura, familia y migración internacional en Vallecillo, Nuevo León." In *El Noreste: Reflexiones*, edited by Isabel Ortega, 105–26. Monterrey: Fondo Editorial Nuevo León.

Zúñiga, Víctor, and Anabela Sánchez. 2010. "Familia y migración internacional en la zona metropolitana de Monterrey: Constantes y variables en los últimos 40 años." In *Cuando México enfrenta la globalización: Permanencias y cambios en el área metropolitana de Monterrey,* edited by Lylia Palacios, Camilo Contreras, and Víctor Zúñiga, 249–69. Monterrey: Universidad Autónoma de Nuevo León/El Colegio de la Frontera Norte.

Index

Founded in 1893,
UNIVERSITY OF CALIFORNIA PRESS
publishes bold, progressive books and journals
on topics in the arts, humanities, social sciences,
and natural sciences—with a focus on social
justice issues—that inspire thought and action
among readers worldwide.

The UC PRESS FOUNDATION
raises funds to uphold the press's vital role
as an independent, nonprofit publisher, and
receives philanthropic support from a wide
range of individuals and institutions—and from
committed readers like you. To learn more, visit
ucpress.edu/supportus.

www.ingramcontent.com/pod-product-compliance
Lightning Source LLC
Chambersburg PA
CBHW020830270326
41928CB00006B/484